CENTENNIAL S.S.
MATH. DEPT.

MATH STORIES FOR PROBLEM SOLVING SUCCESS

Ready-to-Use Activities for Grades 7-12

Jim Overholt

Nancy Aaberg

Jim Lindsey

Illustrated by
Ron Schultz

The Center for Applied Research in Education, Inc.
West Nyack, New York

©1990 by
THE CENTER FOR APPLIED
RESEARCH IN EDUCATION
West Nyack, NY

10 9 8 7 6 5 4 3 2 1

Library of Congress Cataloging-in-Publication Data

Overholt, James L.
    Math stories for problem solving success: ready-to-use activities
for grades 7-12 / by Jim Overholt, Nancy Aaberg, and Jim Lindsey:
illustrated by Ron Schultz.
    Bibliography:
    ISBN 0-87628-570-1
    1. Problem solving.   2. Word problems (Mathematics)
3. Mathematics—Study and teaching (Secondary)   I. Aaberg, Nancy.
II. Lindsey, Jim.   III. Title.
QA63.O89   1989
510′.76—dc20

**THE CENTER FOR APPLIED
RESEARCH IN EDUCATION**
BUSINESS & PROFESSIONAL DIVISION
A division of Simon & Schuster
West Nyack, New York 10995

Printed in the United States of America

ABOUT THE AUTHORS

James L. Overholt, Ed.D. (University of Wyoming, Laramie) has over 20 years' of experience as a public school teacher and educator. He began his career teaching in the public schools of LeSueur and Albert Lea, Minnesota, then served as a mathematics teacher/coordinator and instructor in Elementary and Junior High School Education at the University School, University of Wyoming. Presently Dr. Overholt is Professor of Education at California State University, Chico, where he specializes in mathematics education for both practicing and prospective teachers.

Nancy H. Aaberg, M.Ed. (California State University, Chico) has over 15 years' experience as a public high school mathematics teacher. She began her career in Toms River, New Jersey, then served as a mathematics teacher, athletic director, and activities director in Marysville, California. Presently Mrs. Aaberg is a mathematics teacher and consultant in Yuba City, California.

James F. Lindsey, Ed.D. (University of California, Berkeley) has over 20 years' experience as a teacher and administrator in public schools. He taught in the upper grades of the elementary school, high school music, social studies, and mathematics, and was a principal. In addition, he served as Professor of Education for 21 years at California State University, Chico, at which he is now Professor Emeritus. He has also taught at Christchurch Teachers' College, New Zealand, and at St. Patrick's College, Dublin, Ireland.

About This Resource

The purpose of *Math Stories for Problem Solving Success: Ready-to-Use Activities for Grades 7-12* is to provide interesting, true-to-life situations that will motivate your teenage students to apply mathematics skills toward solving everyday problems. It is designed to be a high-interest/low-vocabulary curriculum supplement for use in any basic mathematics class, grades 7-12. We've found these stories and problems an ideal way to teach problem solving—a perennial concern of math educators—while providing practice in important math skills.

To help you select problem sets that parallel the math topics being taught in your class, a handy Table of Contents/Emphases Matrix is provided at the beginning of the book. An Answer Key in the back furnishes explanations and background information, in addition to answers, and can be helpful to both you and your students. The book has been formatted to make reproducing the student handouts as easy as possible, with spiral binding so that the $8\frac{1}{2}$ x 11 pages will lie flat for photocopying. Also to help you, most of the worksheets have a layout that provides space for students to work out the problems.

You will find that each story has a vocabulary grade level of 4, 5 or 6 according to the Fry Readability Formula[1] and features characters and problems relating to typical student interests and concerns. To build student involvement, the stories feature recurring characters and are ordered as if they occur over a two- or three-year period, but you can also use them out of order without difficulty.

Each short, interest-building story is followed by three related problem sets, all focusing on the same math topics and arranged in order of increasing difficulty. Set A problems are primarily single-step operations; while Set B is of medium difficulty; problems from Set C generally require multistep operations. Therefore, your most able students should work with Set C, those displaying average capability with Set B, and students experiencing difficulty with Set A. However, since all three problem sets have the same mathematical focus, discussions about the topics can include all of the students.

Following the Table of Contents/Emphases Matrix is a short section on teaching the problem solving strategies and support tactics that are so useful to students. And to kick things off, an introductory story whets students' curiosity about Tessa, Jake, and Michael, who all discover that real life is full of math problems.

It is our belief that the stories and math problems in *Math Stories for Problem Solving Success* will help you to motivate those students who think math is something they'll never need out in the real world, by showing them lots of practical and interesting ways they can use it *right now*.

Jim Overholt
Nancy Aaberg
Jim Lindsey

---

[1] Edward B. Fry, *Elementary Reading Instruction* (New York: McGraw-Hill Book Co., 1977), pp. 216–219.

Table of Contents— Emphases Matrix

	Pages
About This Resource	v
Teaching Problem Solving Strategies	xi
A Problem Solving Strategy and Example	xii
Notes for the Teacher	xiii
Time to Go	1

M	= Major Emphasis
m	= minor emphasis
s	= selected problems

	Estimation	Whole Numbers	Decimals	Fractions/Ratios	Percentages	Averages	Statistics & Probability	Using Calculators	Multiple Answers	Money/Interest	Time	Consumer Math	Patterns & Functions	Systematic Lists	Logic	Measurement	Geometry	Map Reading	Graphs & Charts	Research	Projects	Page
Which Way for Jake?	s	s	s	s	s			s	s		M											3
The Caper	s	s					m		s		M											8
A Sigh of Relief	s	s	s		s			s	s			M	m							s		12
Future Forecast	m	s	s	s	s		m							s	s							16
Harper's Surprise	s		s	s	s			s	s	s									s			20
Our Daily Bread	s	M	m			M	M	s	m	m	M	M		m						s	M	24
Sweet Spending		m										m		M	m							29
The County Fair		M	m	m	m		M	m	m	m	M	m			s							33
Square Cents												M		M					m			38
Halloween									s					M					m		s	40
Amazing Measurements	M	m	m	s		m					m					M			M			44
Metric Airplane Contest	M	m	m						m			m	m			M	m	m	m			49
Take Me to Your Liter	M	m	m						m		s	m	M			M	m					53

vii

TABLE OF CONTENTS

	Estimation	Whole Numbers	Decimals	Fractions/Ratios	Percentages	Averages	Statistics & Probability	Using Calculators	Multiple Answers	Money/Interest	Time	Consumer Math	Patterns & Functions	Systematic Lists	Logic	Measurement	Geometry	Map Reading	Graphs & Charts	Research	Projects	Page
Give a Gram	M	m	m			m					s	m	m			M		s		M		58
Measurement Madness	M	m	m			m		m							M							60
The Invitation	M		m				m	s	M		M							m				63
On to D.C.	m			M	s	s		m	M		s							m				67
The Job Crisis		s	M			s		s	M													71
Tickets		s		s		M																75
Jake Turns the Corner		m						s	M	M												79
It's Simply Interest	m		m	M		M	s	M	m	M												82
An Interesting Loan			m	M		M		M	M	M				m								86
Homecoming	s					m	s					s		s		M						90
Pendulum Project	m	m		s		m		m		m		m	m		m			m	M	M		94
Take a Chance				m		M													s	s		98
831 Monroe Street												M	m									102
The Pattern Game								s					M	m				m		s		106
Unlucky Friday	s		M									m						s				110
Lucky Seven						M		m						m	m					m		114
Busing for Bucks			s	M	M	m			M	m												118
Far Out Funds	M		m		m	M	m		M	m												122
Maggie's Secret		s	s	s	s	s		s	s	s	s											126
The Frantic Drive		s	s					s	s	s					M			m				131
Tessa's Grounding	M	m			m	s			M	M	m											136
Geometry in the Park	m	m		s		m						m					M	M	s	m		140
String Triangles	m		m										M	m	M	M			s	m		145
Geometry Project	M	m					s	m	s		m	M		m			M		M	M		149
What's the Score?	m					s	m											M				153
What is the Average?						M		m						m					m	m		157
The Challenge		m				M		s							m					m		161
To the Coach		m				M	m	M	M		M											165

	Estimation	Whole Numbers	Decimals	Fractions/Ratios	Percentages	Averages	Statistics & Probability	Using Calculators	Multiple Answers	Money/Interest	Time	Consumer Math	Patterns & Functions	Systematic Lists	Logic	Measurement	Geometry	Map Reading	Graphs & Charts	Research	Projects	Page
The Pro Game	s	s				s		m		s							M					169
Table for Eight?	M											M	M	M				M				173
Jake's Surprise	m	s	m	m				s		s			s	s								176
Sale by Mail			m					m	M		M											181
A Day at Clear Lake	M	m		s		m	m	m	m	s	M		m							M		184
Survey							M		m											m		188
Summer Plans	s	M	m						m													192
The Dinosaurs Rock	M		m		M	m			M	m	m						M					196
Cassette by Credit			m	M				s	M	M		M										201
Oregon or Bust	m	m						m	M	s	m	s				M		M		M		205

Answer Key (with Explanations) 209

Selected References 237

Teaching Problem Solving Strategies

Whether working with the problems in this book or in textbooks, most students benefit from problem solving guidelines. Formal procedures have not been specified for these lessons, but we do recommend that students use an overall strategy and/or selected support tactics. See, for example, the Sample Problem on the bottom of this page and a detailed explanation of it's solution via a Problem Solving Strategy on the following page. You may, in fact, wish to reproduce copies for your students and work through this problem and other with them. As such, they will begin to understand how such a strategy might be applied to many diferent problems.

One way to begin would be to talk about how the first four steps of this overall strategy could be used to approach problems from one or more of the problem sets. You may, at times, want to direct students to write out information about certain steps in the strategy; for example, you could ask students to isolate the **question**, or list the **important facts**, or write down an **estimate**, and give partial credit for these as well as the correct answers. However, students should generally be able to verbalize the entire strategy as they work independently or in groups to solve the problems in their assigned sets.

Other support tactics can also prove helpful. Some that could be used in selected situations are:

1. drawing pictures and diagrams
2. estimating and checking
3. working backwards
4. using systematic lists
5. looking for patterns
6. orally presenting problems
7. analyzing mathematical vocabulary
8. verifying reasonable answers
9. logical thinking
10. tables, graphs and charts
11. maps and scale drawings
12. writing original problems

We are confident that, when combined with an overall problem solving strategy and appropriate support tactics, this book will help your students to become better mathematical problem solvers.

Sample Problem:

Of the 1,800 students at Central High School 1,000 are boys. What percent of the students are boys?

Problem Solving Strategy	**Example**
1. *Main Idea* (State what the problem is about. This will provide a basis upon which to start working the problem.)	1. *Main Idea:* Students at Central High School
2. *Question* (Tell what is being asked for in the problem.)	2. *Question:* What percentage of the students are boys?
3. *Important Facts* (Note the facts that must be used to solve the problem. Disregard any unnecessary information or identify any information that may be lacking.)	3. *Important Facts:* 1,800 students; 1,000 boys
4. *Relationship* (State verbally how the problem can be solved. Note which type(s) of computation and/or other solution procedures will be used.)	4. *Relationship:* 1,000 is what percentage of 1,800?
5. *Estimation* (Make a reasonable "guess" as to what the solution will be.)	5. *Estimate:* 1,000 is more than half of 1,800, so the result will be over 50%. 60% might be a good guess.
6. *Equation* (If computation is necessary, arrange the important facts in a number sentence. Otherwise, set up the solution sequence to be used.)	6. *Equation:* $1,000 = $ _____ $\% \times 1,800$ or $\dfrac{(?)}{100} = \dfrac{1,000}{1,800}$
7. *Computation or Process* (Compute or carry out the solution sequence.)	7. *Computation:* $1,000 = $ _____ $\% \times 1,800$ so $\dfrac{1,000}{1,800} = $ _____ $\%$; $\dfrac{1,000}{1,800} = .555 = 56\%$ or $\dfrac{(?)}{100} = \dfrac{1,000}{1,800}$; $1,800 \times (?) = 100 \times 1,000$ $\dfrac{1,800 \times (?)}{1,800} = \dfrac{100,000}{1,800}$ $(?) = 55.5\% = 56\%$
8. *Check Your Work* (Compare your answer with your estimate. Is it a reasonable answer for the question that was asked?)	8. *Check:* Over ½ of the students were boys, so I estimated 60%. 56% is between 50% and 60%, so I'm close.
9. *Answer Sentence* (State the solution in a sentence that answers the questions in the problem.)	9. *Answer Sentence:* Approximately 56% of the students at Central High School are boys.

Notes for the Teacher

"Time to Go," the introductory story, is not followed by any mathematics problem sheets. Instead, we suggest that the best way to build student interest in this series of stories and problems is to follow the reading of this first story with a period of class discussion and speculation on the characters and situation. Some open-ended questions might be:

- If you have moved from one school to another one in a different location, how did you feel? What were you worried about?
- Do you know anyone who seems to be like Mike, Tessa or Jake?
- How do you think Tessa will get along at her new school?
- How does Jake, an outsider, feel? What will he do after tonight?
- What can the Samuelsons do to help Tessa and Jake?
- Do you think Mike will resent the Martins and Jake butting into his life?

After this discussion, students will be more curious about these characters and their problems and more interested in solving the related problems with math!

TIME TO GO!

With tears in her eyes, Tessa said good-bye to the small group who gathered early one October morning. Tessa Martin and her mother, Maria, climbed into their pickup and headed for the city as their friends waved farewell. Just two months ago Mr. Martin had suffered fatal injuries in a construction accident. Since then Tessa and her mom had settled business, sold their home and prepared to move closer to Mrs. Martin's family.

Tessa wanted to stay on the ranch where she'd lived all her life. Leaving her friends and familiar surroundings would not be easy. In September Tessa had begun her sophomore year in a high school where she actively participated in school activities. She was content with life there and resented moving away.

The trip, although only two days, seemed forever to Tessa. Uncomfortable with the thought of a new school and new friends, she pouted most of the time. Mrs. Martin felt confident that the Samuelsons, her sister's family, would help make the adjustment easier. Tessa already looked forward to visiting her old friends next summer.

Tessa did not know her cousin Michael very well. It had been almost two years since she last visited her older cousin and she hoped they would find something in common. The trip wore on and Tessa's mind filled with sad thoughts of old friends left behind.

Meanwhile, the Samuelsons prepared for the arrival of their guests. Michael wasn't thrilled about giving up his bedroom to the Martins. His mom assured him that Tessa and her mom would stay with them only until Mrs. Martin found a job and a suitable home.

Mrs. Samuelson planned a small gathering of friends to greet the Martins. Michael only had to stay for dinner before leaving to catch up with some friends at the football game. By six o'clock the Samuelsons became worried about the Martins. Their last phone call indicated an arrival time of four-thirty. Mr. Samuelson, Michael and a few others set out by car to locate the Martins.

Mr. Samuelson finally spotted the Martins' truck. As he approached them he noticed a young man helping to change a tire. Tessa waved and quickly told how lucky they were that the young man, Jake Burton, had come by after their two hours of being stranded by a flat tire and the rusty bolts that had prevented them from removing the wheel.

Jake asked for a lift into town, as he was looking for a new place to settle. His family, he told, had rejected him and sent him out on his own. He needed a place to stay that night before moving on. They all drove back into town. Jake Burton sat quietly through dinner as everyone tried to become acquainted again.

QUESTIONS:

① IN YOUR OWN WORDS, EXPLAIN THE FOLLOWING

a) WHY THE MARTINS WERE MOVING

b) WHO THE SAMUELSONS WERE

c) WHY JAKE BURTON GOT AN INVITATION TO DINNER

d) TESSA'S FEELINGS ABOUT HER NEW HOME

e) JAKES SITUATION AT HOME

WHICH WAY FOR JAKE?

Jake Burton thanked the Samuelsons for dinner and got up to leave. Mr. Samuelson asked where he would be staying. Jake said he didn't know, but he would find a place. They insisted that he stay with them until he could find a job and a place of his own. He was more than happy to accept.

The next morning Jake ate an early breakfast at the Samuelsons'. He started job hunting by 7:45 A.M. He spent 1/2 hour filling out an application form at one store and 3/4 hour at another. At a third store he spent 1/2 hour completing a form and 1/4 hour being interviewed. By 12:30 P.M. he felt downhearted and stopped searching for the day.

Jake decided to really keep at job hunting the second day. He left at 7:15 A.M. and kept searching until 4:30 P.M. That afternoon he decided to go to the public employment office. When he got there he was astonished at the lines of people. In one line there were 18 men and 7 women, in a second line 23 men and 11 women, the third had 16 men and 23 women and the fourth line held 29 women and 3 men.

Jake had searched for 13 days straight without luck. What little money he did have was almost gone. When he had started he had had $88.75, but now he was down to $23.10. Staying with the

3

Samuelsons and eating some of his meals with them had been a big help. But he was beginning to feel like a burden. He just had to get some money and his own place to stay! Something just had to happen!

One afternoon, while job hunting, Jake became very hungry and stopped at a vending center. He skipped lunch in order to save the few dollars he had left. He looked longingly at the vending machines full of sandwiches, candy, soft drinks and fruit. Just then he noticed another young man opening some machines with what looked like a piece of wire. As he watched, the other young man ate a sandwich and drank a coke, and then started to open a candy machine. Jake meant to say don't do that, but instead he asked, "Would you get some for me too?"

"Sure, here's a candy bar. Would you like something to drink too?"

Jake soon learned that the other's name was Zeke. Zeke had lost his job two months earlier. Since then he had been staying with different friends and getting by any way he could.

Which Way for Jake?
Problem Set A

Directions: First read the story "Which Way for Jake?" Information from the story will help you to solve some of the problems below. Write your answer sentences below each problem. Use the back of this page or a separate sheet of paper to show your work.

1. How long did Jake spend job hunting the first day?

2. During his first day, how much time did Jake spend being interviewed and completing application forms?

3. Jake stopped at a lumber yard to check on a job. The manager had him use a measuring tape to mark a board to be cut into pieces of $2\frac{1}{2}$ inches, $18\frac{3}{4}$ inches and $7\frac{3}{8}$ inches in length. What was the total length of the board before being cut?

4. The manager also wanted to know if Jake could measure accurately in metric units, so he had him mark a second board to be cut into lengths of 27.5 cm, 32.65 cm, and 101.87 cm. What is the total length of all the pieces to be cut?

5. At a grocery store, the manager told Jake that they stocked the fresh fruit counter with 9 apples for every 6 peaches. At this ratio, if there were 66 peaches, how many apples should be on the counter?

Which Way for Jake?
Problem Set B

Directions: First read the story "Which Way for Jake?" Information from the story will help you to solve some of the problems below. Write your answer sentences below each problem. Where possible, use the back of this page or a separate sheet of paper to show your work.

1. How many people, total, were waiting in the lines at the public employment office?

2. What was the ratio of women to men in the employment office lines? Refer to Problem 1 above.

3. A free pamphlet in the employment office said that it served 2,600 people each month. If the office was open for business 20 days each month, what is the average number of people it serves each day?

4. The employment pamphlet also claimed that 38% of the people they served got jobs within a month. If they serve 2,600 people in an average month, how many should get jobs?

5. The vending machines sold sandwiches for $.85. The machine only accepted quarters, dimes and nickels. List four coin combinations that you could put into the machine for a sandwich.

Which Way for Jake?
Problem Set C

Directions: First read the story "Which Way for Jake?" Information from the story will help you to solve some of the problems below. Write your answer sentences below each problem. Where possible, use the back of this page or a separate sheet of paper to show your work.

1. After 13 days how much money had Jake spent? On the average, how much money had he spent each day?

2. Jake looked at himself in a mirror and decided his rumpled clothes weren't helping him find a job. He decided to spend approximately 1/3 of his remaining money for a new shirt. Approximately how much will he spend for the shirt? How much money will he have left?

3. The vending machine sold sandwiches for $.85. The machine only accepted quarters, dimes, and nickels. List four coin combinations that you could use to buy a sandwich.

4. Several days later Jake found another temporary job applying lawn fertilizer. The directions said that each bag of fertilizer would cover 200 square feet. The lawn was a rectangle of 65 feet by 95 feet. How many bags of fertilizer would be needed?

5. Jake missed the bus and had to take a taxi to a job interview. The taxi charged 75 cents per mile for the first five miles and 55 cents per mile after that. To get across town to the job interview it turned out to be 11.8 miles. How much will the taxi ride cost? How much should the driver's tip be at 15%?

THE CAPER

The clock read 11:42 P.M. when Zeke crashed a hammer into the window of the Burger Barn. "Hurry up, Jake!" hissed Zeke. "We gotta get that money before someone sees us!"

"I can't get the register open," said Jake. "We better split now before we're caught."

"Listen, if you're chicken it's too late now. We're in this together. Now hurry up!" answered Zeke.

"All right—hold it right there and don't move!" said someone with a gruff voice.

Those words rang through Jake's head as he spent the night in the city jail. Zeke had managed to raise bail, but Jake wasn't as lucky.

"If only I hadn't gone along with Zeke and his dumb idea! I knew we'd never pull that one off," thought Jake.

Jake regretted his connection with Zeke. He'd only been in town a few days, but that was long enough to learn of Zeke's reputation. He had needed the money, though, so he had gone along with the robbery idea.

In the morning Jake learned that his parents had refused to post bail for him. The judge put him on probation and assigned him to a foster home. Jake had to work four hours each day at the Burger Barn to repay them for the damaged cash register and window. He needed to break out of this rut and make something of himself.

Burger Deluxe	$1.15		
Cheese	$ .20		
Fish Burger	$1.45		
Double Burger	$1.75		
Juicy Burger	$ .99		
Cheese	$ .20		
Shake	$ .59	$.69	$.89
Soft Drink	$ .35	$.50	$.65
Fries	$ .49		$.69

California Sales Tax 6%

Name _____   **Period** _____   **Date** _____

The Caper
Problem Set A

Directions: First read the story "The Caper". Information from the story and the illustration will help you to solve some of the problems below. Write your answer sentences below each problem. Where possible, use the back of this page or a separate sheet of paper to show your work.

1. The police arrived at 12:07 A.M. How long were Jake and Zeke in the Burger Barn?

2. The cost for replacing the window was $177.80. Repairs to the cash register totaled $196.95. Estimate the repair cost to the nearest $10. How much did they actually have to repay in all?

3. If Jake planned to repay one-half of the total repairs, how much did he have to repay? (See Problem 2 of this set for information.)

4. Zeke was born in August 1971. Jake was born in May 1973. How much older is Zeke than Jake? Give your answer in years and months.

5. If Jake earned $3.75 per hour, how much did he earn each day?

The Caper
Problem Set B

Directions: First read the story "The Caper." Information from the story and the illustration will help you to solve some of the problems below. Write your answer sentences below each problem. Where possible, use the back of this page or a separate sheet of paper to show your work.

1. A customer ordered a fish burger, large fries and small shake. How much was the total before sales tax?

2. How much more would it cost, before tax, to buy a double burger, small fries and large shake than a juicy burger with cheese, large fries and a large soft drink?

3. You and two friends have each ordered a burger deluxe, small fries and small shake. How much was the total bill before sales tax?

4. List two different orders you could buy for less than $2.50. Each order must include at least one burger and a drink. You do not have to include sales tax.

5. Your bill was $4.61. The cash register was out of quarters. Name two different ways the cashier could have given you the correct change for $5.00.

The Caper
Problem Set C

Directions: First read the story "The Caper." Information from the story and the illustration will help you to solve some of the problems below. Write your answer sentences below each problem. Where possible, use the back of this page or a separate sheet of paper to show your work.

1. A customer placed an order for two fish burgers and two small shakes. After 6% sales tax was added, how much change did she receive from $5?

2. Jake received an order for three juicy burgers with cheese, two large fries and three medium soft drinks. Name three ways Jake could have given the proper change from $20.00. Do not forget that sales tax had to be added.

3. The Burger Barn had twenty tables with four chairs each, six tables of six chairs each and fifteen tables of two chairs each. How many people could be seated at the Burger Barn?

4. Create a table arrangement for the Burger Barn. Use the information in Problem 3 of the set. Draw your arrangement.

5. You are starved, but have only $2.50 to spend at the Burger Barn. Name three possible orders you might place and not exceed the $2.50 limit. Each order must include at least one burger, one drink and sales tax.

A SIGH OF RELIEF

"Mrs. Maria Martin?" called the receptionist. "Right this way, please."

"I need this job," thought Mrs. Martin. "It's what I've been hoping for!"

Mrs. Martin had interviewed for several jobs over the past few weeks, but without luck. This accountant's job was her last hope. The interview began at 2:35 P.M. with the usual questions regarding her past employment and education. By the time she had completed the short written test it was 3:20 P.M. She headed for the Samuelsons', thinking of the house she and Tessa had found last week. They really needed a place of their own, but couldn't afford it without this job. The monthly salary of $1,575 would be a good start on the payments for a new home.

"How can I face Tessa if I don't get this job? And we can't go on staying with the Samuelsons much longer," thought Mrs. Martin.

It would be three days until she heard about the job. During that time Mrs. Martin searched through the newspaper in hopes of another job lead. There just weren't any jobs around that she qualified for and could earn enough money at to raise her family. She had no choice but to wait until she heard about the job.

"Mrs. Maria Martin?" asked a voice on the telephone.

"Yes," answered Maria.

"This is Baker Accounting Firm, and we'd like to inform you that you have the job. We'd like you to report to work in the morning."

"There'll be lots to do now," smiled Mrs. Martin. "I'll begin with arrangements for our new home!"

12

A Sigh of Relief
Problem Set A

Directions: First read the story "A Sigh of Relief." Information from the story will help you to solve some of the problems below. Write your answer sentences below each problem. Where possible, use the back of this page or a separate sheet of paper to show your work.

1. Use the monthly salary and estimate how much Mrs. Martin would make in one year. Now, compute the salary for one year. How close did you come to your estimate?

2. How long was the interview?

3. The original selling price of the Martins' new home was $47,650. The price was reduced by $2,999. What was the final selling price of the home?

4. The lot size of the new home was 90′ by 110′. What was the area of the lot?

5. The realtor earned 6% of the final selling price as commission. With the final selling price you found in Problem 3 of this set, find the amount of commission earned.

A Sigh of Relief
Problem Set B

Directions: First read the story "A Sigh of Relief." Information from the story will help you to solve some of the problems below. Write your answer sentences below each problem. Where possible, use the back of this page or a separate sheet of paper to show your work.

    Measure the rooms in the floor plan below to the nearest 1/4 inch. In this diagram 1/4 inch represents 3 feet.

1. What are the dimensions of bedroom 3? (Give the dimensions in feet.)

2. What is the area of bedroom 3?

3. What are the dimensions, in feet, of bedroom 1?
    What is the perimeter of the room?

4. Tessa's room (bedroom 3) needs new carpeting.
    Sears has carpet on sale for $21.99 per square yard.
    Which of the answers below is the best estimate
    for the price of the carpeting in Tessa's room?
          (a) $4,000   (b) $400
          (c) $1,800   (d) $500
    Explain how you arrived at your estimate to your
    partner or group.

5. What is the actual price for carpeting
    Tessa's room?

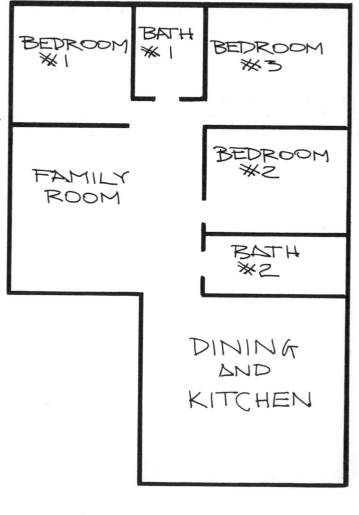

A Sigh of Relief
Problem Set C

Directions: First read the story "A Sigh of Relief." Information from the story will help you to solve some of the problems below. Write your answer sentences below each problem. Where possible, use the back of this page or a separate sheet of paper to show your work.

In the diagram below, 1/4 inch represents 3 feet.

1. How many square yards of linoleum are needed for the two bathrooms?

2. The Martins learned that the average electric bill will be increased by 15% next month. If the current bill is $47.90, how much can they expect the next bill to be?

3. Find the total square footage of the Martins' home.

4. Create and draw a different house plan for the Martins. Find the square footage of the plan you created.

BEDROOM #1 BATH #1 BEDROOM #3 FAMILY ROOM BEDROOM #2 BATH #2 DINING AND KITCHEN

FUTURE FORECAST

The first few days with the Andersons were pretty awkward. Jake couldn't relax with Mrs. Anderson fussing over him and Mr. Anderson lecturing on the value of a good education. It'd been years since the Andersons had had a teenager around the house. They tried to make Jake feel welcome, but as far as Jake was concerned they tried too hard. Dinner time was the worst. Jake wasn't used to table conversation, and Mrs. Anderson insisted upon asking about Jake's future plans.

"What future?" thought Jake. "I owe the Burger Barn several more weeks of work and after that I still won't have any money. How will I ever get a real job?"

Jake returned home after work and looked forward to the solitude of his room.

"We've been invited to the Samuelsons' for dinner tonight, Jake," said Mrs. Anderson.

"You go ahead," answered Jake. "I'll make something here and go to bed early."

"Oh, but they were counting on you. Tessa and her mother will be there too," she replied.

"Well, I'll go to eat, but don't count on me hanging around afterwards!" said Jake as he stormed into his room.

Jake dreaded going there. He felt as though he, Tessa and Michael had nothing in common. High school talk didn't interest Jake, mainly because he wasn't part of it and couldn't decide if he wanted to be. He'd only earned seventy-five credits so far and was tired of school.

"I'm glad you stayed around long enough to talk some with Tessa and Michael," said Mrs. Anderson after returning home.

"Well, it sounds like that high school has some programs where you can work and take a few classes," remarked Jake.

"If I could get the manager of the Burger Barn to let me stay on after the debt was paid off, I might be able to get into that program," he continued. "I sure could use the $3.75 an hour. Besides, I heard after two months you get a raise!"

"I'll talk with him tomorrow. At this point I have nothing to lose!" thought Jake as he went into his room.

16

Future Forecast
Problem Set A

Directions: First read the story "Future Forecast." Information from the story will help you to solve some of the problems below. Write your answer sentences below each problem. Where possible, use the back of this page or a separate sheet of paper to show your work.

1. If Jake needs 220 credits to graduate, how many more does he have to earn in order to graduate?

2. Jake owes the Burger Barn $112.50. Estimate how many hours he still has to work to pay off the debt.

3. On the way to the Samuelsons' Mr. Anderson filled his car with gas. He put in 9.7 gallons and paid $1.13 per gallon. Estimate the total charge. What was the actual charge for gas?

4. Mrs. Anderson made a cherry pie for the Samuelsons and one for her family. One pie required 1³/₄ cups of flour for the crust. How much flour was required for two pies?

5. Mrs. Anderson only had measuring cups of 1/2 cup and 1/4 cup. Name two different ways she could measure out the flour for the pies. Refer to the information in Problem 4 of this set.

Future Forecast
Problem Set B

Directions: First read the story "Future Forecast." Information from the story will help you to solve some of the problems below. Write your answer sentences below each problem. Where possible, use the back of this page or a separate sheet of paper to show your work.

The chart below shows the food served by Mrs. Samuelson and the calories per serving. Estimate the answer to each of the following questions using the chart. Then calculate the actual answer.

Chicken (baked)	187	Pie (cherry)	400
Rice	103	Milk (8 oz)	160
Green beans (per cup)	25	Coffee	5
Bread (wheat)	110		

1. Michael ate two helpings of chicken and rice and one helping of beans, bread and pie. He also drank two glasses of milk. How many calories did he consume?

   Estimate _____   Actual _____

2. Jake had one helping of rice and chicken, two pieces of pie and two cups of coffee. How many more calories did he consume than Michael?

   Estimate _____   Actual _____

3. Tessa had a glass of milk. What else could she have eaten and kept her entire meal under 450 calories?

4. Mrs. Samuelson's diet allowed 1,000 calories per day. She had 378 calories earlier in the day. Her dinner consisted of chicken, rice, pie and coffee. By how much did she go over the 1,000-calories limit?

   Estimate _____   Actual _____

5. If you had your choice of anything on Mrs. Samuelson's menu, what would you choose? How many calories would that be in all?

   Choices _____

   Estimate _____   Actual _____

Future Forecast
Problem Set C

Directions: First read the story "Future Forecast." Information from the story will help you to solve some of the problems below. Write your answer sentences below each problem. Where possible, use the back of this page or a separate sheet of paper to show your work.

1. Jake averages 25 hours of work per week. How much does he earn?

2. Jake said his other high school had 2,500 students and 1,400 were girls. Write the ratio of boys to girls at Jake's other school.

3. Central High School had some classrooms with 20 desks and some with 30 desks. List three possible ways in which the 1,800 students could be seated in the classrooms.

4. Can you find the least number of classrooms needed to house the 1,800 Central High School students? Assume that you must use at least 10 classrooms of 20 desks and 10 classrooms of 30 desks. Discuss your ideas with your partner or group.

5. Can you find the greatest number of classrooms needed to house the 1,800 Central High School students? Assume that you must use at least 10 classrooms of 20 desks and 10 classrooms of 30 desks. Discuss your ideas with your partners or groups.

HARPER'S SURPRISE

Michael and Tessa made their way through the damp and dark evening toward Jed Harper's house. Michael had left his books at Jed's and needed them for the weekend.

Tessa barely noticed the roundabout route they traveled to Jed's. She wanted to get to the 8:15 movie where they planned to meet several friends. The November rains caused mud slides to close off some local roads, so they took a 12½-mile detour to Jed's.

"Hurry up, Michael! It's 7:40. How much farther till we get there?" said Tessa before adding, "I've been wanting to see this movie for months and we can't be late!"

Michael gave her an irritated glance and mumbled something about her not being ready on time.

Finally they reached Jed's, but the house was dark.

"Great—all this way and no one home! I knew that you should have called first!" Tessa exclaimed.

"Relax!" said Michael. "I know they leave the back door open. Come on in with me."

As they approached the living room the clock struck eight. The lights flashed on and Tessa heard voices yell "Surprise!" Michael and some friends had planned the party to celebrate Tessa's sixteenth birthday. The movie could wait for another time, but Tessa didn't mind.

Harper's Surprise
Problem Set A

Directions: First read the story "Harper's Surprise." Information from the story will help you to solve some of the problems below. Write your answer sentences below each problem. Where possible, use the back of this page or a separate sheet of paper to show your work.

1. Michael and Tessa left at 7:15 P.M. and headed for Jed's. How long did they take to get there?

2. Maggie volunteered to bake a cake. She decided to double the recipe. If the original recipe called for 3/4 cup brown sugar, how much brown sugar did she need?

3. Maggie only had a 1/2-cup and a 1/4-cup measuring cup. Name two ways that she could have measured the brown sugar for the cake? Refer to Problem 2 of this set for information to help.

4. The ingredients for the cake included flour ($.89), sugar ($1.69), brown sugar ($.69), vanilla ($.87), milk ($.79), four eggs ($.08 each) and walnuts ($.97). Estimate, to the nearest dime, the cost of the ingredients.

5. Maggie had a 1/4-cup and 1/2-cup measuring cup. How could she have measured out 3³/₄ cups of flour? Can you find at least two different ways?

Harper's Surprise
Problem Set B

Directions: First read the story "Harper's Surprise." Information from the story will help you to solve some of the problems below. Write your answer sentences below each problem. Where possible, use the back of this page or a separate sheet of paper to show your work.

1. Michael traveled 4.3 miles before reaching the detour point. How many miles did Michael actually drive to reach Jed Harper's house? (Include the detour.)

2. When returning home, Michael and Tessa were able to take the normal route (7.8 miles). How far did Michael drive on the round trip to Jed's and back? (See Problem 1 of this set for information to help.)

3. At the party the ratio of boys to girls was 7:5. How many boys were at the party if there were 10 girls?

4. At the party they played a game that required teams of 4. Was it possible for all teams to have the same number of boys and girls? Discuss your answer with your partner or group.

5. There were 9 cans of cola left after the party. If they started with 4 cases of 24 cans each, what percentage of cans remained unopened? Give your answer to the nearest tenth of a percent.

Harper's Surprise
Problem Set C

Directions: First read the story "Harper's Surprise." Information from the story will help you to solve some of the problems below. Write your answer sentences below each problem. Where possible, use the back of this page or a separate sheet of paper to show your work.

1. Alfredo volunteered to make a new tape for the party. How many 1½-minute songs could he put on a 90-minute tape?

2. If Alfredo put the 90-minute tape on at 8:25 P.M., at what time would it end if he played it twice?

3. Michael planned for 30 guests at the party. He also planned for having two plates and napkins per person. Use the information and calculate the total price for plates and napkins. Do not forget 6% sales tax must be added.

Plates	
16/pkg.	$1.19
Napkins	
20/pkg.	$ .79

4. At the party they played a game that required teams of 4. Was it possible for all teams to have the same number of boys and girls? Discuss your answer with your partner or group. (The ratio of boys to girls was 7:5 and there were 10 girls.)

5. Maggie and three friends bought a pair of earrings for Tessa. The earrings sold for $23.70, plus tax. How much was each person's share of the expense?

OUR DAILY BREAD

"We are just about to finish our unit on statistics and probability," said the teacher. "To end the unit I am going to propose one real life problem. You will be gathering a lot of data about bread. So, I'll call the problem 'Our Daily Bread.' You will be finding out about wheat bread, cinnamon toast and French bread. Whether the bread is sliced thick or thin will also be important. You have a key question that you need to answer. It is: how many loaves of bread do the people in our town eat? Now, what will you need to do to solve this problem?"

"We need to know how many people live in our town," said Maggie.

"Yes, and how much bread does a person eat in a day?" suggested Sara.

"And how many days, or weeks, or even years are we considering?" asked Tessa.

"Yes, these are some of the things you will need to know," agreed the teacher. "To begin with I'll tell you that about 60,000 people live in our town. However, if you lived in another community, where could you get an estimate of the number of people?"

"You could contact the Chamber of Commerce, or the Mayor's Office, or maybe the City Library," said Larry.

"That's correct," responded the teacher. "However, you have an estimate of 60,000 people for our town. Now, what else must you do to solve the problem?"

"We need to find out how much bread every person in our town eats," said Joseph.

"We should ask a lot of people how much bread they eat in a day. Then we could add up all their responses and divide by the number of people. That would give us an average," volunteered Dan.

"That would work," said Dianne. "We could each ask a lot of people. Then we could bring our data back on Monday."

"We also need to find out how many slices there are in a loaf of bread," said Jim.

"That shouldn't be too hard," said Terri. "Some of us could go to my dad's grocery store after school. Then we can count the number of slices in loaves of different kinds of bread."

"Will your dad let you open all that bread?" asked Jerry.

"No, but we can count the slices through the clear plastic wrappers," suggested Terri. "Then we could use math to find the slices in an 'average' loaf of bread."

"Your ideas sound good so far," said the teacher. "As Dianne suggested, it would be good to bring your data back by Monday. However, I also think you need to define what you mean by bread. Is raisin toast bread? Are English muffins bread? What about biscuits?"

"I think all of these things should be counted as bread," stated Andrew.

"I agree, and also hamburger and hot dog buns," suggested Matthew.

"I think you are about ready to begin," said the teacher. "I'm going to divide the class into four groups. Each group will be gathering similar data so that we can compare findings next week. Tessa will be the leader for group A, Matthew for group B, Andrew for group C, and Sara for group D. Now, please get your groups together and decide what each person will do. Also decide how your group will keep records."

© 1990 by The Center for Applied Research in Education, Inc.

Our Daily Bread
Problem Set A

Directions: Read the story "Our Daily Bread." You will need to use story information to solve some of these problems. You will also need to gather information from students in your class, other people in your town, your home and one or more grocery stores. Write your answer sentences below each problem. Where possible, use the back of this page or a separate sheet of paper to show your work. You may wish to use a calculator with some problems.

1. Will everyone eat the same amount of bread in a day? Ask 10 people in your class how many slices of bread they each eat each day. Include all bread items such as hamburger buns (2 slices), small biscuits (1 slice), English muffins (1 slice per half), and so on. Then add up all the slices and divide by 10 to get an "average" for those students.

2. Ask 10 or more people in your town to estimate how much bread they each eat in a day. Remind them that muffins, biscuits, buns, and the like count as bread. Add up all the slices and divide by the number of people. This will give you another "average." How does this "average" compare with the "average" you found when you asked the students in your class?

3. How many slices are there in an "average" loaf of bread? Count the slices in 5 or more different kinds of bread loaves. Use the suggestion that Terri gave in the story; count the slices through the clear plastic wrappers. Then divide the total number of slices by the number of loaves to get your "average."

4. You now have data about the "average" number of slices in a bread loaf. You know the "average" amount of bread some people eat per day. Also find the population information in the story. Use this data to estimate how many loaves of bread the people in the "Our Daily Bread" story eat per day.

5. How much does a loaf of bread cost? Find the prices of 5 or more different kinds of bread. Add all of the prices together and divide the total by the number of different breads. This will give you an "average" price. Use this "average" price to estimate how much the people in the "Our Daily Bread" story would spend per day on bread.

Our Daily Bread
Problem Set B

Directions: Read the story "Our Daily Bread." You will need to use story data to solve some of these problems. You will also need to gather information from students in your class, other people in your town, your home and one or more grocery stores. Write your answer sentences below each problem. Where possible use the back of this page or a separate sheet of paper to show your work. You may wish to use a calculator with some problems.

1. How much bread does each person eat in a day? To obtain an estimate, ask the teacher and at least 10 people in your class how many slices of bread they each eat each day. Include all bread items such as hamburger buns (2 slices), small biscuits (1 slice), English muffins (1 slice per half), and so on. Then add up all the slices and divide by the number of people asked, to get an "average" or "mean" for those students.

2. Ask 10 to 20 people in your town to estimate how much bread they each eat in a day. Remind them that muffins, biscuits, buns, and the like count as bread. Make a chart of your findings and use it to determine the "mean," the "median," and the "mode." How does this "mean" compare with the "mean" you found when you asked the students in your class? Is the "mean" the best "measure of central tendency" to make use of in this type of situation, or would the "median" or the "mode" be better?

3. How many slices are there in an "average" loaf of bread? Count the slices in at least 10 different kinds of bread loaves and keep a chart of your findings. Use the suggestion that Terri gave in the story; count the slices through the clear plastic wrappers. Determine the "mean," the "median," and the "mode." Which "measure of central tendency" is probably most useful in situations such as this?

4. You now have data about the "mean," "median" and "mode" for the number of slices in a bread loaf and the amount of bread a number of people eat per day. Use this data, together with the given population information, to estimate how many loaves of bread the people in the "Our Daily Bread" story eat per day. Compare your results when you use "means" only, with those for "medians" only and with those for "modes" only.

5. How much does a loaf of bread cost? Find the prices of 10 or more different kinds of bread. Then divide to get an "average" or "mean" price. Also, determine the price "median" and the price "mode." Use these prices to estimate how much the people in the "Our Daily Bread" story may spend per day on bread. Tell which price outcome you think is the most likely, and why.

Name _____   Period _____ Date _____

Our Daily Bread
Problem Set C

Directions: Read the story "Our Daily Bread." You will need to use story data to solve some of these problems. You will also need to gather information from students in your class, other people in your town, your home and one or more grocery stores. Write your answer sentences below each problem. Where possible use the back of this page or a separate sheet of paper to show your work. You may wish to use a calculator with some problems.

1. How much bread does each person eat in a day? To obtain an estimate, ask the teacher and at least 10 people in your class how many slices of bread they each eat each day. Include all bread items such as hamburger buns (2 slices), small biscuits (1 slice), English muffins (1 slice per half), and so on. Then add up all the slices and divide by the number of people asked, to get an "average" or "mean" for those students.

2. Ask 10 to 20 people in your town to estimate how much bread they each eat in a day. Remind them that muffins, biscuits, buns, and the like count as bread. Chart your findings and determine the "mean," the "median" and the "mode." How does this "mean" compare with the "mean" you found when you asked the students in your class? Is the "mean" the best "measure of central tendency" to make use of in this type of situation, or would the "median" or the "mode" be better?

3. How many slices are there in an "average" loaf of bread? Count the slices in at least 10 different kinds of bread loaves and keep a chart of your findings. (Use the suggestion that Terri gave in the story.) Determine the "mean," the "median" and the "mode." Which "measure of central tendency" is probably most useful in situations such as this?

4. You now have data about the "mean," "median" and "mode" for the number of slices in a bread loaf and the amount of bread a number of people eat per day. Use this data, together with population information for your own community, to estimate how many loaves of bread the people in your town eat per day. Compare your results when you use "means" only, with those for "medians" only and/or with those for "modes" only.

5. What types of bread do most people prefer? Is wheat bread more popular than English muffins? Do more people purchase bread with high fiber content or bread made from processed enriched wheat flour? Does your favorite grocery store sell more hamburger or hot dog buns? Work in a team of three or four to devise as many questions about the differences in bread as you can think of, and then find the answers to them. Finally, chart or graph your results, and present your findings to the class.

"There! We're finished! Thanks so much for helping me bag these leaves. It would have taken me all day," said Tessa. "I've got a great idea," she added. "Let's go down to Mr. Murphy's store and get a snack—my treat!"

Ryan and Jen loved Mr. Murphy's store with all the different sweets. The best part was that everything cost from a nickel to a quarter. They often went there with Tessa. Mr. Murphy greeted them as they rushed to the counter to see what they would buy.

"Forty-five cents for each of you," said Tessa. "Spend it anyway you want." Mr. Murphy helped the children decide.

While Ryan and Jen chose their candy, Tessa gave Maggie a quick call to find out what was going on later.

"OK, I should be home by 6:30 or 7:00—call me then," said Tessa. "Bye."

Ryan and Jen finally decided so they headed to the car. Tessa dropped them off and went straight home. She looked forward to the party later that night.

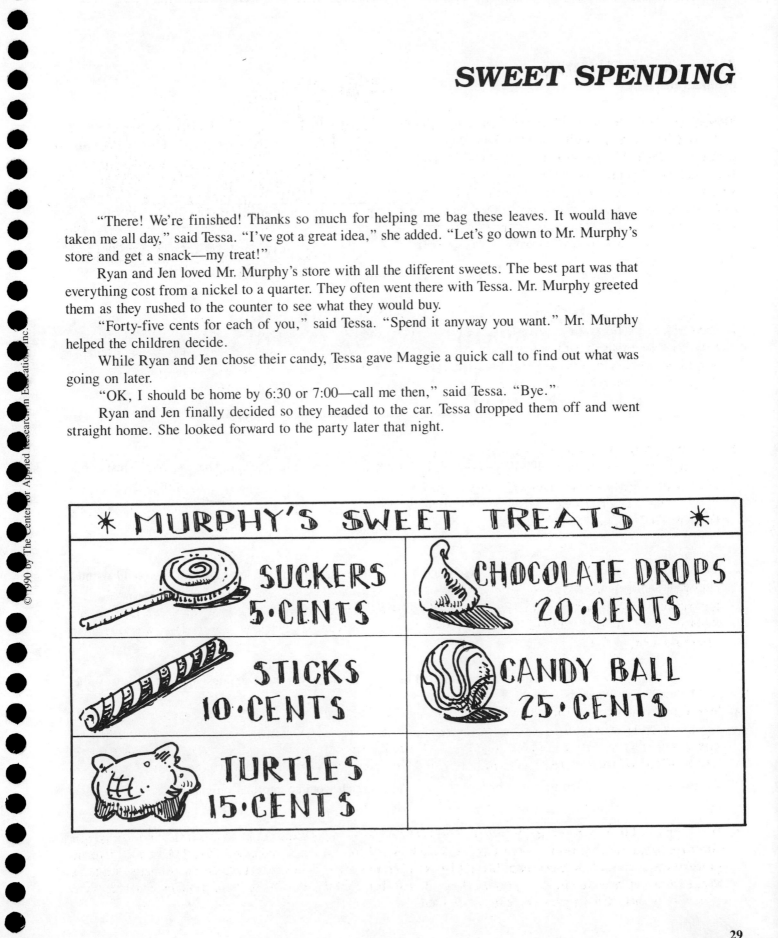

Sweet Spending
Problem Set A

Directions: First read the story "Sweet Spending." Information from the story and the illustration will help you to solve some of the problems that follow. Write your answer sentences below each problem. Where possible, use the back of this page or a separate sheet of paper to show your work.

1. Ryan decided to save 25 cents and spend the rest. List three different ways that he could have spent the rest of his money.

2. Jen wanted to buy a piece of candy for herself and her two friends. What is the least amount she could spend? List what she bought.

3. If Jen wanted to buy a piece of candy for herself and her two friends, what is the greatest amount of money she could spend? List what she bought.

4. List two other ways for Jen to buy 3 pieces of candy. How much would each total purchase cost?

Sweet Spending
Problem Set B

Directions: First read the story "Sweet Spending." Information from the story and the illustration will help you to solve some of the problems that follow. Write your answer sentences below each problem. Where possible, use the back of this page or a separate sheet of paper to show your work.

1. Ryan has 25 cents left in his pocket. List all the possible coin combinations that he might have; do not include pennies.

2. List three ways in which Jen could spend 35 cents, and only buy 3 pieces of candy.

3. If you had 45 cents to spend and wanted to spend it all, list 5 different combinations of candy that you could buy.

Sweet Spending
Problem Set C

Directions: First read the story "Sweet Spending." Information from the story and the illustration will help you to solve some of the problems that follow. Write your answer sentences below each problem. Where possible, use the back of this page or a separate sheet of paper to show your work.

1. List 4 different ways in which you could spend less than 35 cents and buy at least 2 pieces of candy.

2. List 4 different coin combinations that Ryan or Jen received to make 45 cents; do not include pennies.

3. List 8 combinations of candy that you could buy with 45 cents and have no money left.

THE COUNTY FAIR

Tessa approached Maggie after school one day. "I've got two free passes to the fair, and I was wondering if you'd like to go with me?" she asked.

"I would, but I've already told Michael that I'd go with him," said Maggie. "Maybe you could get a date too, and then we could all go together"

"I would like to go with Dan, but he's so shy he'll never ask me," admitted Tessa.

"I think Michael would ask him, if you'd like," suggested Maggie.

"Well, I really do think it would be fun to go with Dan, and Michael, and you," said Tessa. "But would Dan think I was too pushy if we had Michael ask him?"

"Let me ask Michael what he thinks," suggested Maggie. "If he thinks it is all right, I'll have him go ahead and ask Dan."

The next day the two girls met on the way to school. "Michael asked Dan last night, and it's all set for Saturday," announced Maggie.

"That's really great!" responded Tessa. "I didn't know if I should have let Michael ask Dan, but now I'm sure happy I did!"

"There is one small problem, though," said Maggie. "Both guys are kind of broke, so I said that maybe we could split the costs. Would that be OK with you?"

"I've got a little money saved ahead," said Tessa. "How much do you think it will cost each of us?"

"I'm not certain, but if you can walk home with Michael and Dan and me today, we can talk about it on the way," suggested Maggie.

After the last bell, they all met in front of the school. At first they talked about a lot of other things, but finally Michael mentioned the fair costs. "I'm really pretty broke," he admitted. "Since I started driving the family car the insurance went up $182.00. My dad said I had to pay that extra amount. It took almost four-fifths of what I had saved. If we go to the fair, about all I can afford is to pay for myself."

"Why don't we each pay our own expenses," suggested Tessa. "Then we can all go and have a good time!"

"What do you think it will cost each of us?" asked Dan.

"I know that it is $2.00 each to get in the gate," said Maggie. "Tessa has two free passes, but we'll need to buy two more."

"I heard that the ride tickets are $5.00 for 15 tickets, and most of the rides take 4 tickets," volunteered Michael.

"Don't forget, that if Michael drives his dad's car, it will take some gas," reminded Dan. "It's 27 miles from here to the fairgrounds."

"We might want some money for the games too," said Maggie. "This year I hope I can win a teddy bear!"

"And don't forget about food and drinks," reminded Michael. "I can almost taste those egg rolls and the caramel apples. Yum, yum!"

The County Fair
Problem Set A

Directions: Before attempting these problems read "The County Fair." You will need to use story information to solve some of them. Write your answer sentences below each problem. Where possible, use the back of this page or a separate sheet of paper to show your work. Also, where it helps, use a calculator.

1. Maggie, Michael, Tessa and Dan decided to split most of the fair costs as evenly as possible. They started by each contributing $1.00 for gas. When they got to the fairgrounds, they discovered that they had to pay $1.50 for parking. Then, before they could get into the fairgrounds, they had to purchase 2 more gate passes. To the nearest dime, what was each person's share of these expenses?

2. They agreed to start with each couple going on 2 rides. They walked around and looked at each before deciding. Those that Maggie and Michael selected were 3 tickets for one ride, and 4 tickets for the other. Both rides that Dan and Tessa picked were 4 tickets. How many tickets will they need for all the rides?

3. Maggie wanted to play the game where players attempt to win prizes by tossing dimes into milk bottles. If one dime lands in a bottle, a small prize is given. If two do so, a miniature bear is won. With three winning tosses, the player wins a large teddy bear. Maggie wanted a large teddy bear. Michael suggested that they watch some other players for a while, and see how many tosses it would take for each to win a prize. Several gave up before winning, but finally there were 4 winners of large teddy bears. One player had tossed 89 times, another 112, a third only 27, and the last 141. What did it cost each of these players?

4. Michael said that he was getting hungry and Maggie agreed. He ordered two egg rolls and a root beer. Maggie had a small coke and a hot dog. What was the total cost of their food?

Hot dogs	$1.25	Egg rolls	$1.50
Hamburgers	$1.75	BBQ ribs	$2.75
Steak sandwiches	$2.50	Pizza—whole	$8.95
Cokes	$.50 & $1.00	—slice	$1.25
Milk	$ .75	Root beer	$ .75

5. Estimate the total amount of money you think Tessa, Dan, Maggie and Michael will spend to go to the fair. Tell how you got your estimate.

The County Fair
Problem Set B

Directions: Before attempting these problems read "The County Fair." You will need to use story information to solve some of them. Write your answer sentences below each problem. Where possible, use the back of this page or a separate sheet of paper to show your work. Also, where it helps, use a calculator.

1. Maggie, Michael, Tessa and Dan decided to split most of the fair costs as evenly as possible. They started by each contributing $1.00 for gas. When they got to the fairgrounds, they discovered that they had to pay $1.50 for parking. Then, before they could get into the fairgrounds, they had to purchase 2 more gate passes. To the nearest dime, what was each person's share of these expenses?

2. They agreed to start with each couple going on 2 rides. They walked around and looked at each before deciding. The rides they decided on all happened to cost 3 tickets each. How many tickets will they need to purchase, and what will the total be?

3. Maggie wanted to play the game where players attempt to win prizes by tossing dimes into milk bottles. If one dime lands in a bottle, a small prize is given. If two do so, a miniature bear is won. With three winning tosses, the player wins a large teddy bear. Maggie wanted a large teddy bear. Michael suggested that they watch some other players for a while, and see how many tosses it would take for each to win a prize. Several gave up before winning, but finally there were 4 winners of large teddy bears. One player had tossed 89 times, another 112, a third only 27, and the last 141. If Maggie wins after throwing the "mean" of these four players, what will it cost her to win a large teddy bear?

4. Michael said that he was getting hungry and the others agreed. He ordered two egg rolls and a root beer. Maggie had a small coke and a hot dog. Dan ordered two slices of pizza at one stand and went to the other and got a large coke. Tessa ate a hamburger and milk. What was the total cost of their food?

Hot dogs	$1.25	Egg rolls	$1.50
Hamburgers	$1.75	BBQ ribs	$2.75
Steak sandwiches	$2.50	Pizza—whole	$8.95
Cokes	$.50 & $1.00	—slice	$1.25
Milk	$ .75	Root beer	$ .75

5. Calculate, as closely as you can, the amount of money each person has spent at the fair so far. Also estimate the total amount of money you think Tessa, Dan, Maggie and Michael will spend by the time they get home. Explain how you got your estimate.

The County Fair
Problem Set C

Directions: Before attempting these problems read "The County Fair." You will need to use story information to solve some of them. Write your answer sentences below each problem. Where possible, use the back of this page or a separate sheet of paper to show your work. Also, where it helps, use a calculator.

1. Maggie, Michael, Tessa and Dan decided to split most of the fair costs as evenly as possible. They started by each contributing $1.00 for gas. When they got to the fairgrounds, they discovered that they had to pay $1.50 for parking. Then, before they could get into the fairgrounds, they had to purchase 2 more gate passes. To the nearest dime, what was each person's share of these expenses?

2. They agreed to start with each couple going on 2 rides. They walked around and looked at each before deciding. The rides they decided on all happened to cost 3 tickets. How many tickets will they need to purchase? What is the most economical way to purchase them? What will the total cost for the tickets be?

3. Maggie wanted to play the game where players attempt to win prizes by tossing dimes into milk bottles. If one dime lands in a bottle, a small prize is given. If two do so, a miniature bear is won. With three winning tosses, the player wins a large teddy bear. Michael suggested that they watch some other players for a while, and see how many tosses it would take for each to win a prize. Several gave up before winning, but finally there were 5 winners of large teddy bears. One player had tossed 145 times, another 112, a third only 27, the fourth 145, and the last 89. Maggie decided to try for a large teddy bear. If Maggie wins after throwing the "mean" of these 5 players, what will it cost her to win a large teddy bear? If she wins after throwing the "median," what will her cost be? If she has to throw the "mode," what will the total cost come to?

4. Michael said that he was getting hungry and the others agreed. He ordered two egg rolls and a root bear. Maggie had a small coke and a hot dog. Dan ordered two slices of pizza at one stand and went to the other and got a large coke. Tessa ate a hamburger and milk. Sales tax of 6% was also charged. What was the total cost of their food.

Hot dogs	$1.25	Egg rolls	$1.50
Hamburgers	$1.75	BBQ ribs	$2.75
Steak sandwiches	$2.50	Pizza—whole	$8.95
Cokes	$.50 & $1.00	—slice	$1.25
Milk	$ .75	Root beer	$ .75

5. Calculate, as closely as you can, the amount of money each person has spent at the fair so far. Also estimate the total amount of money you think Tessa, Dan, Maggie and Michael will spend by the time they get home. Explain how you got your estimate.

SQUARE CENTS

"When is that bus going to get in?" asked Jen. "I'm getting tired of waiting."

"Soon, I hope," said Tessa. "The agent said there'd been a delay. Maggie's bus should get here soon."

"Well I'm bored," said Jen. "Don't you have any games we could play?"

"Here's a bunch of coins, Jen. Take three pennies, three nickels and three dimes. See if you can arrange them in a square so that every row and column has only one of each coin."

"Oh, Tessa, you always have the dumbest games! I hate to admit it, but I kind of think they're fun," said Jen.

Tessa was so anxious to see Maggie. She was coming into town for a short visit. Tessa hadn't seen her for several months. She was glad that Jen seemed satisfied with the game for now. "When will that bus get here?" Tessa thought. "We've got so much to do and talk about!"

"Tessa, how's this? I think I won the game!" shouted Jen.

"Great," said Tessa, "now are you really ready for a challenge? I'll keep thinking of games until the bus gets here. That should make the time go faster!"

© 1990 by The Center for Applied Research in Education, Inc.

Square Cents
Problem Set A/B/C

Directions: First read the story "Square Cents." You will need some coins, tokens or other manipulatives to help in solving some of the problems below. Information from the story will also help to solve some of the problems. Write your answer sentences below each problem. Where possible, use the back of this page or a separate sheet of paper to show your work.

1. Can you show how Jen arranged the coins to win the game?

2. Compare your coin square with your partner or group. Share the method you used to arrange the coins.

3. Tessa's next game for Jen was to arrange four different kinds of coins (or tokens) into a square, using four of each kind. This time Jen must also work with the diagonals of the square. Every row and column and diagonal could only have one of each coin (token). Use your coins (tokens) and show how Jen could have arranged them.

4. Share your arrangement with your partner or group. Is there more than one possible arrangement? How many different arrangements did your group (or class) find?

5. Discuss your method for arranging the coins (tokens) with your partner or group. Did the same method you used for Problem 1 of this set work for Problem 4? Tell your group or partner about any new methods you discovered.

6. Could you now take five different kinds of coins (tokens) and arrange them into a square? Each row, column, and diagonal must contain only one coin (token) of each kind.

7. How many different arrangements did your group or class find for Problem 6? Were any new methods discovered? Discuss them as a group.

HALLOWEEN

Tessa, Michael and the clown drove to the Goblin Gala together.
Jake gave the hobo his old shoes to wear.
The clown borrowed the costume from Jake.
Michael was not the hobo or the rabbit.
Tessa helped fix the rabbit's ears.
Erin gave the witch a black hat.
Who was wearing the rabbit costume?

"What is this?!?" asked Artie. "How are the readers ever going to figure this out? I asked you to do a story on the Goblin Gala. What do you call this?"

"I decided that this paper needs some really fun and different articles. Maybe we could make a contest out of it. Get some prizes donated and give them to the winners. Don't make me do some boring article telling the details that everyone already knows. You know that over 400 kids went to the Gala this year. Let's try it and see how it goes," begged Maggie.

"Well, what if I don't even know how to solve it?" he asked. "How can we tell who the winner will be?"

"Let me show you a way to solve it. Make a clue box like this—" she drew quickly.

MAGGIE'S CLUE BOX

	Clown	Rabbit	Hobo	Witch
Tessa				
Michael				
Jake				
Erin				

"Label one side with the names of the people in the clues. Label the top of the box with the types of costumes they wore," she said.

"Now, read each clue and mark on the box what information it tells you. For example, the first clue tells you that neither Tessa nor Michael was the clown (since they drove together with the person wearing the clown costume). To show that neither one of them is the clown put an × in the box next to their name, in the clown column.

"The second clue tells that Jake is not the hobo, since he gave that person some shoes to wear. So now the box looks like this.

MAGGIE'S CLUE BOX

	Clown	*Rabbit*	*Hobo*	*Witch*
Tessa	X			
Michael	X			
Jake			X	
Erin				

"Try now to do the next few clues. You'll see that this method really helps to figure out the puzzle," she said. "I'll get going now and get some prizes. I think this could be a fun contest."

Name _____   Period _____ Date _____

Halloween
Problem Set A/B

Directions: First read the story "Halloween." Information from the story and the clue boxes will help you to solve some of the problems that follow. Write your answer as a sentence below each problem and fill in the clue box if necessary. Where possible, use the back of this page or a separate sheet of paper to show your work.

1. Copy the clue box at the end of the story. Mark the box showing the information given in the next two clues.

2. After marking the clue box in Problem 1 of this set, what conclusions can you draw about the costumes worn by Erin and Michael?

3. Use the information from Problems 1 and 2 of this set and the clue box above. Draw a circle in the box showing the costume that Erin wore. If she is the clown, then what costumes was she not wearing? Draw an × in each of those boxes.
   Now mark the box to indicate what costume Michael wore. Also, if you know which costume that Michael wore, then mark an × in the boxes showing that no one else wore the costume.

4. Continue marking the clue box above, using the remaining clues in the story. Who was wearing the rabbit costume?

Halloween
Problem Set C

Directions: First read the story "Halloween." Information from the story and the clue boxes will help you to solve some of the problems in this set. Write your answer as a sentence below each problem and fill in the clue box as necessary. Where possible, use the back of this page or a separate sheet of paper to show your work.

1. Copy and complete the clue box started for you in the story. Use the remaining clues and mark the box. Use the following hints to help in marking the box:
   (a) An × indicates that a person did not wear that costume.
   (b) An 0 indicates that a person wore that costume.
   (c) When you know which costume a person wore, mark the clue box showing that no one else wore the same costume.

   Draw the clue box here:

2. Use the clues below and a clue box to find out what costumes Donna, Craig, Artie, Greg and Sandy wore to the Goblin Gala.
   (a) No one wore a costume that started with the same first letter as their name.
   (b) Greg and Sandy picked up the dancer on their way to the gala.
   (c) Craig loaned the scarecrow a flannel shirt.
   (d) Sandy was neither the ghost nor the artist.
   (e) Donna danced with the scarecrow and the artist.
   (f) Artie drove home with the dancer and the cowboy.

   Draw the clue box here:

AMAZING MEASUREMENTS

The last person just made it to his seat as the bell rang. The teacher waited for everyone's attention. She began, "Ancient measurements are really interesting. Hold one of your arms in front of you. Bend the elbow, but keep your hand outstretched. Look at the distance from your elbow to the tip of your middle finger. This measure was used in building all of the Egyptian pyramids. Put one hand flat on your desk. Keep your fingers together and look at the width. This very old measurement is still being used to measure horses. Another ancient measure was based on the length of the left feet of the first 16 men out of church on a certain Sunday. Does anyone know what any of these three measurements were called?"

"The first measurement you talked about was a cubit. I think it was mentioned in the Bible story about Noah's Ark," suggested Matthew.

"I know the second one! Sometimes we use hands to measure horses," said Tessa.

"Does anyone know the name for the measure of the left feet of 16 men?" asked the teacher. "It is a rod. Also, a rod is supposed to equal 8 cubits, or 16 spans, or a double fathom. These are some other very old measures. Many early measures were based on parts of the human body. Why do you suppose body parts were used? Why didn't they use rulers and other measuring devices?"

"Was it because people didn't always have rulers? But they always had their body parts with them. I know that I sometimes use parts of my body to make approximate measurements," said Dave.

"That's a good deduction," said the teacher. "Body parts were often used in ancient times. They continue to be used for many types of measurement today. In fact, for today's math you will need to use your own body to measure some things at school or at home. You will also need to find the meanings for a number of ancient measurements like fathoms and barleycorns. You already know that the cubit is the distance from the elbow to the tip of your middle finger. So your first task will be to find out how many cubits long and wide our room is."

Amazing Measurements
Problem Set A

Directions: First read the story "Amazing Measurements." Information from the story will help you to solve some of these problems. You will also need to find the meanings for some measurements from math books, encyclopedias, and so on. In addition, one or more boxes of paper clips will be needed. Write your answer sentences below each problem.

1. "Cubit" measurement was used when building the Egyptian pyramids. About how many inches long is a cubit? Measure the length and width of the classroom in cubits.

2. The "fathom" was an ancient Egyptian measurement. It is still in use throughout the world. How long is a fathom? Where will you find fathoms being used today?

3. The "mille" or "statute mile" was set by the Romans. How did they decide on the length of the mile? How many feet long is the mile we use today? What building or landmark is about one mile from the school?

4. The "inch" was also invented by the Romans. It was compared with thumbs, barleycorns, poppyseeds, and even human hairs. Find out as much as you can about each of these inch standards. Share your findings with the class.

5. In the late 1600s the metric measurement system was proposed. Today all but one of the industrial nations use it. Which nation is not using the "meter" in industry? Make a meter chain with paper clips. Measure the length and width of the classroom with it.

Amazing Measurements
Problem Set B

Directions: First read the story "Amazing Measurements." Information from the story will help you to solve some of these problems. You will also need to find the meanings for some measurements from math books, encyclopedias, and so on. In addition, one or more boxes of paper clips will be needed. Write your answer sentences below each problem.

1. The basic unit of measure for building the Egyptian pyramids was the "cubit." What is the perimeter, in cubits, of an Egyptian pyramid? About how many inches long is a cubit?

2. Nautical measurement still includes the ancient Egyptian "fathom." About how long is a fathom? Explain how one span, one fathom and one cable's length are related.

3. The "mille" or "statute mile" that the Romans set is still used today. How did they decide on the length of the mile? How do a "statute mile" and a "meridian mile" compare? What buildings or landmarks are about one statute mile from the school? What is about one meridian (nautical) mile from your school?

4. Find out what Irish thumbs, English barleycorns, and the more precise use of poppyseeds and human hairs had to do with the inch. Share your findings with the class.

5. Here are some other very early measurements. Use resource books to find as much as you can about them. Construct several of these measurement units with paper clip chains. Share your findings with the class.

span   palm   rod   yard   furlong   league   acre

Amazing Measurements
Problem Set C

Directions: First read the story "Amazing Measurements." Information from the story will help you to solve some of these problems. You will also need to find the meanings for some measurements from math books, encyclopedias, and so on. In addition, one or more boxes of paper clips will be needed. Write your answer sentences below each problem.

1. The basic unit of measure for building the Egyptian pyramids was the "cubit." What is the distance around an Egyptian pyramid? How does this perimeter relate to the "meridian mile"?

2. Nautical measurement still includes the ancient Egyptian "fathom." Approximately how long is a fathom? Explain the nautical unit system that is used today.

3. The "mille" or "statute mile" that the Romans established is still used today. How did the Romans decide on the length of the "mille" or "statute mile"? How do a "statute mile" and a "nautical mile" compare? How was the nautical (meridian) mile derived?

4. Find out what Irish thumbs, English barleycorns, and the more precise use of poppyseeds and human hairs had to do with the inch. Share your findings with the class.

5. Use references to find as much as you can about the following measurement units. Construct several of them with paper clip chains. Share your findings with the class.

ell   span   rod   furlong   league   chain   acre

cord   board foot   peck   gill   hogshead   long ton

THE METRIC AIRPLANE CONTEST*

Tessa and Dan were teasing each other as they came into the classroom. When they looked up, they noticed that the teacher had put a metric chart on the chalkboard. "What is Mr. Kenyon going to have us do metrically today?" Tessa wondered aloud.

"I sure don't know! But he did say that we would each be constructing something," replied Dan.

METRIC LINEAR MEASUREMENTS

Value	Prefix	Symbol	Linear Measure
1,000	kilo-	km	kilometer
100	hecto-	hm	hectometer
10	deca-	dam	decameter
1		m	meter
0.1	deci-	dm	decimeter
0.01	centi-	cm	centimeter
0.001	milli-	mm	millimeter

Mr. Kenyon waited for attention. "First, we need to have a short review of metric length measurements," he said. "Then, each of you will be constructing paper airplanes. For the remainder of today's class period and most of tomorrow's, we will be doing paper airplane mathematics.

"OK, let's begin the review. How long is a meter? Andrew?"

"A meter is 100 centimeters long," responded Andrew.

"That's correct of course. What I really want to know is whether each of you remembers the approximate length of a meter. Hold your hands in the air, about a meter apart. Keep them in exactly that position while I get a meter

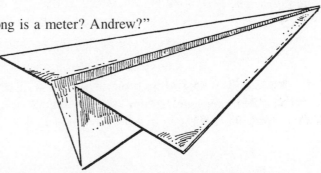

stick. Let me quickly check each of your meter estimates. You are all very close. Great!

"Now, someone show me a body part that is about one centimeter? Tessa?"

"The fingernail on my little finger is about one centimeter across," said Tessa.

"You're correct," responded Mr. Kenyon. "How would you write the term centimeter on your math paper?"

"Well, I might put the whole word or I could just write 'cm,' " said Tessa.

"Wouldn't you write 'cm' and a period?" asked the teacher.

"No, just 'cm' since it's a symbol, rather than an abbreviation," answered Tessa.

"A good explanation," said Mr. Kenyon. "OK, who can point out something that is a decameter?"

*James L. Overholt, *Dr. Jim's Elementary Math Prescriptions: Activities/Aids/Games to Help Children Learn Elementary Mathematics.* Copyright © 1978 by Scott, Foresman and Company, p. 188. Used by permission.

"OK, but how many meters is that?" asked the teacher.

"The chart on the board says that deca- means 10. So a decameter is 10 meters," responded Larry.

"Great! And next, where do we use kilometers?" asked the teacher.

"So we might make use of kilometers when traveling in an automobile. How many meters are in a kilometer? Also, is a kilometer longer or shorter than a mile?" asked Mr. Kenyon.

"A kilometer has 1,000 meters and it's shorter than a mile. Actually it's about 6/10 of a mile," volunteered Joseph.

The review session continued for several more minutes. Then Mr. Kenyon said, "OK, it's time to start the 'Metric Paper Airplane Contest.' You will each receive several sheets of typing paper. With them you may construct as many airplanes as you wish. However, each person may enter only one airplane in Category A and one in Category B. Category A is for those airplanes attempting to fly the farthest. Category B airplanes will try to land on a target that is 10 meters away. There is, however, one further requirement. Before an airplane may be entered in the contest, a plan for it must be submitted to me. The plan must include:

1. A sketch of the airplane.

2. Length of the plane.

3. Width at the tail.

4. Depth at the tail.

5. Area of the wing surfaces.

6. Notation of special features.

7. Record of greatest distances flown during testing.

8. Record of test flights for accuracy.

9. Any other important information."

Mr. Kenyon allowed time for a short class discussion about "the best ways" to make paper airplanes. Not everyone agreed, but a lot of good ideas were shared. After a short time the paper was passed out. Everyone began designing, folding and cutting out their paper airplanes.

Metric Airplane Contest
Problem Set A/B/C

Directions: First read "The Metric Airplane Contest" story. It will provide information needed for some of these questions. You will also need some typing paper, a metric ruler, a pencil and scissors.

1. Use your own height to review some common metric measurements. With a meter stick, find how tall you are. Write your centimeter height on this chart. Also figure your height for each of the other listed measurements.

_____	kilometers
_____	hectometers
_____	decameters
_____	meters
_____	decimeters
_____	centimeters
_____	millimeters

2. Choose the best metric unit (mm, cm, dm, m, dam, hm or km) for each of the following situations. Measure and compute the areas. If this is not possible, give a good estimate.

   Our classroom floor is _____ sq. _____.

   The cover of my math book is _____ sq. _____.

   The basketball court covers _____ sq. _____.

   Our town has an area of _____ sq. _____.

   The sole of my shoe has an area of about _____ sq. _____.

3. Use a sheet of typing paper. What is its metric length, width, diagonal measure and area? Decide on a basic form for your first paper airplane and begin to construct it. Any folded shape is allowed. You may cut off extra material, but you may not add anything. You may construct as many airplanes as you wish, but only two may be entered in the contest.

4. There will be two categories in our Metric Airplane Contest. You may enter only one airplane in each category. Category A will include airplanes attempting to fly the greatest distance. Category B airplanes will try to land on a target that is placed 10 meters away. Before an airplane may be entered in either category, however, a plan for it must be given to the teacher. The plan must include:

   (a) A sketch of the airplane.
   (b) Length of the plane.
   (c) Width of the tail.
   (d) Depth at the tail.
   (e) Area of the wing surfaces.
   (f) Notation of special features.
   (g) Record of greatest distances flown during testing.
   (h) Record of test flights for accuracy.
   (i) Any other important information.

Metric Airplane Contest
Problem Set A/B/C (Cont'd)

5. It is time for our Metric Airplane Contest. Get ready to tally the results. Keep a record of them on charts like those that follow:

CATEGORY A: AIRPLANES FLYING THE FARTHEST

Name	Distance Flown	Features of the Plane
:	:	
:	:	

CATEGORY B: MOST ACCURATE AIRPLANES

Name	Distance From Target	Features of the Plane
:	:	
:	:	

Which of the metric airplanes flew the greatest distances? Did certain features seem to allow them to fly farther than other airplanes? If so, what features were they? Which airplanes were the most accurate in landing? Did they have features different from those flying long distances? If so, what were the differences?

*TAKE ME TO YOUR LITER**

Maggie and Michael arrived a few minutes early for math class. They saw the metric volume chart on the chalkboard. Then they noticed the plastic bottles and containers and the bucketful of water on the front table.

"It looks like Mr. Kenyon really meant it," chuckled Maggie.

"Meant what?" asked Michael.

"He said we'd be all wet if we came to math class today," Maggie reminded.

METRIC VOLUME/CAPACITY MEASUREMENTS

Value	Prefix	Symbol	Volume Measure
1,000	kilo-	kl	kiloliter
100	hecto-	hl	hectoliter
10	deca-	dal	decaliter
1		l	liter
0.1	deci-	dl	deciliter
0.01	centi-	cl	centiliter
0.001	milli-	ml	milliliter

At the start of class Mr. Kenyon said, "Today each of you will have to Take Me to Your Liter."

"That's a pretty bad joke," said Sara.

"It sounds that way, but it's really not," responded Mr. Kenyon. "First we will have a short review of the common metric volume and capacity measures. Then you will actually be using these containers and the water to try to get a liter. All right, let's begin the review. Look at the Metric Volume/Capacity Chart on the chalkboard. Which two of these volume measures are the most commonly used?"

"The liter and the milliliter are the two that most people would use," answered Dan.

"That's correct," said the teacher. "Now, how much space is occupied by a liter, and how large is a milliliter?"

"A liter is the same as a cubic decimeter," said Susan.

"That's correct, but what are some things from our daily lives that are a liter?" asked Mr. Kenyon.

"The container for a quart of milk is almost a liter," suggested Matthew.

"Sometimes my mom buys 1-liter and 2-liter bottles of soda at the grocery store," responded Terri.

"OK, these give us a pretty good idea of a liter, but what about a milliliter?" asked Mr. Kenyon.

"It only takes up about as much space as a small marble," suggested Joseph.

*James L. Overholt, *Dr. Jim's Elementary Math Prescriptions: Activities/Aids/Games to Help Children Learn Elementary Mathematics*. Copyright © 1978 by Scott, Foresman and Company, p. 189. Used by permission.

"I'll accept Joseph's estimate, but what two things did we use in class when we talked about milliliters?" questioned the teacher.

"We used medicine droppers," said Tessa. "Some of them had 'ml' stamped on them and some were marked 'cc.' I also remember that the water from a 1-milliliter medicine dropper exactly filled a hollow 1-centimeter cube. So we decided that a milliliter and a cubic centimeter had the same capacity."

"Good," responded Mr. Kenyon. "Now, who remembers how many milliliters there are in a liter? Juan?"

"I'm pretty sure there are 1,000," said Juan.

"That's correct," said the teacher. "We also need to review how many milliliters there are in each of the measures we have listed. Let's make a chart to get our information organized."

Measure	Number of Milliliters
ml	1
cl	10
dl	100
l	1,000
dal	10,000
hl	100,000
kl	1,000,000

The review session continued for several more minutes. Then Mr. Kenyon said, "It is time to start the Take Me to Your Liter Contest. I'm going to put you in teams of five. Your team will have a liter container. Each two competing teams will share a water bucket, some small metric liquid measuring devices, and three specially marked dice:

- Stickers labeled 'ml,' 'cl,' 'dl,' 'ml,' 'cl' and 'dl' have been placed on the surfaces of one of the dice.

- The stickers on the second die are labeled '+,' '−,' '+,' '+,' '−' and '+.'

- The third is a regular die with one to six dots on each of the surfaces.

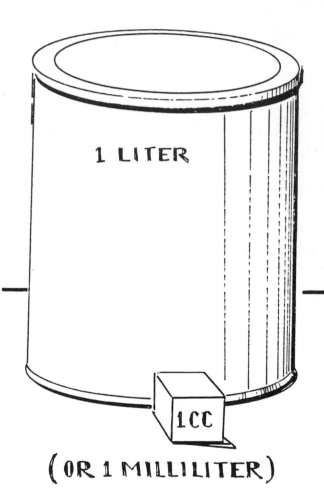

1 LITER

1 CC

(OR 1 MILLILITER)

"When it is your turn, you will roll the three dice to see how much water to add to or subtract from your team's liter container. For example, the dice you rolled might show ' + ,' 4 dots and 'dl.' You would then use one of the liquid measuring devices to add 4 deciliters (400 ml) to your team's liter container. Another time you might roll ' − ,' 6 dots and 'ml.' Then you would have to take 6 milliliters of water out of your team's liter container. However, even if your team rolls the subtract sign several times you can't have less than zero amount of water. OK, let's get into teams and get started."

Take Me to Your Liter
Problem Set A/B/C

Directions: First read the "Take Me To Your Liter" story. It will provide information needed to answer some of the questions. You will need a liter container for each team. Each two competing teams will also need a water bucket, some metric liquid measuring devices (for ml, cl, and dl), and three dice (one regular, a second marked "ml," "cl," "dl," "ml," "cl," "dl," and a third with "+," "−," "+," "+," "−," and "+").

1. As a quick review, answer the following questions. If you aren't sure, have another class member or the teacher check as you pour the indicated amounts of water into a liter container.

   1 cl = _____ ml   3 dl = _____ ml
   1 dl = _____ ml   5 cl = _____ ml
   1 l = _____ ml   5 dl = _____ ml

2. Choose the metric unit (ml, cl, dl, l, dal, hl, kl) that is most often used to measure each of the following:

   Gasoline is sometimes measured in _____.
   You can get Coke in 2 _____ bottles.
   Liquid medicine is often measured in _____.
   A quart of milk is nearly a _____.
   A cubic centimeter or cc is the same as a _____.

3. It is time for the Take Me To Your Liter Contest. Get together with your team members and get all the needed materials. Your team needs a liter container. The competing teams will share a bucket of water, liquid measuring devices and the three specially marked dice. Use the following chart to keep a record of your team's water levels. Your team will try to be the first to get a liter. The teacher will need to check each team member's records before declaring a winner. If you are on a winning team, you may cut out the Take Me To Your Liter badge and wear it for the rest of the day!

Take Me to Your Liter
Problem Set A/B/C (Cont'd)

	Dice readings:			Water added or subtracted:	Total volume:
	(1)	(2)	(3)		
1.					
2.					
3.					
4.					
5.					
6.					
7.					
8.					
9.					
10.					
11.					
12.					
13.					
14.					
15.					
16.					
17.					
18.					
19.					
20.					

GIVE A GRAM

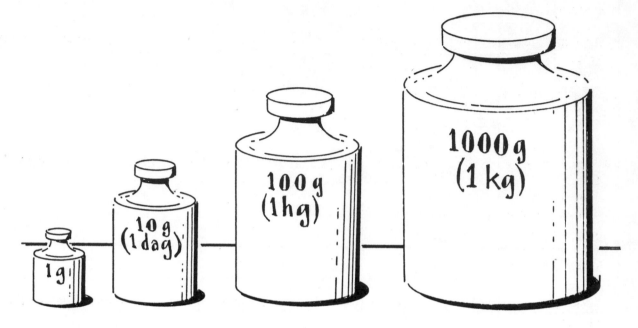

METRIC MASS (WEIGHT) MEASUREMENTS

Value	Prefix	Symbol	Mass Measure
1,000	kilo-	kg	kilogram
100	hecto-	hg	hectogram
10	deca-	dag	decagram
1		g	gram
0.1	deci-	dg	decigram
0.01	centi-	cg	centigram
0.001	milli-	mg	milligram

The teacher set out some metric items. He had a pan balance, some metric mass pieces (weights) and a metric bath scale. He said, "We've been studying about metric weight, or, more correctly, metric mass. We've also been using the chart to help with some problems. Now I want to see if you are able to use these measurements in daily life. So your assignment for tomorrow is to bring in four objects. The objects should weigh a gram, a decagram, a hectogram and a kilogram. These can be store-bought items or things from nature. Also, see if you can locate other things that measure a decigram, a centigram, and a milligram. Remember that metric consumer goods will likely be marked only in grams or kilograms. So you will need to remember, for example, that 10 grams and a decagram are the same.

"We still have about five minutes of class time. Before class is over I want everyone to come up and handle the mass pieces. This will give you some idea of which item to pick for each mass. If you'd like, you can also find your own metric mass by using the bathroom scale."

Give A Gram
Problem Set A/B/C

Directions: First read the story titled "Give a Gram." It will provide information needed to answer some of the following questions. You will also need a pan balance and metric mass pieces from 1 to 1,000 grams, or a metric scale. If available, a metric bathroom scale can be used with the final question.

1. As a quick review, answer the following questions. If you aren't sure, use the pan balance and the mass pieces, or the chart, to find out.

   1 kg = _____ g   1 g = _____ mg   500 g = _____ kg
   1 hg = _____ g   1 dg = _____ mg   2 hg   = _____ g
   1 dag = _____ g   1 cg = _____ mg   10 g   = _____ dag

2. Choose the metric unit (mg, cg, dg, g, dag, hg, kg) that is most often used to measure each of the following:

   Your own weight is measured in _____.
   Medicine is often measured in _____.
   The mass of a cubic centimeter of water is one _____.
   An automobile is weighed in _____.
   A metric ton (tonne) equals 1,000 _____.

3. What is the difference between mass and weight? Use a reference book to find out. Where are weight and mass the same?

4. Bring objects from home that you think have masses of a gram, a dekagram, a hectogram and a kilogram. Find their actual masses using the pan balance and the mass pieces, or a metric scale. Use the chart below to keep a record.

Intended Mass	Object	Actual Mass	Grams + or −
_____ 1 g _____	_____	_____	_____
_____ 1 dag _____	_____	_____	_____
_____ 1 hg _____	_____	_____	_____
_____ 1 kg _____	_____	_____	_____

5. Assume the average weight for each person in your class is 43 kg. All together, how many kg does the class weigh? Does your class weigh a metric ton? If a kilogram is approximately 2.2 pounds, how many pounds does the entire class weigh? (Optional: Divide your own weight in pounds by 2.2 to find your approximate mass in kilograms. Has your teacher provided a metric bath scale? If so, use it to check your actual mass. How does it compare with your calculated mass?)

MEASUREMENT MADNESS*

On the way to class, Tessa and Matthew talked about the Friday night game. But when they came into their math classroom the overhead projector was on. It showed a spinner surrounded by different metric measurements. Some of the measurements were rather odd.

"I wonder what the teacher is up to today?" said Matthew. "We sure have had some different kinds of assignments lately."

"I know," agreed Tessa. "I never had a teacher before who had us fly paper airplanes. And what about that Take Me to Your Liter game."

The teacher called for attention and began to give directions. "We need to have a quiz today. However, it's going to be a different kind of quiz! For this quiz everyone will use the spinner on the overhead projector. You will also need your metric ruler, and one of the Measurement Madness papers that I'm passing out now.

"Look first at the Measurement Madness paper. You will be drawing line segments on this paper according to whatever the spinner stops at. The line segments will be connected end to end. Everyone will begin at the intersection of the Start × and try first for figure A, then figure B, and so on, in order. To count, a line segment must end within a figure. Thus, a line segment that is too long may be drawn through a figure, but it doesn't count as ending within. So you must try again on the next spin. Let's consider a couple of examples so that you can understand exactly what I mean. What if the first spin pointed to 3 cm? Could you get from the Start × to figure A?"

"No, it would be too short," said Larry.

"That's correct," agreed the teacher. "However, if we were actually playing, each person would have to draw a 3-cm line segment on their paper. You would have the choice of drawing it straight toward figure A, or in some other direction. It would have to be a straight line segment, and it could not go off the paper. OK, suppose the next spin was 18 cm. What would you have to do now?"

"I'd have to connect it to the end of the 3 cm segment," said Joseph. "But, if I draw it in a straight line, wouldn't I go off the paper?"

"Yes, if you had drawn the 3-cm segment straight toward figure A, and now you continued in a straight line with the 18-cm segment, you would go off the paper," agreed the teacher. "But you can change direction at the end of each segment. In fact, in this case, you would have to."

"Does that mean that we can turn a corner, either to the left or right, at the end of every line segment?" asked Dan.

"That's correct," answered the teacher. "Are there any other questions? If not, let me explain how I'm going to give grades for this Measurement Madness activity. The first 10 people to get to the G circle get an A grade, the next 10 win a B grade, and the rest get C grades. OK, let me make the first spin so you can see how long your first line segment must be."

*James L. Overholt, *Dr. Jim's Elementary Math Prescriptions: Activities/Aids/Games to Help Children Learn Elementary Mathematics.* Copyright © 1978 by Scott, Foresman and Company, p. 186. Used by permission.

Name _____   **Period** _____   **Date** _____

Measurement Madness
Problem Set A/B/C

Directions: First read the story titled "Measurement Madness." It will explain how to use this page together with a metric ruler, a pencil and a spinner. (You may want to make a paper clip spinner and use the spinner chart shown on the next page.) As you do the activity, label each line segment with the Spin Number and the Metric Measurement; for example, if the second spin was for 14 cm, label that line segment as (2—14 cm).

 **START**

 D

 F

 A

 G

 E

 C

 B

Making A Measurement Madness Spinner

Directions: This spinner chart may be used as you play the Measurement Madness Activity. A simple spinner can be devised with a paper clip and the point of a pencil. Lay the paper clip on the chart so that one end overlaps the center point of the chart. Put your pencil point through the end loop of the paper clip and hold it on the center point of the chart. Use your other hand to flip the paper clip. The paper clip spinner will randomly point to the different measurements.

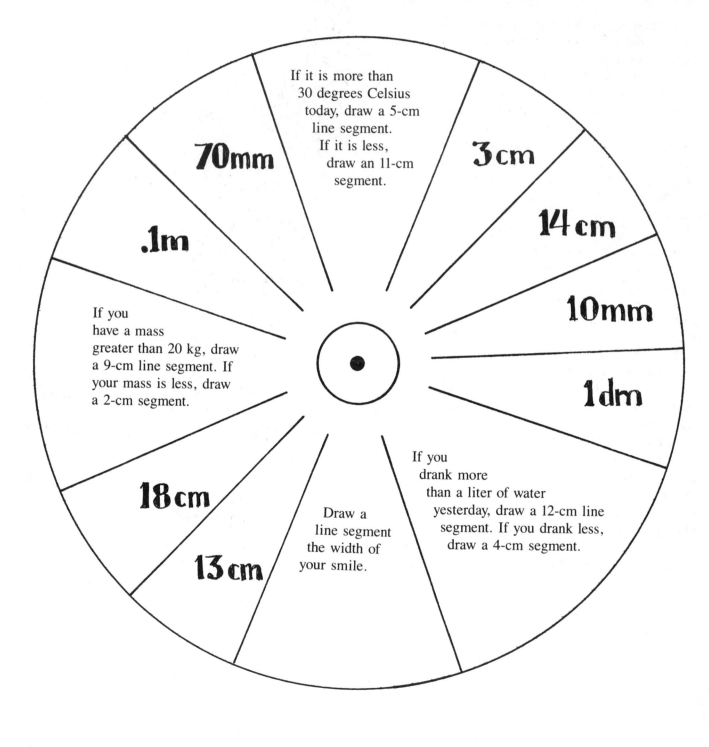

THE INVITATION

Michael saw one of his friends, Bill Brown, at the end of second period. Bill had never looked so excited.

"What's up, Bill?" he asked.

Bill was full of news. At the beginning of second period, he had walked into the band room. Both the principal, Mr. Boss, and Mr. MacNamara, the band director, were waiting. As soon as the band settled down, Mr. Boss started talking.

He said, "We have an announcement for you! Congressman Dull called this morning. You, the Central High School Band, are invited to Washington, D.C. You are invited to be in the inaugural parade on January 20."

When the yelling and screaming stopped, Mr. MacNamara asked if they wanted to go. All 70 members of the band yelled "Yeah!" and they were off again.

As Mr. MacNamara pointed out, there was much to do. Permission had to be granted. They would need to practice during Christmas vacation. At least six parent volunteers would need to go with them.

The band members were too excited to care right then. The principal picked up the baton. Mr. MacNamara grabbed a trumpet. The period ended with a wild playing of the school fight song.

During the next few days things calmed down. An "On to D.C." Committee was formed. Members were elected by the band and the band parents, and it included Mr. MacNamara.

The Invitation
Problem Set A

Directions: Read the story "The Invitation." One of the first jobs of the "On to D.C." Committee was to estimate costs. Do as they did and use your calculator. Write your answer sentences below each problem. Where possible, use the back of this page or a separate piece of paper to show your work.

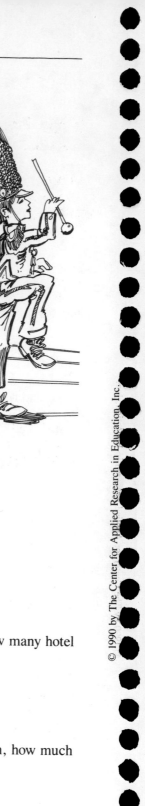

1. If all the band members, Mr. MacNamara and six volunteer parents went, how large a group would this be?

2. A travel agent could get them a group rate of $99 each way. How much would airfare for the whole group cost?

3. They couldn't march from the airport to the hotel in Washington. Chartered buses would cost $150 per trip. It would take two buses each way. How much would it cost for buses between the airport and hotel and back?

4. Five band members could share each hotel room. The adults would need another four rooms. How many hotel rooms would be needed?

5. It was decided to allow time for sightseeing. The group would stay three nights. At $50 per room, how much would the hotel cost (number of rooms × $50 × 3 nights)?

The Invitation
Problem Set B

Directions: Read the story "The Invitation." Use your calculator for the estimates, as the "On to D.C." Committee did. Write your answer sentences below each problem. Where possible, use the back of this page or a separate piece of paper to show your work.

1. In addition to the band members, Mr. MacNamara and six volunteer parents would go on the trip. A travel agent got them a group rate of $99 each way per person. What was the total airfare?

2. The group would have to travel by bus to the airport in Jackson City. Enough parents would drive so that only one bus was needed. It would cost $566 each way. The group would also need two buses each way to go from the airport to the hotel and back in Washington. These would cost $150 per one-way trip. How much would buses cost altogether.

3. The Centerville group would stay three nights in Washington. This would allow sightseeing. Band members would stay five to a room. Adults would need four more rooms. At $50 per room, how much would the hotel cost each night?

4. The hotel said they would provide dinners for two nights at $5 per person. They would also serve a $2.25 breakfast on two mornings. These would be at set times and set menus, and they would charge for everybody. What would the meals add to the hotel bill?

5. What would be the total hotel bill for three nights and four meals for the group?

The Invitation
Problem Set C

Directions: Read the story "The Invitation." Do as the "On to D.C." Committee did in making their estimates. Use your calculator. Write your answer sentences below each problem. Where possible, use the back of this page or a separate piece of paper to show your work.

1. The band will go by bus to the Jackson City Airport. Some parents will drive so that only one bus, at $566 each way, will be needed. The group airfare will be $99 each way per person. The band, Mr. MacNamara and six volunteer parents will fly. If buses between airport and hotel cost $300 each way, what will be the cost of transportation?

2. By staying three nights in Washington, they will be able to do some sightseeing. Hotel rooms will cost $50 each per night. Five band members will share each room. Four rooms will be used by adults. What will be the total cost of hotel rooms?

3. The hotel gave a package deal on meals. They will provide two breakfasts at $2.25 each and two dinners at $5.00 each. These will be at set times and set menus, and they will include the whole group. One box lunch on Inauguration Day will be provided at $1.25. What will the meals for the whole group cost?

4. What is the total cost of items listed so far?

Transportation	$_____
Hotel	$_____
Meals	$_____
Total	$_____

5. Members of the "On to D.C." Committee agreed on the following policy: Personal expenses, one lunch and food at the rest stops would be paid by individuals. Meals on the plane, of course, had no charge. If you were going as a member of the band, how much money would you need to take?

Personal	$_____
Lunch	$_____
Bus stop food	$_____
Other eating	$_____
Total	$_____

Bill Brown was a student member of the "On to D.C." Committee. He agreed with the estimate of $21,000 to cover transportation, food and rooms. The Committee faced the problems of (1) Where can we cut costs? and (2) How can we raise the money? They only had six weeks to raise the money. The final decision to accept had to be made by then. Advance reservations and deposits had to be made by then also.

The committee decided to go to the school board meeting to ask for help. It would be great if school buses could be used to go to and from the Jackson City Airport. The board was so proud of the band that they agreed. This saved $566 each way.

The six parent volunteers said they would pay for their meals. As a matter of fact, they would prefer to bring some money of their own so that they could eat at times and places of their choice. This cut costs by $15.75 per volunteer.

These savings were welcome. It still left a lot of money to be raised. November and December were not good months for car washes.

Bill and several other members of the Committee called on the editor of the Centerville *Trumpet*. He said, "With a paper named the *Trumpet*, we've got to help. We'll start a fund. Daily contributions will be listed. We'll start it off with a $500 donation."

Other Committee members listed merchants and community service groups. Members divided the list. They would use their personal contacts to ask for help. Student members would talk to the Student Council. Everyone was fired up.

On to D.C.
Problem Set A

Directions: Read the story "On to D.C." Do the problems in order. In Problem 5 show the rough proportion. Write your answer sentences below each problem. Where possible, use the back of this page or a separate piece of paper to show your work.

1. How much would be saved by using the school buses?

2. How much will expenses be cut by parent volunteers paying for their meals?

3. How much will these two cuts save?

4. What amount will still have to be raised (to the nearest dollar)?

5. The *Trumpet* showed a thermometer every day. It showed the progress of the band fund. After one week $3,320 had been raised. Fill in the proper space on the thermometer/graph.

On to D.C.
Problem Set B

Directions: Read the story "On to D.C." Do the problems in order. In Problem 4 show the rough proportion. In Problem 5 round off to the nearest dollar. Write your answer sentences below each problem. Where possible, use the back of this page or a separate piece of paper to show your work.

1. How much will be saved by using the school buses and cutting payment for parent meals?

2. What amount will still have to be raised?

3. Other donations were added to the one from the *Trumpet* during the first week. The total for the week came to $3,320. How much more had been added?

4. The *Trumpet* showed a thermometer every day to record donations. Show the amount ($3,320) by filling in the space on the thermometer/graph.

5. The committee had six weeks to raise the money. To meet their goal, how much should they average per week? Mark the goals for each of the weeks at the side of the thermometer.

On to D.C.
Problem Set C

Directions: Read the story "On to D.C." Do the problems in order. Write your answer sentences below each problem. Where possible, use the back of this page or a separate piece of paper to show your work.

1. The School Board helped with the bus to and from Jackson City. The parent volunteers decided to pay for their meals. These savings were deducted from the original $21,000 goal. To the nearest dollar, what was the new fund-raising goal? Write it at the top of the thermometer.

2. As promised, the *Trumpet* ran a thermometer/graph in each day's paper to show the amount raised to date. Show how it looked on the day the fund had $4,862 by filling in the approximate space.

3. If $4,000 came in the first week, how much per week would they need to average during the rest of the time (to the nearest dollar)?

4. The Associated Students voted $200. The Band Boosters put in all $193 of their money. The Teachers' Union donated $200. What percentage of the total fund came from these sources altogether?

5. Part way through the end of the sixth week, the fund totaled $17,822.
   As far as the Committee could see, there were no other sources of money. On the Friday of that week, an "anonymous donor" said that he or she would make up the rest. It was truly "Off to D.C.!" How much did this person give? About what percentage of the total was this?

THE JOB CRISIS

Jake finally decided to enroll in school. He made arrangements with the Burger Barn to stay on after he repaid the robbery debt. With the job, he qualified for the work program where he attended four classes each day and went to work. Tessa and Michael were excited about getting Jake interested in school again. He could graduate with three more semesters.

When Jake arrived at work Friday night he found the manager waiting for him. "Jake, could you come into my office for a minute?" he asked.

"Sure," he answered. "Is there something wrong?" said Jake.

"I'm afraid I have to change my mind on the work arrangements, at least for now," replied the manager. "I'm just overstaffed now and I don't think it's fair to hire you and cut everyone's hours," he added.

"But I need this job for my work program," Jake replied.

"I know and I'm sorry; probably things will pick up in a few months. You'll be the first one to be rehired," said the manager. "I'll call you as soon as I can get you back on the schedule," he added.

"Great," thought Jake. "Now what do I do?"

He talked it over with the Andersons that night. Mr. Anderson had been trying to get Jake to consider the carpentry trade. Mr. Anderson had his own business and needed a new man. Jake had no interest or experience in that type of work. Besides, he felt uncomfortable with the job offer since he didn't want charity.

The job would pay $3.35 per hour and Jake would work from 12:45 to 4:30 every afternoon. He would have a 15-minute break. At Mr. Anderson's suggestion Jake planned to save 25% of his pay. All this seemed fair to Jake. Besides, he had nothing else in sight.

They agreed that Jake would try it until the Burger Barn called. Then he would have the option of choosing the job he liked better. At this point at least he had a job.

© 1990 by The Center for Applied Research in Education, Inc.

The Job Crisis
Problem Set A

Directions: First read the story "The Job Crisis." Information from the story will help you to solve some of the problems below. Write your answer sentences below each problem. Where possible, use the back of this page or a separate sheet of paper to show your work.

1. Jake started to work for Mr. Anderson. How much would he make after 23 hours?

2. During the first 3 weeks Jake worked 18, 22 and 27 hours. How many hours did he average per week (to the nearest tenth of an hour)?

3. Jake earned an average of $68.25 per week with Mr. Anderson. His average pay at the Burger Barn would have been $83.00. How much less per week was he earning with Mr. Anderson? About how much less per month would you estimate? $20? $60? $80?

4. Jake had a 12-foot board that needed to be cut down to 9′7″. How much had to be cut off?

5. Jake cut a 40′ strip of molding into 7′ pieces. How many pieces did he have? How long was the remaining piece?

The Job Crisis
Problem Set B

Directions: First read the story "The Job Crisis." Information from the story will help you to solve some of the problems below. Write your answer sentences below each problem. Where possible, use the back of this page or a separate sheet of paper to show your work.

1. Jake purchased 5 pounds of nails at $1.49 per pound. How much was the total charge?

2. Mr. Anderson calculated that he needed nine shingles per square foot. How many shingles would be required for 240 square feet?

3. The shingles cost $85 per box, with 100 in a box. How many boxes did he need for the job in Problem 2 of this set? What is your estimate for the price of the shingles? $900? $1,200? $1,900?

4. The lumber bill came to $827.55. How much sales tax was added? (Use a 6% sales tax.)

5. Jake deposited two checks in the bank. One was for $56.77 and the other $39.68. If Jake kept $15 for himself and put the rest in the bank, how much did he deposit?

The Job Crisis
Problem Set C

Directions: First read the story "The Job Crisis." Information from the story will help you to solve some of the problems below. Write your answer sentences below each problem. Where possible, use the back of this page or a separate sheet of paper to show your work.

1. A set of cabinets required nine doors priced at $5.99 each and six doors priced at $9.29 each. After 6% sales tax was added, what was the total cost for the doors?

2. Create a set of cabinets that use all the doors mentioned in Problem 1 of this set. Draw your creation and share it with your partner or group.

3. Jake rode his bike to school and work each day. It was 3.7 miles from home to school and 2.9 miles from school to work. If he traveled the same route to and from work, how many miles did he travel in 5 days?

4. Mr. Anderson charged $453.75 in supplies. After sales tax and the down payment of 15%, how much was the balance he owed?

5. The lumber company had a 25% discount day. Mr. Anderson's bill came to $514.66, plus tax. How much could he save by buying on sale day?

TICKETS

Michael hated selling raffle tickets. Each baseball player had fifty to sell. It was lucky for him that Mr. Samuelson offered to take some to sell at work. The prizes were OK but he didn't like asking people for money. First prize, a trip to Disneyland, included two days of unlimited food and rides, plus a nice place to stay. Coach Watson said they should tell people that the probability of winning was good. He said that would sell more tickets.

Until then Michael didn't even know what "probability" even meant. Coach Watson explained that it was the chance of being drawn for a prize. If you bought one ticket and there were one hundred sold, the chance that you would be drawn for first prize was 1/100. The more tickets a person bought, the better his chance of being drawn. Since there were more fourth prizes than others, the probability of winning a pizza was greater than any other prize.

They needed to sell lots of tickets to get the new uniforms for this season. Despite the hassle of selling the tickets, Michael knew the new uniforms would look a lot sharper than those old ones.

"No time like now to get started!" said Michael. "Who can resist a chance like this!!"

Name _____

Address _____

Phone # _____

#536

First Prize: Weekend for 4 to Disneyland
Second Prize (4 given): VCR
Third Prize (10 given): 10-speed bicycle
Fourth Prize (35 given): Jumbo pizza
   prizes donated by local merchants
Donation $2.00 to Central High School Athletics

Tickets
Problem Set A

Directions: First read the story "Tickets." Information from the story and the illustration will help you to solve some of the problems that follow. Write your answer sentences below each problem. Where possible, use the back of this page or a separate sheet of paper to show your work.

1. How many prizes would be given in all?

2. The team planned to sell $1,200 worth of tickets. How many tickets did they have to sell?

3. What fractional part of the tickets sold will win a prize?

4. The fractional part of tickets sold that win a prize shows the probability that someone will win a prize if they buy one ticket. If you bought one ticket, what is the probability of winning first prize? (*Hint:* Use Problem 2 of this set to see the total number of tickets sold.)

5. What is the probability that you will win first or second prize if you buy one ticket?

Tickets
Problem Set B

Directions: First read the story "Tickets." Information from the story and the illustration will help you to solve some of the problems that follow. Write your answer sentences below each problem. Where possible, use the back of this page or a separate sheet of paper to show your work.

1. Assume $1,200 worth of tickets were sold. What percentage of the tickets sold will win a prize?

2. What fractional part of the tickets sold will win a prize? What is the probability of winning a prize? Refer to Problem 1 of this set. Assume that all the tickets were sold.

3. What is the probability that your ticket will win first or second prize?

4. What is the probability that your ticket will win third prize?

5. Your chance of winning is doubled if you buy two tickets instead of just one. Write the following probabilities based on the purchase of two tickets:

    (a) Probability of winning first prize = _____

    (b) Probability of winning any prize = _____

    (c) Probability of not winning any prize = _____

Tickets
Problem Set C

Directions: First read the story "Tickets." Information from the story and the illustration will help you to solve some of the problems that follow. Write your answer sentences below each problem. Where possible, use the back of this page or a separate sheet of paper to show your work.

1. Assume that $1,200 worth of tickets were sold. What is the probability of winning first prize with one ticket?

2. What is the probability of winning first prize with two tickets?

3. What is the probability of winning any prize with one ticket?

4. What is the probability of winning any prize if you bought two tickets?

5. Discuss your answers to the questions above with your group. Write your method for answering the questions.

JAKE TURNS THE CORNER

You can't lose them all! Things had started to go better for Jake Burton. He had paid his debt at last. The job seemed to be going OK. The Samuelsons were great, and so were Tessa, Maggie and the others. Best of all, Jake was making friends of his own age. He decided to stay in Centerville.

Like everyone else, he had bills to pay. Jake was complaining to Charlie about the time it took just to go around paying them. He either had to hide his cash or carry it around. There were things in a catalog he wanted to buy. He had to buy a money order to pay for them.

Charlie said, "Why don't you go to the bank? You could open a checking account. It's a lot easier."

Jake said, "Who? Me? I've never had a checking account."

After thinking about it, Jake went to the bank one Friday after work. He selected a "no minimum balance" account. His only charges would be 15¢ per check. He would get a statement each month. He could then check his record against the bank's. Jake began his account by depositing $100 he had in cash.

He then got his paycheck. It looked like this:

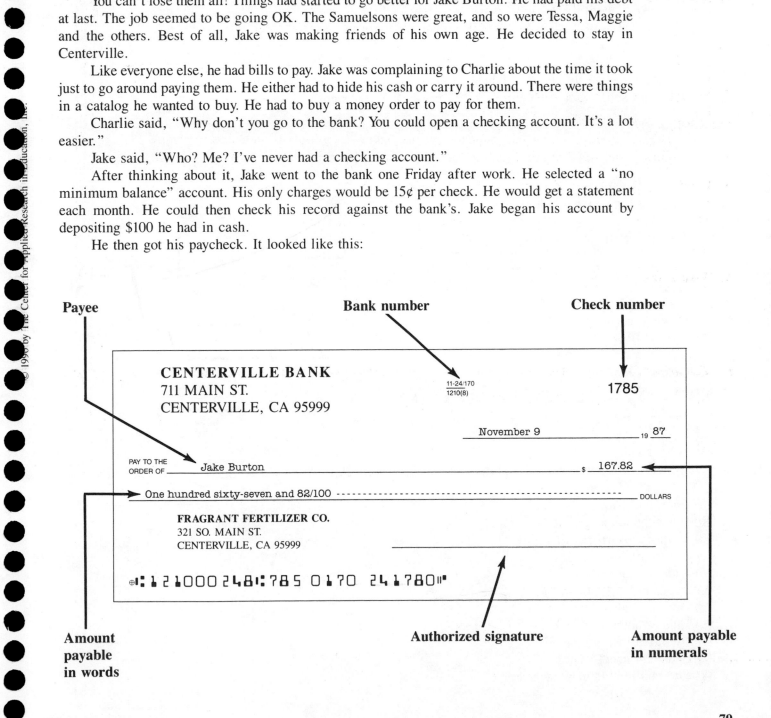

Payee   **Bank number**   **Check number**

CENTERVILLE BANK
711 MAIN ST.
CENTERVILLE, CA 95999

11-24/170
1210(8)

1785

November 9 _____ 19 87

PAY TO THE
ORDER OF ____ Jake Burton _____ $ 167.82

One hundred sixty-seven and 82/100 --- DOLLARS

FRAGRANT FERTILIZER CO.
321 SO. MAIN ST.
CENTERVILLE, CA 95999

⑯:121000248:785 0170 241780⑯

Amount payable in words   **Authorized signature**   **Amount payable in numerals**

Jake Turns the Corner
Problem Set A/B/C

Directions: Read the story "Jake Turns the Corner." Some of the problems ask for answers. Others ask you to fill out checks or deposit slips. Write directly on the checks and slips. For number 5, write your answer sentence below each problem. Where possible, use the back of this page or a separate piece of paper to show your work.

1. Jake decided to deposit his paycheck. He took it to the bank on November 10. He wrote his name on the back to endorse it. Jake also wanted $30 in cash. What was his net deposit?

2. Fill in Jake's deposit slip. Enter (a) the date, (b) the bank number of the paycheck, (c) the paycheck amount, (d) the total, (e) subtract cash received, (f) the net deposit, (g) sign Jake's name.

```
┌─────────────────────────────────────────────────────────────────────────────┐
│                          DEPOSIT SLIP                                         │
│                                                                               │
│  CENTERVILLE BANK          11-24/170   USE OTHER SIDE FOR ADDITIONAL LISTING  │
│  711 MAIN ST.              1210(8)     BE SURE EACH ITEM IS PROPERLY ENDORSED │
│  CENTERVILLE, CA 95999                 ┌──────────────────────────┬────┐      │
│                                        │      CURRENCY            │    │      │
│  DATE _____ 19 ____      │ CASH ────────────────────┤    │      │
│                                        │      COIN                │    │      │
│  _____          │ LIST CHECKS SINGLY       │    │      │
│   SIGN HERE FOR LESS CASH IN TELLER PRESENCE │                    │    │      │
│                                        │                          │    │      │
│  JAKE BURTON                           │ TOTAL FROM OTHER SIDE    │    │      │
│  123 NORTH ST.                         │ TOTAL                    │    │      │
│  CENTERVILLE, CA 95999                 │ LESS CASH RECEIVED       │    │      │
│                                        │ NET DEPOSIT              │    │      │
│  ⑉:121000248|:785 0170  241104|⑈        └──────────────────────────┴────┘      │
└─────────────────────────────────────────────────────────────────────────────┘
```

3. After making his deposit, Jake paid his rent. He wrote a check for $115. His landlady was Barbara Allan. Fill out Jake's check stub.
   (a) Enter the date
   (b) Enter the amount
   (c) To payee (Barbara Allan)
   (d) For (rent)
   (e) Old balance ($100)
   (f) Deposit (see Problem 2)
   (g) Add (e) and (f) for total
   (h) Enter amount of check
   (i) Subtract to find total
   (j) Enter 15¢ check charge
   (k) Subtract to find new balance

```
┌──────────────────────────┐
│ _____ 19 ____  │
│ 101                       │
│ $ _____   │
│ TO _____   │
│ FOR _____   │
│           │ DOLLARS │CENTS│
│ OLD       │         │     │
│ BALANCE   │         │     │
│ DEPOSITED │         │     │
│ TOTAL     │         │     │
│ THIS CHECK│         │     │
│ TOTAL     │         │     │
│ IF SPEC. CHECKING        │
│ CHECK CHARGE             │
│ NEW       │         │     │
│ BALANCE   │         │     │
└──────────────────────────┘
```

Jake Turns the Corner
Problem Set A/B/C (Cont'd)

4. Fill out the check Jake wrote to Barbara Allan. Be sure you fill in (a) the date, (b) the payee, (c) the amount in numerals, (d) the dollar amount in words, the cents amount as "no/100," (e) sign Jake's name.

CENTERVILLE BANK
711 MAIN ST.
CENTERVILLE, CA 95999

11-24/170
1210(8)

101

_____ 19 ____

PAY TO THE
ORDER OF _____ $ _____

_____ DOLLARS

JAKE BURTON
123 NORTH ST.
CENTERVILLE, CA 95999

_____

⑆:121000248⑆:785 0170 241104⑈

---

5. Jake's check was for his net pay. Fragrant Fred had taken out deductions for the following:

Social security	$ 16.79
Unemployment insurance	$ 2.38
Workmen's compensation	$ 2.38
Income tax	$ 50.63
Total deductions	$ _____
Net pay	$167.82
Gross pay	$ _____

These were listed on the paycheck stub. Add the deductions listed above. What was Jake's gross pay (net pay plus deductions)?

IT'S SIMPLY INTEREST

"I need your help," said Mr. Samuelson one night after dinner. "A man I do business with has offered me a big contract. I'll need to borrow $100,000 for supplies. I'll make a good profit when he pays me. Meanwhile, we're going to be short of money."

"How will you get the money?" Michael asked.

"I can borrow from the bank. My business property will be the security. Since I can't pay them back until the contract is over, I'll take a simple interest loan."

Mr. Samuelson went to the bank. He showed a copy of the contract to the manager. His credit was good since he had paid back earlier loans on time. He also turned over the deed to his business property.

Mr. Buck, the bank manager, said he would lend the $100,000. The interest rate would be 12%. The payment of the loan plus interest would be due in three months.

Mr. Samuelson called the man who had offered the contract. At Mr. Buck's suggestion, a lawyer looked over the contract. It seemed fair, so both parties signed.

Michael asked his father about the difference between simple and compound interest. "It's simple," his father smiled. "In simple interest, I just pay the rate for the amount of time I use the money. If it were compound, I'd also pay interest on the interest."

Name _____   **Period** _____   **Date** _____

It's Simply Interest
Problem Set A

Directions: Read the story "It's Simply Interest." Do the problems in order. Write your answer sentences below each problem. Where possible, use the back of this page or a separate piece of paper to show your work.

1. What fraction of a year is three months (or 90 days)?

2. If the 12% loan is for three months, what percentage will Mr. Samuelson actually pay as interest?

3. How much interest will he pay at the end of three months?

4. How much would he pay the bank altogether after three months (loan plus interest)?

5. How much would the interest be if the loan were for a year?

Name _____ **Period** _____ **Date** _____

It's Simply Interest
Problem Set B

Directions: Read the story "It's Simply Interest." Do the problems in order. You will need answers from the earlier problems to do the later ones. Write your answer sentences below each problem. Where possible, use the back of this page or a separate piece of paper to show your work.

1. Figure the fraction of the year covered by Mr. Samuelson's loan. What percentage of the loan amount will he pay in interest?

2. How much will Mr. Samuelson pay the bank after 3 months (loan plus interest)?

3. If he could get an extension on the loan and pay it in six months, what would he owe the bank (principal plus interest)?

4. Assume Mr. Samuelson wanted to extend the loan. Mr. Buck said the bank wouldn't extend it. Since Mr. Samuelson had a good record, the bank would replace his original loan on September 1, when the 3-month loan was due. The amount of the new loan would be what he owed on that date. (See your answer to Problem 2.) This would be a new 3-month loan. How much interest would he owe on the new loan?

5. In Problem 4, the interest was compounded. This means that interest was paid on interest. How much more would interest cost if it were compounded quarterly than if simple interest were paid, as in Problem 3? (Hint: Use the answers to Problems 2, 3 and 4.)

Name _____   **Period** _____   **Date** _____

It's Simply Interest
Problem Set C

Directions: Read the story "It's Simply Interest." Do the problems in order. Your calculator will be useful. Write your answer sentences below each problem. Where possible, use the back of this page or a separate piece of paper to show your work.

1. How much interest will Mr. Samuelson pay after three months?

2. At simple interest, what interest would be paid for a year?

3. If the interest were compounded quarterly, what would a year's interest cost?

	Beginning Balance	*+ Interest*	*= New Balance*
First quarter	$100,000	$3,000	$103,000
Second quarter	$103,000	$3,090	$106,090
Third quarter	$ _____	$ _____	$ _____
Fourth quarter	$ _____	$ _____	$ _____
	Total interest	$ _____	

4. What is the difference in interest cost between simple interest and compound interest?

5. If, after three months, Mr. Samuelson had paid off half the loan and all of the interest due, how much additional interest would he owe after six months? (Reminder: Since he had already paid the interest to date, he would only pay simple interest for the second three months.)

An Interesting Loan
Problem Set B

Directions: Read the story "An Interesting Loan." Remember that interest is usually stated in terms of a rate for a year. Do the problems in order. Write your answer sentences below each problem. Where possible, use the back of this page or a separate sheet of paper to show your work.

1. When he bought the bike, Michael paid 6% sales tax. How much did he pay for the bike altogether?

2. He came up with $20.39 for the bike. How much did he have to borrow from his dad?

3. How much interest did he pay for the six-month loan?

4. What would be the total amount he would pay his father on September 1 (loan plus interest)?

5. If Michael gets part-time work, he could pay his dad off in three months. How much interest would he pay if he did this?

Name _____   Period _____   Date _____

An Interesting Loan
Problem Set C

Directions: Read the story "An Interesting Loan." Do the problems in order. Your calculator will be very helpful. Use estimates so that your decimal placement will make sense. Since your calculator only goes to eight decimal places, you will need to round off final numbers. Remember that interest rates are stated on an annual basis. Write your answer sentences below each problem. Where possible, use the back of this page or a separate piece of paper to show your work.

1. If Michael buys the bike, adds 6% sales tax and pays $20.39 of his own money, how much will he borrow from his dad?

2. Figure the six-month interest on the loan. When it is added to the list price and the sales tax, what is the full cost of the bike?

3. Michael decided to put money from odd jobs into a bank account. He didn't have to pay back his dad until September 1. The account paid 6% interest. Interest was compounded daily. If he started with $100, he would get 1.6434 cents interest the first day. The computer would multiply the balance ($100) by the rate (.06) by the time (1/365 of a year). How much interest would be earned the second day?

4. How much interest would be earned the third day? (Add the interest for the first two days to $100. Multiply by .06 and divide by 365. Note: The computer will deal with more decimal places than your calculator. It will "compound" interest on interest every day. Therefore the "yield" is higher than on "simple interest," which remains constant each day.)

5. Why would Michael be smarter to put the money in the bank until the loan was due rather than pay back his father early?

HOMECOMING

"June is here!" thought Tessa. "Finally I can get back to the ranch and see all my old friends." Tessa put her head back as the plane started the 652-mile flight. She had many thoughts running through her head.

The trip had been long in coming. She spent many hours babysitting to earn $350 for the trip. It'd been almost a year now since Tessa had seen her old friends. During that time she made many new friends, but there was something special about the thought of going "back home."

Tessa and her mom had bickered about the length of the trip and how she'd get there. Finally it was resolved that Tessa would fly to Arizona. The length of the trip would be three weeks. Now all she could think about was catching up on the latest news and spending time with good friends.

The plane landed at 1:47 P.M. Tessa waved to several friends as she entered the airport. They never stopped talking while the baggage arrived and they headed toward the car. During her stay Tessa soon realized that life in her home town had continued on as usual after she left. Her friends laughed about incidents she hadn't been part of and spoke of people she didn't know. Tessa found that the only thing she felt a part of was the past. The present was filled with new names and faces, all of which made Tessa very sad.

July 7 arrived and Tessa said good-bye to her old friends once again. This time she had a better appreciation for old friends and new as she headed "back home."

Homecoming
Problem Set A

Directions: First read the story "Homecoming." Information from the story will help you to solve some of the problems below. Write your answer sentences below each problem. Where possible, use the back of this page or a separate sheet of paper to show your work.

1. A one-way economy ticket cost $119.00. If the return flight cost the same, how much would Tessa pay for the entire plane trip?

2. How much money did Tessa have left after paying for her round-trip ticket? (See Problem 1 of this set for information to help.)

3. On what date did Tessa leave for Arizona?

4. Tessa purchased two new shirts. The total cost was $11.98 and she gave the clerk $20.00. The clerk had no $5.00 bills in the register. Name two ways in which the clerk could have given Tessa the correct change.

5. If the bus would have taken 741 miles, how many more miles would she have to travel round trip by bus than round trip by plane?

Homecoming
Problem Set B

Directions: First read the story "Homecoming." Information from the story will help you to solve some of the problems below. Write your answer sentences below each problem. Where possible, use the back of this page or a separate sheet of paper to show your work.

1. Use the chart and determine how much was charged for parking the car. They arrived at the airport at 1:35 P.M. and left at 2:50 P.M.

AIRPORT PARKING	
First hour or part	$2.00
Each additional hour or part	$ .50

2. Refer to Problem 1 of this set. What would have been the latest time they could have left the airport and still paid the same fee as they paid in Problem 1?

3. What would be the maximum amount paid for parking one full day at the airport?

4. Tessa considered traveling to Arizona by air ($119.00 one way) and back by bus ($77.45 one way). How much more would she have saved with this plan over a round-trip flight?

5. Tessa averaged 20 hours of babysitting per week. How much money did she earn, on an average, if she earned $1.50 per hour? How many weeks would it take to earn the money for the trip?

© 1990 by The Center for Applied Research in Education, Inc.

Homecoming

Problem Set C

Directions: First read the story "Homecoming." Information from the story will help to solve some of the problems below. Write your answer sentences below each problem. Where possible, use the back of this page or a separate sheet of paper to show your work.

1. Refer to the chart. If Tessa's home was 32 miles from the airport, how much would it cost to take the Airport Shuttle Bus, one way?

AIRPORT SHUTTLE BUS	
First 20 miles	$ 5.00
Each additional mile	$ .20
Maximum charge	$15.00

2. Use the Airport Shuttle Bus chart above and indicate how many miles must be traveled in order to pay the maximum fare.

3. Use the phone chart and determine the cost of a call placed at 1:05 P.M. on Friday and ended at 1:37 P.M. the same day.

	First 3 Minutes	Each Additional minute
Mon.-Fri. 8 A.M.-11P.M.	$.95	$.21
Mon.-Fri. after 11 P.M. Sat., Sun. all day	$.35	$.09

Homecoming
Problem Set C (Cont'd)

4. If the phone call in Problem 3 of this set were placed on a Saturday instead of a Friday, what would be the difference in price?

5. What would be the maximun charge for a 20-minute call? On what day and at what time might that call be made?

PENDULUM PROJECT

Dan and Michael walked into math class at the same time. "I see now what the teacher meant. He said we would be 'free swinging' in math class today," said Michael. Swinging from the light fixture was a long pendulum. A short one was hanging from a chart stand, and a pendulum diagram was on the chalkboard.

The teacher began, "Where are pendulums used in our daily lives?"

"Our grandfather clock, at home, has a pendulum that helps it to keep time," answered Robin.

"My aunt has a cuckoo clock that has a pendulum," added Eric.

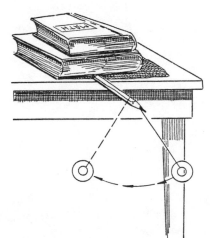

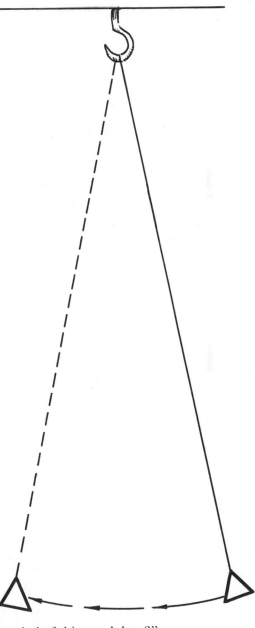

"Are the playground swings in the park pendulums?" asked Andy.

"Yes, swings in motion are pendulums," answered the teacher. "Can you also tell me the name of the pendulum that is probably the most famous? No one? OK, I'll leave that as a research question for you.

"Now, look at this small pendulum," said the teacher. "It has a 1-foot cord with a *bob*, or weight, attached to it. Watch as I hold the bob back, and then let go of it. It swings in an *arc* going away from me, and another coming back. A complete swing back and forth is called the *period of the pendulum*. How could we find the time for the period of this pendulum?"

"We could use a stopwatch. Then we could find how long it takes to make one swing back and forth," said Jerry.

"It might be more accurate to do it for a longer time. We could count the periods for a minute. Then we could divide to figure out how long each one took," suggested Terry.

"Good suggestions," said the teacher. "You will be finding the periods of several pendulums today. However, I need to ask some related questions first. Will the period for a pendulum change as it slows down and begins to make smaller arcs? Will the length of the cord make a difference? What about the type of bob? Also, does the weight of the bob cause the period of the pendulum to change?"

The teacher continued, "You will be making your own pendulum. I'll provide the string and some washers to use for bobs. Fasten the bob to one end of your string. Measure a certain length and fasten that point of your string to a pencil. Lay the pencil on your desk top with the pendulum hanging over the side. To keep it in place, set several books on the other end of the pencil. Then do some experiments with your pendulum. Organize your findings in a list or chart. When you have finished, you should know the answers to the questions that I asked."

Pendulum Project
Problem Set A/B/C

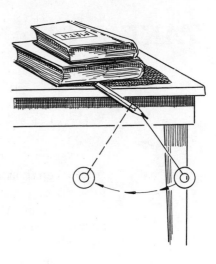

Directions: First read the story "Pendulum Project" and notice the diagram. You will need a yard stick (or meter stick), a watch that displays seconds, and an encyclopedia or other reference books. It will also be helpful to have a scale that can weigh the pendulum bobs in ounces (or grams). Otherwise, use bob items that all weigh the same (such as washers).

1. Construct your pendulum and try several experiments. Be certain that you only change one item at a time. (For example, when trying different string lengths, do not change the pendulum bob. Or when experimenting with bobs of different weights, be certain to keep the cord length the same.) Record your findings in a systematic list or chart like the one that follows. Share your findings with the teacher and the class.

Length of Cord	Bob Material	Bob Weight	Length of Arc	Period of the Pendulum

2. Measure the length of the arc when a pendulum first swings. Measure it again after 30 seconds, 60 seconds, and once more at 90 seconds. What happens to the length of the arc? Does the time for the period of the pendulum change? Explain why this happens.

3. When the length of the cord is kept the same, what does a heavier pendulum bob cause? On the other hand, when the bob is kept the same, what does a longer cord cause?

4. Use the same bob for each of these pendulums. Find the period for a pendulum with a 1-foot cord. What is the period when the cord is lengthened to 4 feet? If you can, find the periods for pendulums with 9- and 16-feet cords. State a rule that we could use to tell what the period of any pendulum might be.

5. Use encyclopedias and other research materials to help you answer the following questions:
   (a) What is probably the world's most famous pendulum? What does it demonstrate about the earth?
   (b) What are the twin pendulums that regulate the speed of some engines called?
   (c) What pendulum-like device is often used by musicians to keep a steady rhythm?
   (d) Why don't the pendulums in grandfather and cuckoo clocks stop?
   (e) What five principles of physics does a swinging pendulum demonstrate?

TAKE A CHANCE

"Step right up and take a chance—only 25 cents!" cried the carnival worker. "Spin the wheel for a prize. Who will be the lucky one tonight?"

Tessa and Michael walked around the county fair and listened as people begged them to put their money down and spin for prizes. Tessa would sure love to have the telephone or the TV for her room!

"Come on, Michael, let's try for the TV!" begged Tessa. "No, you know there's hardly a chance you'll win!" said Michael. "I'm gonna try," said Tessa, "you watch—I'll bet I win!"

"You're wasting your money," said Michael. "Tell you what," answered Tessa. "If you're right I'll treat to the roller coaster, but if I win—you buy the tickets."

Tessa spun the wheel. "OK—go ahead and laugh! It sure looked easier to win than that! Maybe I should try again."

"Come on," laughed Michael. "I'm ready for that roller coaster ride."

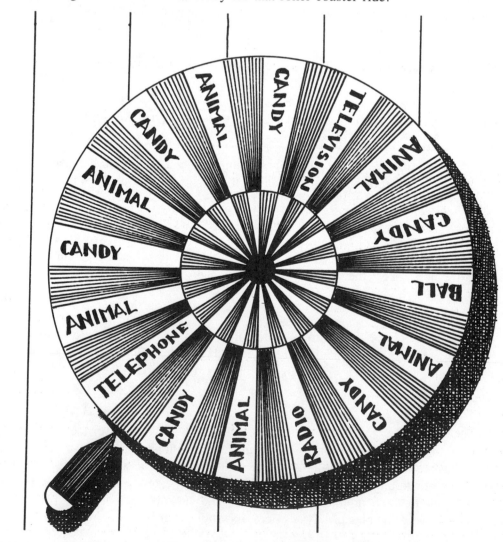

Take a Chance
Problem Set A/B

Directions: First read "Take a Chance." Information from the story and the illustration will help you to solve some of the problems that follow. Write your answer sentences below each problem. Where possible, use the back of this page or a separate sheet of paper to show your work.

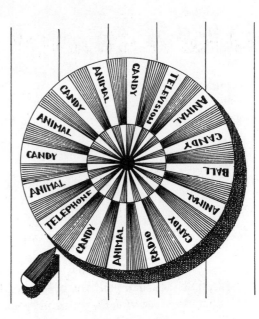

1. Count the segments on the wheel. How many show a TV as the prize? What fractional part of the spaces are marked "TV"?

2. The probability that Tessa would win the TV on one spin is written as the fractional part of the prizes that are marked "TV." (Refer to Problem 1 of this set.) How could you show the probability that Tessa would win a TV? What is the probability that Tessa would win a telephone on one spin?

3. What was the probability that Tessa would win any prize on one spin?

4. What was the probability that Tessa would not win a prize on one spin?

5. What was the probability that Tessa would not win a TV on one spin?

6. Copy the prize names shown on the wheel in the story onto strips of paper, one prize per strip. Make a blank strip for each segment of the wheel that does not have a prize written on it. Now put all of these strips into a hat or bag. Work with your group. Have each member draw out one strip at a time and record the results on the frequency chart below. *Be sure to put the strip back into the hat or bag after recording it.* Continue this until you and each of your group members have chosen a paper 10 times. Record the prizes drawn onto the frequency chart below:

Prize Drawn	Tally	Total	Number of Times Drawn
Telephone			
TV			
Candy			
Animal			
No prize			
Total			

Name _____   Period _____   Date _____

Take a Chance
Problem Set C

Directions: First read the story "Take a Chance." Information from the story and illustration will help you to solve some of the problems that follow. Write your answer sentences below each problem. Where possible, use the back of this page or a separate sheet of paper to show your work.

1. Count the segments of the wheel. How many show a TV as the prize? What fractional part of the segments are marked "TV"?

2. The probability that Tessa would win the TV on one spin is written as the fractional part of segments that are marked "TV." How could you write the probability that Tessa would spin for a TV on the first spin? Also, write the probability that Tessa would spin for a telephone on the first spin.

3. Arrange your own probability experiment. Use either a spinner like the one in the problem, or simply cut 36 strips of paper and write a prize name on them. (Be sure to have enough blank papers to represent the parts of the wheel that represent no prize.) Put the papers in a hat, sack or box.
   Now predict what you think the probability of drawing or spinning each prize would be. Complete the following:
   (a) Probability of spinning (drawing) a TV = _____
   (b) Probability of spinning (drawing) a telephone = _____
   (c) Probability of spinning (drawing) candy = _____
   (d) Probability of spinning (drawing) an animal = _____
   (e) Probability of spinning (drawing) no prize = _____

4. Have each classmate spin the wheel 10 times (or select 10 pieces of paper, one at a time). *Be sure to have them put the paper back into the sack after they read it.* Record the results on the frequency chart below:

Prize Drawn	Tally	Total	Number of Times Drawn
Telephone			
TV			
Candy			
Animal			
No prize			
Total			

Take a Chance
Problem Set C (Cont'd)

5. How do your actual results compare with the predicted probabilities found in Problem 3 of this set? Explain.

6. Have each classmate spin the wheel (or select paper) 10 more times. Add the results to the previous results. Compare the actual results with the predicted probability again. Now how do they compare? Explain.

7. What do you think would happen if each classmate spun the wheel (or drew paper) 10 more times? 100 more times? Write your predictions and share them with your neighbor or group.

831 MONROE STREET

"There's the house! 831 Monroe," cried Tessa.

"But there's no one home," said Maggie. "Are you sure you have the right address? Why didn't you bring the invitation, Tess? Let's keep driving and see what we find. I'm sure that Juanita's grandmother's house is on this street," she added.

"Well we're bound to find cars in front of the house somewhere," Tessa said.

"Not necessarily. I told Juanita that we would be over early to help set up. We're already later than I said," said Maggie.

"Well I know the address has an eight and a three and a one in it. I just can't remember the order," answered Tessa.

"Great!" said Maggie. "I wonder how many houses fit that description? This is a pretty long street, you know."

By the time Maggie and Tessa arrived, Juanita had everything set up. "What happened to you two?" she asked. "I thought you weren't coming."

"It's my fault," said Tessa. "You know me and numbers! I had the wrong address. I never knew that so many addresses used the same numbers."

831 Monroe Street
Problem Set A

Directions: First read the story "831 Monroe Street." Information from the story will help you to solve some of the problems that follow. Write your answer sentences below each problem. Where possible, use the back of this page or a separate sheet of paper to show your work.

1. List three different house addresses that Maggie and Tessa could have been looking for.

2. List all the possible two-digit addresses that could be made using 8, 3 and 1. Each digit can be used once in a number.

3. What system did you use (or could you have used) in Problem 2 of this set? Discuss your system with your neighbor or group. Was it different from the system(s) used by other members?

4. Use either your system or that of one of your group members to do the following problem: List all the possible three-digit numbers that can be made using the digits 8, 3 and 1. Each digit can be used only once in each number.

831 Monroe Street
Problem Set B

Directions: First read the story "831 Monroe Street." Information from the story will help you to solve some of the problems that follow. Write your answer sentences below each problem. Where possible, use the back of this page or a separate sheet of paper to show your work.

1. Make a systematic list of all the possible three-digit house numbers that Tessa and Maggie could have been looking for.

2. What system did you use for listing the addresses in Problem 1 of this set? Discuss your system with your neighbor or group. Did you learn of any other systems that you could have used? Explain.

3. Systematically list all the possible three-digit house numbers using 2, 7 and 5. Each digit can be used only once in a number.

4. Predict how many more numbers you could have made in Problem 3 of this set if you could have used each digit twice in a number. Test your prediction by listing the numbers systematically.

831 Monroe Street
Problem Set C

Directions: First read the story "831 Monroe Street." Information from the story will help you to solve some of the problems that follow. Write your answer sentences below each problem. Where possible, use the back of this page or a separate sheet of paper to show your work.

1. Make a systematic list of all the possible three-digit addresses that Tessa and Maggie could have found on Monroe Street. Each digit may only be used one time in a number.

2. Describe the system you used to generate the list in Problem 1 of this set. Share your system with your group or neighbor. Did you learn of any systems different from yours? Explain.

3. Predict how many more three-digit addresses you could list using the same digits as in Problem 1 of this set if this time you can repeat the digits two times in a number. Test your prediction by systematically listing the numbers.

4. Predict how many more three-digit numbers could be generated using your system if now you may use the digits any number of times in the numbers. Test your prediction by systematically listing the numbers.

THE PATTERN GAME

"OK," said Ms. Wagner, "I'd like to show you a new game. I will put some numbers on this chart. Your job is to take the top number and see if you can find out how I got the number below it."

"You mean we have to find the rule?" asked Brian.

"This reminds me of a function machine," added Beth.

"You're both right. Now think carefully about how a function machine works. It takes a number and changes it into another number with the help of a rule," she said.

"Great!" moaned Marco, "I can never get these."

"I love this game," answered Maggie. "We played it a lot last year. I always try to see if I can see a pattern because sometimes the rule is hard to find."

"Remember, you try to figure out how I got from the top number to the one below it. If you think you know, come up and fill in one of the blank spaces," said Ms. Wagner.

0	1	2	3	4	5	6	7
1		5			11		15

The class members filled in the rest of the chart like this:

0	1	2	3	4	5	6	7
1	3	5	7	9	11	13	15

While discussing their strategies, they found at least two different ways to fill in the empty boxes.

"I just added each number on top to the one that comes after it. That gave me the one on the bottom," said Aaron.

"I just filled in the odd numbers on the bottom," added Maggie.

"Good!" said Ms. Wagner, "now I'm going to give you another chart. This time I'll mix up the numbers on the top. If you get stuck and can't figure out the bottom numbers, rewrite the chart with the top numbers in numerical order. That way you might find it easier to see the pattern. Remember that each number on top is matched with the one below it. If you move the top number to a new location, you must also move the bottom one. So give this one a try."

1	7	3	0	5	2	4	6
2				10		8	

The Pattern Game
Problem Set A

Directions: First read "The Pattern Game." Information from the story and the pattern games will help you to solve some of the problems that follow. Write your answer sentences below each problem. Where possible, use the back of this page or a separate sheet of paper to show your work.

1. Copy and complete the last problem that Ms. Wagner gave. Remember to use the hint given by Ms. Wagner if you get stuck.

2. Describe in words what you did to complete the table above. Discuss your ideas with your group or neighbor.

3. Complete this pattern game:

2	0	6	3	5	1	4	7
4				25		16	

    Describe in words how you completed the table above. Share your ideas with your group or neighbor. Did you learn of any methods different from yours? Explain.

4. Make up a number pattern game like the one in the story. Give it to your group or neighbor to complete. Discuss the solution when finished.

The Pattern Game
Problem Set B

Directions: First read "The Pattern Game." Information from the story and the pattern games will help you to solve some of the problems that follow. Write your answer sentences below each problem. Where possible, use the back of this page or a separate sheet of paper to show your work.

1. Copy and complete the last problem that Ms. Wagner gave. Remember to use the hint given by Ms. Wagner if you get stuck. Now describe in words what you did to complete the table. Discuss your ideas with your group or neighbor.

2. Complete the pattern game below.

1	5	3	6	0	2	7	4
	15				6		12

   Describe in words what you did to complete the table. Discuss your ideas with your group or neighbor.

3. Complete the pattern game below.

12	4	6	2	5	9
10				3	

   Describe in words what you did to complete the table. Discuss your ideas with your group or neighbor.

4. Make up a pattern game like the one in the story. Give it to your group or neighbor to complete. Discuss the solution when finished.

The Pattern Game
Problem Set C

Directions: First read "The Pattern Game." Information from the story and the pattern games will help you to solve some of the problems that follow. Write your answer sentences below each problem. Where possible, use the back of this page or a separate sheet of paper to show your work.

1. Copy and complete the last problem that Ms. Wagner gave. Remember to use the hint given by Ms. Wagner if you get stuck. When finished, describe in words what you did to complete the table. Discuss your ideas with your group or neighbor.

2. Complete the pattern game below:

2	5	8	0	1	3	7	4	6
6			2		8			14

   Describe in words what you did to complete the table. Discuss your ideas with your group or neighbor. Did you learn of any methods different from the one you used? Explain.

3. Complete the pattern game below:

9	2	7	15	0	5	12
	6		19		9	

   Describe in words what you did to complete the table. Discuss your ideas with your group or neighbor. Did you learn of any methods different from the one you used? Explain.

4. Make up a pattern game like the one in the story. Give it to your group or neighbor to complete. Discuss the solution when finished.

UNLUCKY FRIDAY

It was after eleven one foggy Friday night. The recent summer storm had caused rain on and off all day. Jake left work at the Burger Barn and headed out over the back roads. He'd thought about the safety of the wet roads, but decided to risk it since he was in a hurry to get to Michael's house. They had to load all their gear so they could leave early in the morning for the lake. Having arranged for the next day off, Jake looked forward to the lake party.

As he started out, Jake realized the slick roads would be a challenge. He had recently earned enough money for the down payment of $195 and insurance on his Honda. His $3.75-per-hour job would allow him to make the monthly payments. Thoughts of tomorrow's party caused Jake's mind to wander. Suddenly he realized he was quickly approaching a slow-moving hay truck. As he tried to slow it down, the motorcycle skidded and threw Jake off. He landed against a tree. The hay truck continued on, the driver unaware of Jake's accident.

Still rather dazed, Jake awoke about thirty minutes later. He picked up the wrecked bike from the roadside and checked out the damage. Scrapes down one side, a cracked mirror, and a broken chain appeared to be the extent of the damage. Now all he could do was hope someone came along soon to help.

Meanwhile, Michael worried that Jake had had trouble and called Jake's house. His foster parents hadn't heard from him, but would go out and start looking. The fog made it difficult for Mr. and Mrs. Anderson to see. They finally found Jake after an hour's search. They loaded the motorcycle into the pickup and headed for the hospital.

Jake's injuries included broken ribs, scrapes and a concussion. He missed the lake party and work for over a week. The thought of paying for repairs depressed him, especially since he'd now have to work overtime to earn the extra money.

On top of everything else, Jake had just had a tune-up. He thought sadly of the $45.05 in labor plus parts. When would his luck improve?

Unlucky Friday
Problem Set A

Directions: First read the story "Unlucky Friday." Information from the story will help you to solve some of the problems below. Write your answer sentences below each problem. Where possible, use the back of this page or a separate sheet of paper to show your work.

1. Jake lost 38 hours of work while recuperating. How much pay did he lose?

2. The balance owed on Jake's Honda (including interest) is $566.40. How long will it take him to pay it off if he pays $120 per month?

3. Motorcycle insurance costs $275 per year. If Jake saved $167.50, how much more would be needed to pay the insurance?

4. The insurance company told Jake that he could pay his $275 insurance under Plan A or Plan B. Plan A requires Jake to pay the $275 in one payment. Plan B requires Jake to pay four payments of $75 each. How much more will Jake pay under Plan B than Plan A?

5. Each year Jake will have to pay for insurance ($275), license ($32.25) and registration ($29.87). What are the total expenses?

Unlucky Friday
Problem Set B

Directions: First read the story "Unlucky Friday." Information from the story will help you to solve some of the problems below. Write your answer sentences below each problem. Where possible, use the back of this page or a separate sheet of paper to show your work.

1. If Jake works overtime he receives 1½ times his regular pay. How much does he earn for overtime pay?

2. If Jake works 8 hours at regular and 2 hours of overtime, how much will he earn in all? Refer to Problem 1 of this set for information to help.

3. Jake plans to earn $50 in overtime pay. Estimate how many hours he will have to work. 5 hours? 10 hours? 15 hours? Refer to Problem 1 of this set for information to help.

4. Jake can either work 16 hours at regular pay and 7 hours overtime or 25 hours of regular pay and no overtime. Which schedule will pay the most money? Refer to Problem 1 of this set for information to help.

5. Jake earned $93.59 one week. How many hours (to the nearest tenth) did he work at regular pay?

Unlucky Friday
Problem Set C

Directions: First read the story "Unlucky Friday." Information from the story will help you to solve some of the problems below. Write your answer sentences below each problem. Where possible, use the back of this page or a separate sheet of paper to show your work.

1. Parts for the tune-up included 2 cans of oil at $1.19 each, 2 spark plugs at $1.40 each, points at $6.00 per set and a condenser at $3.50. What was the total charge for parts?

2. A tune-up at the motorcycle shop costs $26.50 per hour for labor. How many hours did Jake pay for? Give your answer to the nearest tenth of an hour and don't forget to consider the amount paid for the parts. (Refer to Problem 1 of this set to help.)

3. Jake must start saving money for a new set of tires. He plans to save $15 per week. How many weeks must he save if the front tire costs $36.95 and the rear tire costs $41.29? Jake had estimated 5 weeks. How close was he?

4. Jake found a sale on oil. If he buys 2 cans, he gets 1 free. How many cans of oil will Jake be able to get with $7.50 if the cans cost $1.30 each?

5. Before the tune-up, Jake traveled 94.5 miles on 2.1 gallons of gas. After the tune-up Jake traveled 90.9 miles on 1.8 gallons of gas. What was the increase in miles per gallon after the tune-up?

LUCKY SEVEN

"Not seven again!" cried Jen, "I think you're cheating!"

"Guess I'm just lucky," answered Ryan.

"Tessa, is it really luck that he gets seven so often, or is he cheating?" asked Jen.

"I'm not sure," answered Tessa. "Let's finish this game and we'll experiment some."

Ryan really bragged about his luck after beating Jen for the fourth straight game. The worst of it for Jen was the fact that the loser had to do the dishes.

While Tessa helped Jen in the kitchen, Ryan started experimenting with the dice. He used a red die and a green die, tossing them one hundred times and recording the total showing each time like this:

	Red	Green	Total
Time 1	5	3	8
Time 2	4	2	6
Time 3	3	5	8
Time 4	1	6	7
Time 5	3	4	7

"There's got to be more than luck here," said Ryan. "I think I figured out why the seven comes up more often. Hey Jen, see if you can figure it out. I'll even give you a hint."

"I don't need your hints, Ryan. I'll figure out if you've been cheating or not!" she added. "Come on Tessa, help me with this. I'll roll and you record. I'm determined to beat him at this game yet!"

Lucky Seven
Problem Set A

Directions: First read the story "Lucky Seven." Information from the story and the illustration will help you to solve some of the problems that follow. Write your answer sentences below each problem. Where possible, use the back of this page or a separate sheet of paper to show your work.

1. During Ryan's experiment he found that seven could be rolled in several different ways. List all the combinations that would give Ryan a total of seven. Use the method shown in the chart in the story.

2. List all the ways in which you could roll a four. Use the method shown in the chart in the story.

3. List all the ways in which you could roll a six using the method shown in the chart in the story.

4. Can you state why Ryan always picked seven as his number in the game with Jen? Explain your idea to your group or neighbor. Now predict how many ways you could roll a ten. Test your prediction making a table similar to the one in the story.

Lucky Seven
Problem Set B

Directions: First read the story "Lucky Seven." Information from the story and the illustration will help you to solve some of the problems that follow. Write your answer sentences below each problem. Where possible, use the back of this page or a separate sheet of paper to show your work.

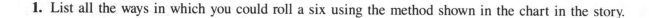

1. List all the ways in which you could roll a six using the method shown in the chart in the story.

2. Complete the chart below by adding the top and side numbers to fill in each box. How many boxes are in the chart?

Green Die

	1	2	3	4	5	6
1	2	3				
2	3	4	5			
3	4	5	6			
4						
5						
6						

Red Die (labels for rows 3 and 4)

3. How many boxes contain a sum of seven in the chart in Problem 2 of this set? Can you tell why Ryan always wanted the number seven in the game he played with Tessa? Discuss your idea with your group or neighbor.

4. Count the total number of boxes above. What fractional amount of those boxes show a sum of seven? What is the probability of rolling a sum of seven using two dice?

Lucky Seven
Problem Set C

Directions: First read the story "Lucky Seven." Information from the story and the illustration will help you to solve some of the problems that follow. Write your answer sentences below each problem. Where possible, use the back of this page or a separate sheet of paper to show your work.

1. Complete the chart below by adding the top and side numbers to fill each box. How many boxes are in the chart?

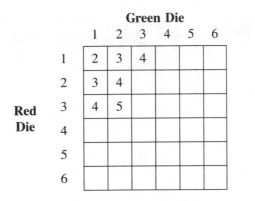

Green Die

		1	2	3	4	5	6
	1	2	3	4			
	2	3	4				
Red	3	4	5				
Die	4						
	5						
	6						

2. What fractional part of the boxes show a sum of five? What is the probability of rolling a sum less than five?

3. Use the chart to find the probability of rolling an even sum.

4. What is the probability of rolling a seven or higher?

5. Can you see why Ryan picked seven so often? Discuss your ideas with your group or partner.

BUSING FOR BUCKS

Easter had come and gone. Michael still didn't know how he was going to get a summer job. He needed the money to pay back his father and to buy the clothes he really wanted next fall. His friend, Bill Brown, had the same problem—no summer job.

Bill and Michael decided to go see Ms. Landers in the counseling office. They talked to her after school that day. She pointed out that neither had any particular skills or job records. A call had just come in from the Far Out Resort. They would need two more busboys for that summer.

The resort was located in the mountains outside of Summit City. It had a dormitory for employees as well as a discount meal plan. The pay would be $3.35 per hour plus tips. A phone number at the Summit City Office was provided. Bill called and made an appointment.

Mrs. Brown drove them to the interview in Summit City. They filled out job applications. Both were interviewed by Ms. Grubb, the dining room manager. They gave her letters of reference from Ms. Landers. Bill also had one from Mr. MacNamara, the band director. Michael had one from his coach. Their records as hard workers and their interview performance made a hit with Ms. Grubb. They got the jobs.

It was agreed that they would work 7:30–9:30, 12–2 and 6–8 six days per week. Each waitress had one busboy working her tables. Waitresses usually paid busboys 20% of their tips if they did a good job. That money would be in addition to their base pay. The first day of work would be June 15. The jobs would end after lunch on Labor Day. Michael decided he would work out the conflict with football practice later.

Busing for Bucks
Problem Set A

Directions: Read the story "Busing for Bucks." Do the problems in order. Write your answer sentences below each problem. Where possible, use the back of this page or a separate piece of paper to show your work.

1. How many hours did they work per week?

2. What was their base pay per week?

3. Each waitress served 5 tables with a total of 30 people per meal. What was the average number of people served per table each meal?

4. On the average, people paid $5 for breakfast and the same for lunch. Dinners ran around $10. If tips to waitresses averaged 15%, how much did they receive per person each day?

5. If the 30 people gave the average tip each day, how much did a waitress give a busboy?

Busing for Bucks
Problem Set B

Directions: Read the story "Busing for Bucks." More information will be found in the problem statements. Use your calculator. Write your answer sentences below each problem. Where possible, use the back of this page or a separate piece of paper to show your work.

1. Add up the weekly total of hours worked. At $3.35 per hour, what was the base pay?

2. Waitresses generally served about 30 people at each meal. Meal prices averaged $5 for breakfast and for lunch. Dinners were around $10. How much per day did waitresses get in tips at 15% of the gross each day?

3. If busboys did a good job, waitresses generally gave them 20% of their tips. How much per day did the busboys get in tips?

4. What was the average daily income of the busboys from base pay plus tips?

5. What was the average weekly income of the busboys?

Busing for Bucks
Problem Set C

Directions: Read the story "Busing for Bucks." Information will also be found in problem statements. Your calculator will be helpful. Write your answer sentences below each problem. Where possible, use the back of this page or a separate piece of paper to show your work.

1. Add up the weekly total of hours. How much is the busboy's base pay?

2. People paid about $10 for dinner and $5 for each of the other meals. Each waitress served about 30 people per sitting. People usually tipped 15% of the bill. How much per day did waitresses average in tips?

3. Busboys who did a good job were usually paid 20% of tips the waitress received. In an average 6-day week, how much did busboys receive altogether from base pay plus tips?

4. How much per hour did a busboy average?

5. Charlie, one of the other busboys, was sick one day. Bill had to work on his day off. He was paid "time and a half (1.5)" of his base pay for work that day. Tips were average. How much did Bill make for working on his day off?

FAR OUT FUNDS

Bill and Michael had been working at the Far Out Resort for a couple of weeks. Although taking the summer jobs meant no vacation, it was a change. With the split shifts, there was time for swimming, short hikes, reading and games in the Rec Hall. They also planned to visit Centerville by bus every two weeks on their day off. They worked hard, but decided they were having a good time.

One night after dinner they were talking about the summer. Bill said, "This job is OK. We're having some fun and making good money."

Michael said, "Yeah, I like it too. Just for the fun of it, let's figure out how much we'll really net for the summer."

"I figure that with the base pay and tips, I've earned about $450 these first two weeks. We'll work about ten weeks. That's about $2,250!" said Bill.

"I guess that's pretty close," replied Michael. "Don't forget, though, that we have a lot of expenses, too."

"Like what?" Bill asked.

"Well," answered Michael, "for openers, there's our food, bus fare, laundry, phone calls to the girls and whatever they take out of our checks. We also have to pay income taxes."

Far Out Funds
Problem Set A

Directions: Read the story "Far Out Funds." The boys are
making estimates. In doing these problems, accept Bill's estimate of income. Do the problems in order. Write your answer
sentences below each problem. Where possible, use the back of
this page or a separate piece of paper to show your work.

1. How much per week is their estimated income?

2. Employees are charged $2.50 for breakfast, $2.75 for lunch
   and $3.75 for dinner. How much per day would they pay for
   meals?

3. If they wish, employees can buy a $55 meal ticket good for a week. This amount is deducted from their
   paychecks. What would they save each week with the ticket if they ate every meal there?

4. The Samuelsons drove them up to the resort on June 14. The Browns picked them up on Labor Day. After the
   first week, the boys took the bus to Centerville every other week on their day off. How many bus trips did they
   take to Centerville that summer?

5. Bus fare from Summit City to Centerville was $17.42 round trip. How much did they each spend on bus fare
   that summer?

Far Out Funds
Problem Set B

Directions: Read the story "Far Out Funds." The boys are making estimates. In doing these problems, accept Bill's estimate of income. Do the problems in order. Write your answer sentences below each problem. Where possible, use the back of this page or a separate piece of paper to show your work.

1. Employees are charged for meals eaten at the resort. Their prices are $2.50 for breakfast, $2.75 for lunch and $3.75 for dinner. How much would meals cost for a week?

2. If they wish, employees can sign up for a $55 meal ticket per week. This amount is taken out of their paycheck each week. Which is the best deal if Bill and Michael go home for one day every two weeks?

3. The Samuelsons drove the boys up to the resort on June 14. The Browns drove them home on Labor Day. Michael and Bill took the bus home every other week after the first week. At $17.42 round trip, what did they each spend on bus fare that summer?

4. You remember that the base pay was $3.35 per hour for 36 hours per week. Unemployment, Social Security and other deductions took $12.60 out of their checks each week. How much was the net paycheck for base pay each week?

5. If they signed up for meal tickets, what would be left of the base paycheck?

Far Out Funds
Problem Set C

Directions: Read the story "Far Out Funds." The boys are making estimates. In doing these problems, accept Bill's estimate of income. Do the problems in order. Write your answer sentences below each problem. Where possible, use the back of this page or a separate piece of paper to show your work.

1. Employee meals cost $2.50 for breakfast, $2.75 for lunch and $3.75 for dinner. Another option was a weekly meal ticket for $55. This amount would be deducted from the weekly paycheck. Which was the better deal if they were to be gone for one day every two weeks?

2. Michael jotted down the following estimate of expenses, based on their first two weeks:

	First 2 Weeks	10 Weeks
Deductions for Social Security, unemployment insurance, etc.	$25.20	$_____
Meals (see Problem 1)	$_____	$_____
Bus fare (if they go home every other week)	$17.42	$_____
Launderette	$ 3.50	$_____
Phone calls to Centerville	$ 6.00	$_____
Personal	$10.00	$_____
Total reductions from income		$_____

3. If Bill's estimate on income and Michael's estimate on expenses are correct, about what will Bill and Michael each net from their summer work (to the nearest $100)?

4. Michael still owed his dad $278.10 for the off-road bike loan. He paid back his dad when he got home. If their estimated net was correct, and he spent $200 on clothes, what is your estimate (to the nearest $100) of what he could put into the bank?

5. Bill wanted to get a new trombone. He was playing in another group besides the school band. The new trombone cost $635.95, including tax. If he spent about $200 on clothes, what is your estimate (to the nearest $100) of what he could put into the bank?

MAGGIE'S SECRET

The students of Central High School poured into the gym for the football rally. Tonight Central played East High School to decide the championship. Michael and other team members sat together and listened as the cheerleaders and fans got ready for the big game. He was the only starter of the ten sophomores. He looked more excited than the 17 seniors. The five freshmen on the team could hardly sit still.

Michael waited after the rally for Maggie and Tessa. Michael dated Maggie and was anxious to make plans for the dance and party after the game.

"Hi Tessa, where's Maggie?" asked Michael.

"Oh, she had to run some errands, but she'll be at the game," lied Tessa.

Actually, Tessa hadn't seen Maggie all day. She called at noon but no one was home. Luckily Michael had a team meeting at 12:45, so he remained unaware of her absence. It wasn't until 5:30 that Michael could call Tessa.

"Well, tell her I'll meet her after the game. A bunch of us are going to Jed's after the dance. You can come too if you want," said Michael.

"OK, we'll see you later," replied Tessa. "Now, where can I start looking for Maggie?" she thought.

Tessa called Maggie's friends. No one had seen her. Her stepmother said Maggie left for school around 7:30 A.M. She had no idea where she might be.

Maggie had family problems. She and her stepmother often argued. Maggie's dad spent a lot of time away with his sales job so it was hard to talk with him about the problem. He pointed out to her that his commission was 12%. He had to sell a lot to make a living.

Game time arrived and Tessa still had no clues. She knew she had to meet Michael afterwards and tell him. How she dreaded that! Suddenly the phone rang.

"Tessa, this is Maggie. I called to say I'm all right but I'm not coming home, at least for a while," Maggie said. "Tell my dad I'll be in touch and tell Michael that I'm sorry I didn't have time to talk with him about this," she added.

"Maggie—tell me where you are!" cried Tessa. There was no response. The line was dead.

Maggie's Secret
Problem Set A

Directions: Read the story "Maggie's Secret." Information from the story will help you to solve some of the problems below. Write your answer sentences below each problem. Where possible, use the back of this page or a separate piece of paper to show your work.

1. Michael had to attend a team meeting at 12:45. How much later was his call to Tessa?

2. Maggie called a friend in Westfalls. The call cost $.55. Maggie had 3 dimes, 2 quarters and 5 nickels in her purse. Name three combinations of coins Maggie could have used to pay for the call.

3. Maggie went to the bus station to buy a ticket to Westfalls. The ticket cost $15.70. How much change did she get back from $20?

4. Name two different money combinations that would have given Maggie the correct change in Problem 3 of this set.

5. The bus left at 11:20 A.M. and arrived in Westfalls at 1:05 P.M. How long did it take to ride to Westfalls?

Maggie's Secret
Problem Set B

Directions: First read the story "Maggie's Secret." Information from the story will help you to solve some of the problems below. Write your answer sentences below each problem. Where possible, use the back of this page or a separate sheet of paper to show your work.

1. Maggie's dad was paid by commission on all his sales. If his sales totaled $4,250 this month, how much commission did he earn?

2. Maggie counted the people on the bus and found there were 36 men. If the ratio of men to women was 4:3, how many women rode the bus that day?

3. There were 60 people on the bus as they entered Edgewater. After they stopped, a dozen people got off and 5 new people got on. How many people were on the bus when it left Edgewater?

4. Maggie sat with a man who had 15 grandchildren. Five of them were 18, three were 17 years old, one was 16, three were 13, two were 9 and one was 7. What was the average age, to the nearest tenth of a year, of his grandchildren?

5. The man said that he always gave his grandchildren money for their birthday. If he gives each grandchild $1 for each year of their age, how much money will he have to spend next year for all 15 grandchildren? Refer to Problem 4 of this set for information to help.

Maggie's Secret
Problem Set C

Directions: First read the story "Maggie's Secret." Information from the story will help you to solve some of the problems below. Write your answer sentences below each problem. Where possible, use the back of this page or a separate sheet of paper to show your work.

1. Maggie's dad earned $480 in commission last month. How much were his total sales?

2. During the past four weeks Maggie's dad traveled 347 miles, 299 miles, 318 miles and 325 miles. To the nearest tenth of a mile, how many miles did he travel on the average?

3. Maggie earned $12 each week for cleaning house and helping with chores. She had to put 60% in the bank each week, and the rest she could keep. How much money did Maggie get to keep for herself each week?

4. Maggie learned that Westfalls had had a population of 35,300 before the local mill closed. Then 18% of the population had moved out of town. How many people remain in Westfalls?

5. Maggie's friends met her at the bus station and took her to lunch. The pizza cost $8.95 and the three cokes cost $.65 each. How much was the total bill, including sales tax at 6%?

THE FRANTIC DRIVE

After the phone call Tessa rushed to get her coat on and find the car keys. She had just gotten her license and knew that her mother would never let her take the car that far alone. But there wasn't time to argue the importance of this trip. She had to get going to make it before the bus left.

Maggie had called and said that she had decided to go live with an aunt in Oregon. She planned to leave on the next bus, which left in an hour and a half. Tessa tried to talk her into coming home before making her final decision. Maggie insisted this would be best for her entire family. Tessa knew it would take her about an hour and a half to drive into Westfalls. Then she had to find the bus station. Maggie didn't know that Tessa was coming. Tessa figured she'd have more luck talking with Maggie in person.

While driving, Tessa tried to relax but the rush hour traffic was nerve-racking. She kept thinking that this trip would probably be her first and last for quite awhile after her mom found out. Tessa's mind wandered back to Maggie and how she would ever persuade her to stop running. She had family problems that needed to be worked out. The question was how to get Maggie back to Centerville to deal with them.

As Tessa's mind wandered back to the road she noticed red lights behind her. Surely she couldn't have been speeding! But as she glanced at the speedometer it read over 60 mph. Tessa pulled over and searched for the registration and her license. The officer wrote the ticket after a stern talk about driving within the speed limits. All Tessa could think of was missing that bus. The bus was due to leave at 6:22 P.M.

She finally reached Westfalls and found the bus station. Maggie was shocked to see her. In her confusion of anger and happiness with her friend, Maggie decided to return to Centerville for a short stay before going to Oregon. She left for Westfalls on October 27. Tessa was to see Maggie return in November. She hoped that with Michael's help Maggie would stay for a long while.

© 1990 by The Center for Applied Research in Education, Inc.

Map of Westfalls

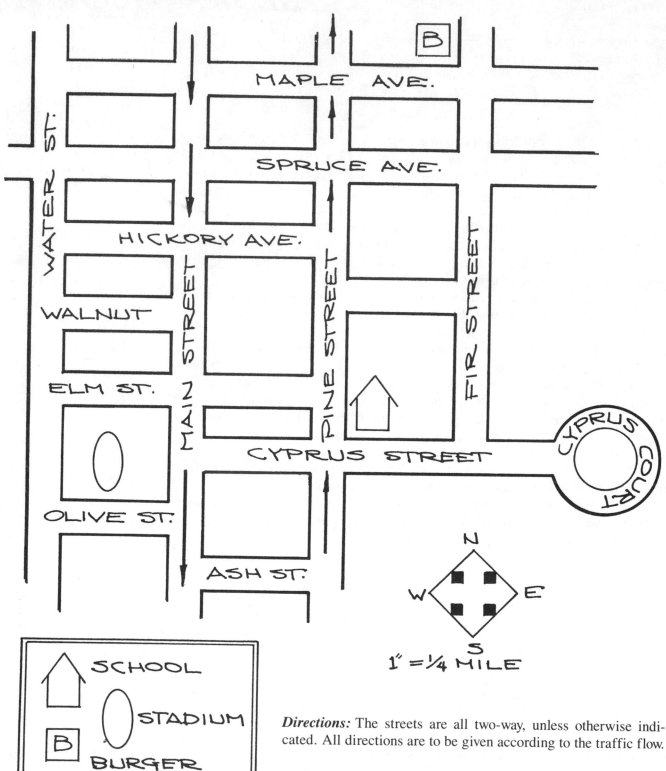

Directions: The streets are all two-way, unless otherwise indicated. All directions are to be given according to the traffic flow.

1" = ¼ MILE

The Frantic Drive
Problem Set A

Directions: First read the story "The Frantic Drive." Information from the story will help you to solve some of the problems below. Write your answer sentences below each problem. Where possible, use the back of this page or a separate sheet of paper to show your work.

1. Maggie's bus was due to arrive in Oregon at 8:10 A.M. How long did the trip take?

2. Before leaving Westfalls Tessa called her mom. The cost was $.55. List three combinations of coins that she could have used to make the call.

3. Maggie left Centerville to go to Westfalls. She was gone for 21 days. When did she return?

4. The girls stopped on the way home to get a hamburger. Their order came to $6.97. Name two combinations of money that would have given them the correct change from $10.

Burger deluxe	$1.15		
cheese	.20		
Fish burger	$1.45		
Double burger	$1.75		
Juicy burger	$ .99		
cheese	.20		
Shake	.59	.69	.89
Soft drink	.35	.50	.65
Fries	.49		.69
California sales tax 6%			

5. Name two combinations of a burger, drink and fries that would cost under $3. (You do not have to worry about sales tax.)

The Frantic Drive
Problem Set B

Directions: First read the story "The Frantic Drive." Information from the story will help you to solve some of the problems below. Write your answer sentences below each problem. Where possible, use the back of this page or a separate sheet of paper to show your work.

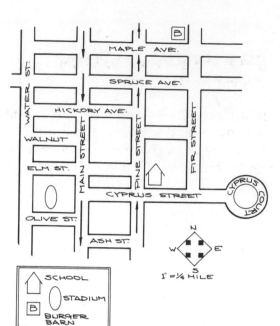

1. Tessa arrived in Westfalls at the corner of Pine and Ash. She was told to go north on Pine for three blocks and turn left. Then go two blocks and turn right. The bus station was two blocks north of there. On what corner was the bus station?

2. How many miles away from her starting point was the bus station?

3. The school was between Oak and Cyprus on Pine Street. Give directions for someone driving from the school to the stadium located between Elm Street and Olive on Water Street. Give directions for someone walking from the school to the stadium.

4. Maggie stayed with some friends on the corner of Cyprus Court and Cyprus Street. She took a taxi to the bus station and paid $.85 per mile. If she received $8.30 in change from $10.00, how many miles did she travel by taxi?

5. You are on the southeast corner of Oak and Pine. Hickory is closed off to all vehicles. Give two different sets of driving directions to the corner of Walnut and Water.

The Frantic Drive

Problem Set C

Directions: First read the story "The Frantic Drive." Information from the story will help you to solve some of the problems below. Write your answer sentences below each problem. Where possible, use the back of this page or a separate sheet of paper to show your work.

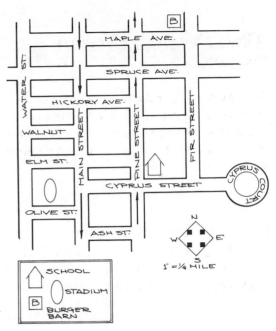

1. You are on the NE corner of Maple and Fir. How far is it to the bus station at Maple and Water?

2. The Burger Barn opened a new store on Maple between Fir and Pine. Estimate the distance from the school to the Burger Barn.

3. You are on the southwest corner of Elm and Main. Elm Street and Water Street are blocked off for road repairs. Give directions to the bus station. You are traveling by car.

4. You are on the southeast corner of Hickory and Main. Drive one block west, two blocks north and two blocks east. Where are you? Give a shorter set of directions to the same location.

5. The entrance to the stadium is on Olive Street. How far from the bus station is the stadium entrance?

TESSA'S GROUNDING

"I want to talk to you and I think you know what it is about," said Tessa's mother.

Tessa knew, all right. She had taken the car to Westfalls without permission. Getting the speeding ticket only made things worse.

At first she had thought about lying. It really had been an emergency. Maybe she could say that she had tried to call her mother. Things had gotten so messed up. Tessa decided to tell the whole truth and to hope for the best.

Her mother said all the things she expected:

"Did you know how much I worried?

"Did you know I thought the car was stolen and I almost called the police? I telephoned the courthouse and the judge said the fine for your speeding ticket will be $47. How will you pay it?"

Tessa didn't try to answer. When her mother stopped, she said she knew she had broken the rules. She was sorry to have upset her mother. She asked for understanding. Tessa had been so worried about Maggie. All she could think to do was to drive to Westfalls and it really had worked.

Tessa's mother listened. After things calmed down, her mother said, "I know you wanted to help Maggie. I'm glad you told me everything. You did break an important house rule and you did get a speeding ticket. You are grounded until the first of December. You will not be able to drive again until you have paid me back for the speeding ticket."

Tessa's Grounding
Problem Set A

Directions: Read the story "Tessa's Grounding." Do the problems. You may use your calculator. Write your answer sentences below each problem. Where possible, use the back of this page or a separate piece of paper to show your work.

1. How long would it take to pay her mother back? About how many hours at $2 per hour would it take?

2. She thought back to sitting she had done. The Smiths and Taylors each had called her about twice a month. Saturday nights were usually 4-hour jobs. If this pattern held up, how many weeks of babysitting would it take to pay her mother back?

3. The insurance bill for the family car this year is $421. If rates go up 5% next year, how much would the cost be?

4. Paying off the ticket wasn't the only problem. Tessa's mother said the ticket would raise insurance rates. The ticket penalty adds 10%. What would the full cost be for next year (based on your answer to Problem 3)?

5. How much more would car insurance be next year compared with this year?

Tessa's Grounding
Problem Set B

Directions: Read the story "Tessa's Grounding." Do the problems. You may use your calculator. Write your answer sentences below each problem. Where possible, use the back of this page or a separate piece of paper to show your work.

1. About how many hours of babysitting at $2 per hour would it take to pay the fine?

2. Tessa tried to figure out how long it would take to pay the loan. She checked her calendar for the last two months. Her records showed:

September 3	Smiths	2 hours
September 5	Taylors	2½ hours
September 7	Bakers	4 hours
September 14	Smiths	4 hours
September 17	Taylors	4 hours
September 23	Smiths	2 hours
October 5	Smiths	2 hours
October 8	Smiths	4 hours
October 10	Taylors	2½ hours
October 11	Bakers	4 hours
October 22	Smiths	2 hours
October 25	Taylors	4 hours

How many hours did she babysit during these two months?

3. What was her total income for the two months?

4. What was Tessa's average monthly income?

5. If the average income held for November, about how many more hours would it take to pay her mother?

Tessa's Grounding
Problem Set C

Directions: Read the story "Tessa's Grounding." Your calculator will be useful in doing these problems. Write your answer sentences below each problem. Where possible, use the back of this page or a separate piece of paper to show your work.

1. Tessa reviewed her babysitting records for the last two months. She found:

September 3	Smiths	2 hours
September 5	Taylors	2½ hours
September 7	Bakers	4 hours
September 14	Smiths	4 hours
September 17	Smiths	2 hours
September 23	Taylors	2 hours
October 5	Smiths	4 hours
October 8	Smiths	4 hours
October 10	Taylors	2½ hours
October 11	Bakers	4 hours
October 22	Smiths	2 hours
October 25	Taylors	4 hours

   What was her average monthly income for the two-month period at $2 per hour?

2. She also tried to estimate her monthly spending. Two movie tickets per month cost $4.00 each. She guessed she had a 35-cent soft drink every day. About once a week she met friends at the Burger Barn. That usually cost $2.25. About what did she spend each month? $21? $28? $34? $37?

3. About how many hours of sitting did it take to pay for this?

4. Tessa decided she wanted to be able to drive again in a month and a half. About how much would she have to save out of her earnings in November to meet this goal? How much more would she have to save by the middle of December to finish paying her mother back (to the nearest dollar)?

5. Assume Tessa's income average held up. About how much could she afford to spend in November and still pay her mother the budgeted amount (as planned in Problem 4)?

GEOMETRY IN THE PARK

As class began, the teacher was saying, "Our mathematics work for today will involve some applied geometry. You will need clipboards, paper and pencils. I will provide also some yardsticks and long measuring tapes. As soon as everyone has their materials ready, we will be going down the street to the city park. That is where we will start today's geometry study. Everyone stay together! OK, let's go!"

"What do you thinks he's going to have us do?" asked Terri.

"I don't know, but this sure is different than sitting in the room to do math," said Dave.

"I think it's kind of neat to be going outdoors to do math," said Tessa.

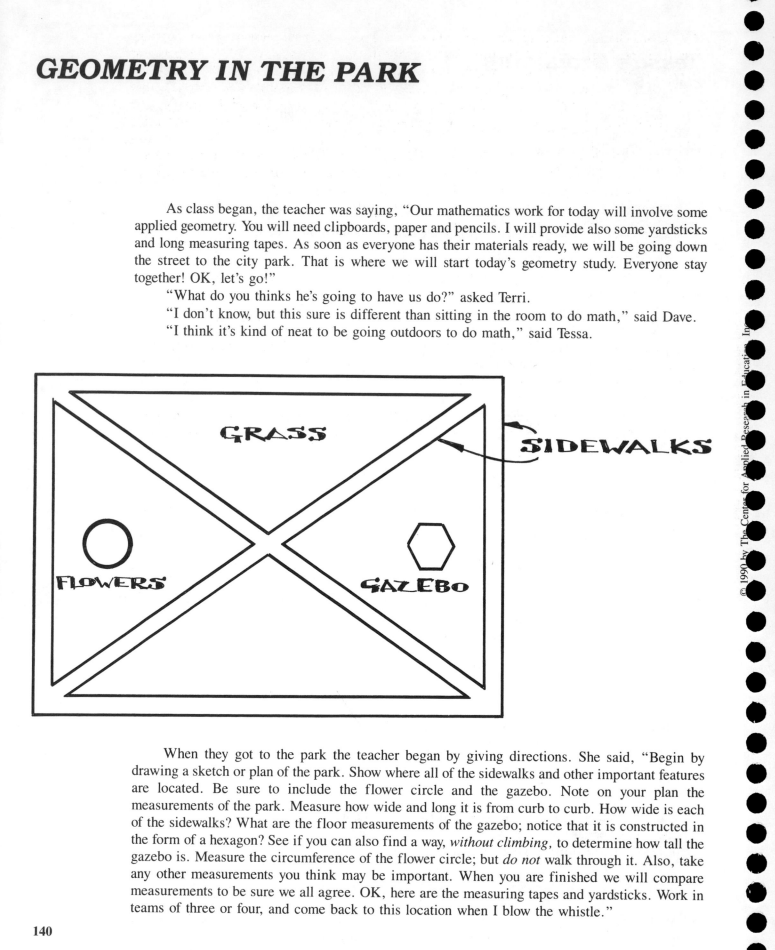

When they got to the park the teacher began by giving directions. She said, "Begin by drawing a sketch or plan of the park. Show where all of the sidewalks and other important features are located. Be sure to include the flower circle and the gazebo. Note on your plan the measurements of the park. Measure how wide and long it is from curb to curb. How wide is each of the sidewalks? What are the floor measurements of the gazebo; notice that it is constructed in the form of a hexagon? See if you can also find a way, *without climbing,* to determine how tall the gazebo is. Measure the circumference of the flower circle; but *do not* walk through it. Also, take any other measurements you think may be important. When you are finished we will compare measurements to be sure we all agree. OK, here are the measuring tapes and yardsticks. Work in teams of three or four, and come back to this location when I blow the whistle."

Tessa, Dianne, Terri and Dave worked together. They took turns measuring and recording their findings. They measured the sidewalks and found that they were all 6 feet wide. The park was 300 feet wide and 400 feet long. It was 62 feet and 10 inches around the flower circle. The gazebo measured 24 feet across between opposite vertexes and 21 feet between the flat surfaces. They decided that they had all of the measurements they needed except the height of the gazebo.

"How do you suppose we can figure out the height of the gazebo?" asked Dave. "The teacher says we can't climb it."

"We could set a long pole beside the gazebo. Then we could lay the pole on the ground and measure it," suggested Tessa. "The only problem is, I don't see any long poles around here."

"That gives me an idea!" exclaimed Dianne. "How tall are you, Tessa?"

"I'm 5 feet tall," said Tessa. "But how will that help?"

"Look, the gazebo is making a shadow, and so are you," explained Dianne. "We can measure both the gazebo shadow length and yours. We already know your height. So, now we can set up a ratio, like the teacher had us do in math class. Do you get it?"

"I think I might see what you're doing," said Tessa. "Is it like when we had to figure out the lengths of the sides of similar triangles?"

"That's it," agreed Dianne.

"OK, I've measured Tessa's shadow. It's 9 feet long," said Dave.

"When we measure the gazebo shadow, shouldn't we measure from the very center of the gazebo, since that's right under the highest point?" questioned Terri.

"Let's try it. Help me stretch this long measuring tape out," said Dave. "OK, it comes to 45 feet."

After a short time the teacher blew her whistle. As soon as everyone returned they compared measurements. Then they returned to their classroom and continued with the rest of the geometry activity.

Geometry in the Park
Problem Set A

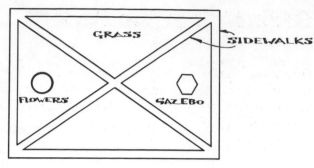

Directions: First read "Geometry in the Park." You will need to use some of the information to solve the problems. Where possible, use the back of this page or a separate sheet of paper to show your work. Write your answer sentences below each problem.

1. How many square feet of land are contained in the park?

2. How many square feet of sidewalks are along the edges of the park? Also estimate how many square feet of sidewalks cross the park.

3. Draw a floor plan for the gazebo. Next draw lines through its center that connect the opposite vertexes. Six triangles will be created. State at least two geometric terms that describe the triangles.

4. The students found that it was 62 feet and 10 inches around the flower circle. Use this measurement and the circle circumference formula to find the diameter.

5. Find the information about the gazebo shadow. Also note Tessa's height and shadow length. Draw a simple diagram of Tessa, the gazebo and the shadows. Use this information to estimate the height of the gazebo.

Geometry in the Park
Problem Set B

Directions: First read "Geometry in the Park." You will need to use some of the information to solve the problems. Where possible, use the back of this page or a separate sheet of paper to show your work. Write your answer sentences below each problem.

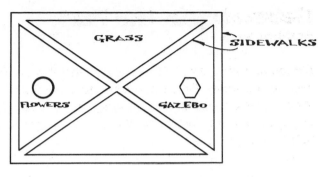

1. How many square yards of land are contained in the park?

2. Estimate the number of square yards of grass area in the park. Tell how you got your answer.

3. Draw a floor plan for the gazebo. Next draw lines through its center that connect the opposite vertexes. Six triangles will be created. State three geometric terms that describe the triangles.

4. The students measured and found that it was 62 feet and 10 inches around the flower circle. Find the diameter, radius and area of it. Use the formula for circle circumference.

5. Locate the information about the gazebo shadow. Also note Tessa's height and shadow length. Use this information to estimate the gazebo's height. Then calculate the height of the gazebo.

Geometry in the Park
Problem Set C

Directions: First read "Geometry in the Park." You will
need to use some of the information to solve the problems.
Where possible, use the back of this page or a separate sheet
of paper to show your work. Write your answer sentences
below each problem.

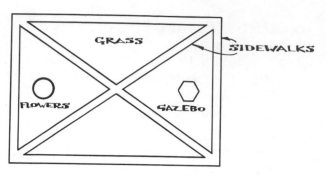

1. What is the surface area, in square yards, of all the
   sidewalks in the park? Tell how you got your answer.

2. How many square yards of grass area are in the park? Tell how you arrived at your answer.

3. Locate the shadow information in the story. Use it to estimate and then calculate the height of the gazebo.

4. The students found that it was 62 feet and 10 inches around the flower circle. They also found that the hexagon-
   shaped floor in the gazebo measured 24 feet across between opposite vertexes. Which covers the greater area,
   the flower circle or the gazebo floor?

5. Do the same kind of geometry and measurement at a park in your town. You will need measuring tapes, pencils
   and paper. Begin by drawing a sketch or plan of the park. Include sidewalks, playground equipment, buildings
   and any other important features. How long and wide is the park? What is the total area of the park? How much
   space has grass on it? How high is the tallest piece of playground equipment? Keep a record of these and other
   important measurements. Share your findings with your teacher and class.

STRING TRIANGLES*

"We are just about finished with this geometry unit," the teacher was saying. "There is just one more problem that you need to try and solve. It is a problem about triangles. To do it you will need two pieces of string from 30 to 60 inches long, scissors and masking tape. Two or three of you will be working together. Each group will construct string triangles on a flat surface. You can do it on a desk or table top, on the floor or on the classroom bulletin board. I want some of you to start with equilateral triangles. Other groups will construct isosceles triangles. Some will make right triangles. Also, a few of you will construct scalene triangles. As soon as you have decided on one or two partners you may come up and get string, tape and scissors. Then I'll show you how to begin." After a few minutes everyone had picked partners and was ready to start.

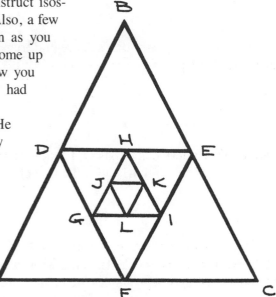

The teacher began making a string figure. He was saying, "Notice how I have stretched my longest string into a triangle. Then I taped it at each vertex. I'll write the letters A, B and C on these tapes in order to label my triangle. Next, I'll find the midpoints of the sides and label them D, E and F. Now I'll need some more string and tape. With it I'll connect these midpoints to form a new smaller triangle DEF. If I was to continue, I'd need to find the midpoints of the sides of this new triangle. Then I'd make an even smaller third triangle, which I'd label GHI. Finally, I'd find the midpoints of the sides of triangle GHI. From these I would construct a fourth, and still smaller triangle. I'd label this central triangle JKL.

"Does anyone have any questions about how to start?" asked the teacher.

"I can get started, but I'm not sure I can remember everything we need to do," said Sara.

"Right now several of you are probably unsure. But go ahead and try, and I'll help if you get stuck. OK, I want you six to begin with isosceles triangles. The eight of you in the back are to construct equilateral triangles. These two groups are to make right triangles. Everyone else is to construct scalene triangles. Go ahead and start. I'll move from group to group to check your progress. When you've finished your string constructions I'll have several questions to ask each group," said the teacher.

*James L. Overholt, *Dr. Jim's Elementary Math Prescriptions: Activities/Aids/Games to Help Children Learn Elementary Mathematics*. Copyright © 1978 by Scott, Foresman and Company, p. 212. Used by permission.

String Triangles
Problem Set A

Directions: Be sure to follow the directions in the "String Triangles" story. The diagram will also help. Your group will need string, masking tape, a pencil and a scissors. Then construct your triangle. When called for, write your answer sentences below each problem.

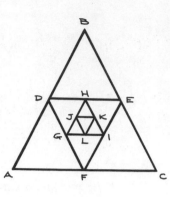

1. Use your string and tape to make a large isosceles triangle. Then divide it in the same way that was done in the story. Label each vertex.

2. Finish making your string triangles. Locate the central triangle JKL. How many triangles the size of JKL are in ABC?

3. You subdivided triangle ABC once at points D, E and F. How many triangles the size of DEF are in ABC? Next you made triangle GHI. How many triangles the size of GHI are in ABC?

4. Name one triangle that is congruent to JKL. Name another triangle that is similar to it but that has an area four times greater. How do the areas of triangles JKL and ABC compare?

5. How many triangles, the size of the central one, will there be each time you subdivide? State a rule that we can use to find out.

String Triangles
Problem Set B

Directions: Read the directions in the "String Triangles" story. The story diagram will also help with Problems 1, 2, 3 and 4. Your group will need string, masking tape, a pencil and a scissors. With it, construct your right triangle. When called for, write your answer sentences below each problem. Finally, note the different directions for Problem 5.

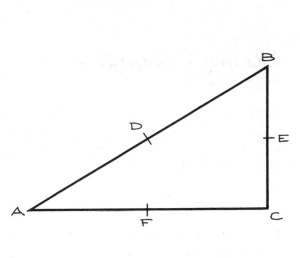

1. Use your string and tape to make a large right triangle (see above). Subdivide it in the same manner as in the story. Label each vertex. Locate the central triangle JKL. How many triangles the size of JKL are contained in ABC?

2. You divided triangle ABC once at points D, E and F. How many triangles of that size had you made? You subdivided again to make triangle GHI. How many the size of GHI are in ABC? How do the areas of triangles DEF and GHI compare? Also compare their areas with triangle ABC.

3. Find the midpoints of the sides of triangle JKL. Construct an even smaller central triangle MNO. How many triangles the size of MNO are in triangle ABC?

4. How many triangles, the size of the central one, will there be each time you subdivide? State the "best rule" that can be used to find out.

5. Construct a new string triangle PQR and extend outward as shown below. Extend line PQ to S such that QS = PQ; also extend PR to T so that RT = PR. How many triangles the size of PQR will fit into PST? Next construct extensions from S and T such that SU = PQ and TV = PR. Now how many triangles the size of PQR are contained in PUV? How many will there be if you extend again and make an even larger triangle PWX? If you were to extend still another time, what do you predict will happen?

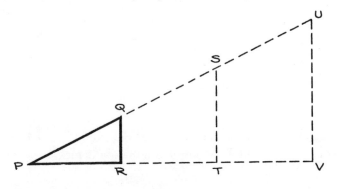

String Triangles
Problem Set C

Directions: Read the directions in the "String Triangles" story. The story diagram will also help with Problems 1, 2 and 3. Your group will need string, masking tape, a pencil and a scissors. With it, construct an obtuse scalene triangle. When called for, write your answer sentences below each problem. Finally, note the different directions for Problems 4 and 5.

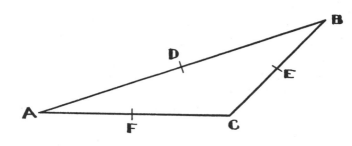

1. Use your string and tape to make a large obtuse scalene triangle (see above). Subdivide it in the same manner as in the story. Label each vertex. Locate the central triangle JKL. How many triangles the size of JKL are contained in ABC?

2. You subdivided triangle ABC once at points D, E and F. How many triangles of that size had you constructed? You subdivided again to make triangle GHI. How many the size of GHI are in ABC? How do the areas of triangles DEF and GHI compare? Also compare their areas with triangle ABC.

3. Find the midpoints of the sides of triangle JKL. Construct an even smaller central triangle MNO. How many triangles the size of MNO are in triangle ABC? How many triangles, the size of the central one, will there be each time you subdivide? State the "best rule" that can be used to find out.

4. Construct a new string triangle PQR and extend outward as shown below. Extend line PQ to S such that QS = PQ. Also extend PR to T so that RT = PR. How many triangles the size of PQR will fit into PST? Next construct extensions from S and T such that SU = PQ and TV = PR. Now how many triangles the size of PQR are contained in PUV? How many will there be if you extend again and make an even larger triangle PWX? If you were to extend still another time what do you predict will happen?

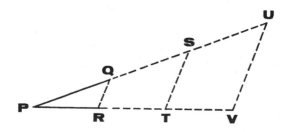

5. How many triangles the size of PQR will result each time you extend your triangle outward? Make a chart and record your findings. State the "best rule" for predicting the outcomes.

GEOMETRY PROJECT

Michael and his friend Dan walked out of math class together. "Wow, I don't know if I can make a bridge that strong with just toothpicks and glue!" sighed Michael.

"I don't know if I can either," said Dan. "Why not work together? Mr. Kenyon said we could work together in groups of up to four people, if we want to."

"Good idea, and let's get Maggie and Tessa to help too," said Michael.

When they met Maggie and Tessa in the hallway, Dan asked, "Did Mr. Kenyon assign your classes to build toothpick bridges too?"

"He sure did, and he said they had to be at least 6 centimeters wide and 45 centimeters long. Besides that, they must support at least one kilogram. We have to do all of that to get a 'C' for this geometry unit," said Tessa.

"Why don't we work together? Then we can split the cost and the work," suggested Michael.

"Sure, but how will we know what shape to make the bridge?" asked Tessa.

"I'm not certain, but Mr. Kenyon has talked about how stable and strong triangles are. Remember when he took the class to that old garage across from the school? Then he showed us how the framework in the walls had been reinforced with triangles. I bet we will end up using triangles as part of our bridge!" said Dan.

"Dan and I can find some information, and maybe some pictures, about bridges in the school library next period," volunteered Michael.

"Great, then Tessa and I can get the three boxes of round toothpicks and the fast drying glue after school today," said Maggie.

"OK, then we can get together to plan and work on our bridge tomorrow evening at 7:00 P.M.," they agreed.

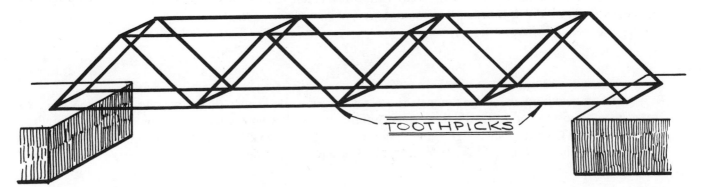

TOOTHPICK BRIDGE

TOOTHPICKS

Geometry Project
Problem Set A

Directions: First read the story "Geometry Project." You will use some of the story information as you solve these problems. You will also need to get information from other sources such as a grocery store, a hobby shop and a library. Write your answer sentences below each problem. Finally, you will need round toothpicks and fast drying glue.

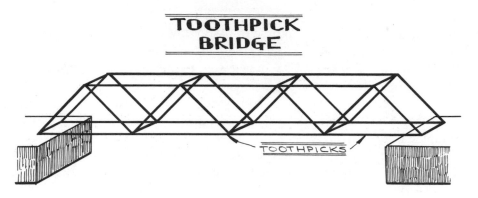

1. Build triangle, square and pentagon frameworks with toothpicks and glue. When dry, push directly on the vertexes of each to test which has the greatest stability and strength. What did you find out?

2. Use books from the library to find bridge-building information and pictures (especially those that show the frameworks). What geometric shape provides strength and stability in many of these bridges? Share the information that you found with your class.

3. On a large sheet of paper draw a side view of your toothpick bridge. Check the story to find how long your bridge needs to be. Remember to allow for some overlap where the toothpicks will be glued together.

4. To build the bridge that you have designed, what will the actual cost be for toothpicks, glue and a piece of cardboard for the floor? Remember that your bridge will have the same framework on both sides and that it must also have a number of cross beams.

5. Build your own toothpick bridge, or get a group together to build one. Remember to check the story for dimensions. Since this project will take some extra time, you will probably have to do some of the work outside of class. To get a C grade your bridge must support one kilogram, two kilograms for a B and three kilograms for an A. Extra points will also be given for a pleasing design, if it is painted, for decorations as flags, or other "extra" features.

Geometry Project
Problem Set B

Directions: First read the story "Geometry Project" below. You will use some of the story information as you solve these problems. You will also need to get information from other sources such as a grocery store, a hobby shop, and a library. Write your answer sentences beside each problem. Finally, you will need round toothpicks and fast drying glue.

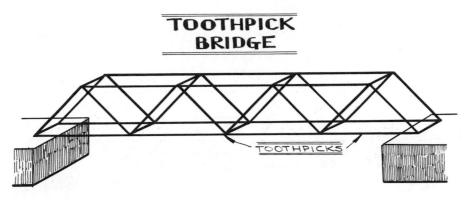

1. When constructing the frameworks for bridges or buildings, what common geometric shape will provide the greatest stability and strength?

2. Use reference books to find bridge building information and pictures (especially those that show the frameworks). What geometric shape provides strength and stability in many of these bridges? Share the information that you found with your class.

3. On a large sheet of paper draw a side view of your toothpick bridge. Will you put your support framework above or below the bridge floor? Check the story to find how long your bridge needs to be. Also allow for some overlap where the toothpicks will be glued together.

4. If the bridge you designed was to be built of metal beams, each five meters in length and costing $7.23, what would the cost for your bridge framework be? Remember that your bridge will have the same framework on both sides and that it must also have a number of cross beams.

5. Build your own toothpick bridge, or get a group together to build one. Remember to check the story for dimensions. Since this project will take some extra time, you will probably have to do some of the work outside of class. To get a C grade your bridge must support one kilogram, two kilograms for a B, and three kilograms for an A. Extra points will also be given for a pleasing design, if it is painted, for decorations as flags, or other "extras."

Geometry Project
Problem Set C

Directions: First read the story "Geometry Project." You will use some of the story information as you solve these problems. You will also need to get information from other sources, such as your home, a grocery store, a hobby shop, a lumber yard, a building supply store and a library. Write your answer sentences below each problem. Finally, you will need round toothpicks and fast drying glue.

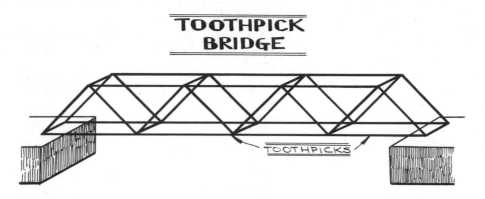

1. Using toothpicks, glue and a bathroom scale, design an experiment to test the strength of two-dimensional shapes (such as triangles, rectangles and pentagons) and three-dimensional frameworks (including triangular- and rectangular-based pyramids, cubes, rectangular solids, and so on). Record the results in a chart and be ready to share them with the class.

2. Use references to find bridge building information and illustrations. What geometric shape provides strength and stability in many of these bridges? Share the advantages and disadvantages of this shape.

3. Draw a side view of your toothpick bridge. Use a scale of 1 cm = 3 cm. Allow for some overlap where the toothpicks will be glued together. Check the story to find what the length of your bridge needs to be.

4. What would it cost to actually build your bridge over a small stream? Assume that the beams in your bridge will be of 2 in. by 4 in. lumber, each 6 ft. long. You will also need large nails and some 3/4-inch plywood for the bridge floor.

5. Build your own toothpick bridge, or get a group together to build one. Since this project will take extra time, you will probably have to do some of the work outside of class. To get a C grade your bridge must support one kilogram, two kilograms for a B, and three kilograms for an A. Could you build one that could support four kilograms or five? What would the maximum be? Extra points will also be given for a pleasing design, if it is painted, for decorations as flags, and other "extras."

"...and make sure your group is ready on Monday to present the report to the class," said Ms. Tandon.

"We shouldn't have put it off for so long," complained Tessa. "We really need to get busy now!"

"Listen," said April, "let's just split up the work and each take a part. Actually this graph is kind of interesting. Everyone always talks about SAT scores, but now I see what they've been saying."

"Well let's get going," added Raj. "You know the big game and dance are this weekend. I don't want to be stuck inside the whole time with this project!"

"I'll do anything but the predictions," said Jason. "I find them really hard to do. Or maybe I could work with someone else and learn what that is all about," he added.

The four finally agreed on what they would do. Ms. Tandon gave each group a graph. They had to come up with eight questions, four observations and two predictions based on the information in the graph. In addition, they had to prepare a general report on the graph and present it orally to the class.

"At least this graph makes me feel better," said Jason. "My scores are about average, according to this."

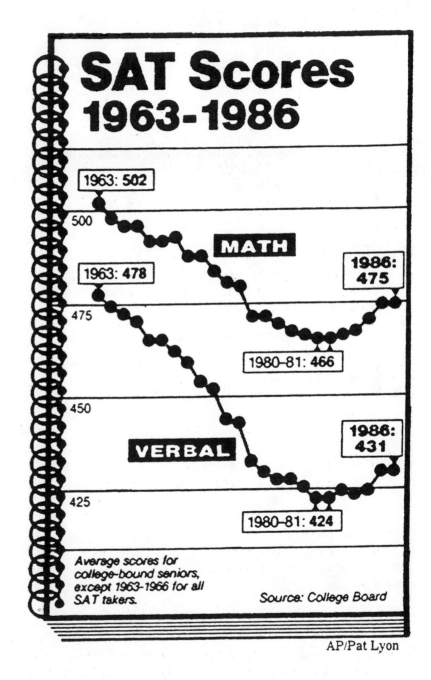

AP/Pat Lyon

*Yuba-Sutter Appeal Democrat, September 22, 1986, p. A-3. Used by Permission of the Associated Press.

What's the Score?
Problem Set A

Directions: First read the story "What's the Score?" Information from the story and the illustration will help you to solve some of the problems that follow. Write your answer sentences below each problem. Where possible, use the back of this page or a separate sheet of paper to show your work.

SAT Scores 1963-1986

1963: 502

500

MATH

1963: 478   1986: 475

475

1980-81: 466

450

VERBAL   1986: 431

425   1980-81: 424

Average scores for college-bound seniors, except 1963-1966 for all SAT takers.   *Source: College Board*

AP/Pat Lyon

1. What do the dots on the graph represent? How many years are covered by the graph?

2. What was the difference in the average math and verbal SAT scores in 1963?

3. Approximately what was the average SAT math score in 1975?

4. Make two observations about average SAT scores using the graph.

What's the Score?
Problem Set B

Directions: First read the story "What's the Score?" Information from the story and the illustration will help you to solve some of the problems that follow. Write your answer sentences below each problem. Where possible, use the back of this page or a separate sheet of paper to show your work.

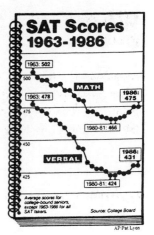

1. Estimate the difference in the average SAT math and verbal scores in 1983.

2. Approximately what is the difference in the average SAT math and verbal scores in 1969?

3. Make two observations about the average SAT math and verbal scores using this graph.

4. Make two predictions about the average SAT math and verbal scores in 1990.

What's the Score?
Problem Set C

Directions: First read the story "What's the Score?" Information from the story and the illustration will help you to solve some of the problems that follow. Write your answer sentences below each problem. Where possible, use the back of this page or a separate sheet of paper to show your work.

SAT Scores 1963-1986

1963: 502

500

MATH

1963: 478   1986: 475

475

1980-81: 466

450

VERBAL   1986: 431

425   1980-81: 424

Average scores for college-bound seniors, except 1963-1966 for all SAT takers.   *Source: College Board*

AP Pat Lyon

1. Are there any trends in the average SAT scores that are shown by the graph? Name two that you see.

2. Make two predictions about average SAT math and verbal scores in 1990 using the graph.

3. What observations can you make about the average SAT math and verbal scores over the past 24 years? State three observations.

4. Make up three questions from the graph and share them with your neighbor or group.

WHAT IS THE AVERAGE?

The project in Mr. Wills' Civics class gave the students a good look at the students in Central High School. One group wanted to know what the "average" student was like in age, height and weight. They separated their results into boys and girls.

Mr. Wills explained that there are several ways of looking at the "average." They are called the mean, the median and the mode. The mean age is calculated by adding up all the age results and dividing by the number of people in the survey. The median is the middle age, when lined up from the lowest to highest. The mode age is the one that occurs most often.

There are so many ways to look at the average, he explained, because very high or very low numbers tend to make the mean less accurate. An easy way to work with averages is to make a frequency chart. There the results are organized in a systematic way. Also, the median and mode are easy to evaluate.

Age	Number of Students	Total Students	Total Age
19		3	$3 \times 19 = 57$
18		13	$13 \times 18 = 234$
17		27	$27 \times 17 = 459$
16		15	$15 \times 16 = 240$
15		23	$23 \times 15 = 345$
14		15	$15 \times 14 = 210$
13		5	$5 \times 13 = 65$
Total	101	101	1,610

What is the Average?
Problem Set A

Directions: First read the story "What Is the Average?" Information from the story and the illustration will help you to solve some of the problems below. Write your answer sentences below each problem. Where possible, use the back of this page or a separate sheet of paper to show your work.

1. Use the frequency table in the story and find the mode age.

2. Use the frequency table in the story and find the median age.

3. Use the frequency table in the story and find the mean age.

4. Survey your classmates to find their age. Put your results in a frequency table.

What Is the Average?
Problem Set B

Directions: First read the story "What Is the Average?" Information from the story and the illustration will help you to solve some of the problems below. Write your answer sentences below each problem. Where possible, use the back of this page or a separate sheet of paper to show your work.

1. Find the mean, median and mode age using the frequency chart in the story.

2. Survey your class members to find their average height in inches. Put your results in a frequency table.

3. Using the frequency table in Problem 2 of this set, find the mean height in inches.

4. Using the frequency table in Problem 2 of this set, find the median and mode height in inches.

What Is the Average?
Problem Set C

Directions: First read the story "What Is the Average?" Information from the story and the illustration will help you to solve some of the problems below. Write your answer sentences below each problem. Where possible, use the back of this page or a separate sheet of paper to show your work.

1. Conduct a survey of your classmates to determine their average age and height.

2. Compile the results into a frequency table.

3. Find the mean, median and mode responses for your classmates' ages and heights.

4. Draw a bar or line graph to show the results of either the ages or heights of your classmates.

THE CHALLENGE

With the championship game only one week away, the Central High *Times* sports staff was doing a lot of last-minute research. Jason, the sports editor, decided to run a feature article on the football team and their winning season. He assigned Tessa to the article. He told her to find lots of statistics to show how Central was favored over Bishop in the championship game.

Coach Russell told her that the team's strength included yards rushing, averaging over 175 yards per game. They were also strong on defense, holding the opponent to less than two touchdowns per game. He also told her about scouting reports and how the Bishop Tigers had scored over 20 points each game this season.

Game	Score		Yards Passing		Yards Rushing	
1	Central 16	North 12	Central 121	North 95	Central 125	North 100
2	Central 8	West 0	Central 115	West 60	Central 100	West 65
3	Central 24	South 14	Central 132	South 121	Central 150	South 160
4	Central 21	Dayton 17	Central 125	Dayton 132	Central 175	Dayton 170
5	Central 28	East 21	Central 152	East 125	Central 200	East 140
6	Central	Bishop	Central	Bishop	Central	Bishop

"Should be a real tough game for us," said Mr. Russell. "Bishop has a great offense and we have a great defense. Our team is really hoping for a championship season. Make this a good story and encourage everyone to come out to the game. Take this sheet of statistics with you to use in the story."

Tessa also interviewed Ryan, the quarterback, Mack, the kicker, and Craig, the center. The team was really excited about the game. Craig predicted that they would hold Bishop to ten points or less. Ryan thought that they would score at least two touchdowns. Mack had a streak going with ten straight points after kicks. He predicted that he would make every point after kick he tried.

Tessa wrote the article and turned it in to Jason. Now that she had learned so much about the team, even she was excited about the game.

Name _____   Period _____ Date _____

The Challenge
Problem Set A

Directions: First read the story "The Challenge." Information from the story and the statistics charts will help you to solve some of the problems that follow. Write your answer sentences below each problem. Where possible, use the back of this page or a separate sheet of paper to show your work.

Touchdown (TD) = 6 points
Point After (PAT) = 1 point
Field Goal (FG) = 3 points
Safety (S) = 2 points

1. Use the chart at the top of this page and determine the final score of the game:

Central: 2 TD 1 PAT 1 FG
Bishop: 1 TD 2 FG

2. Use the statistics chart in the story to find the average number of yards rushed by the opponents. Give your answer to the nearest tenth of a yard.

3. Use the score chart in the story to find the average number of points scored by the Tigers this year, including the Bishop game. Give your answer to the nearest tenth of a point.

4. Use the score chart in the story and find out, on an average, how many more points did the Tigers score than their opponents? Give your answer to the nearest tenth of a point.

5. Use the score chart in the story and the chart at the top of this page. List three different ways in which the Tigers could have scored their points in the first game. (Hint: The only way to score a PAT is to score a TD first.)

The Challenge
Problem Set B

Directions: First read the story "The Challenge." Information from the story and the statistics charts will help you to solve some of the problems that follow. Write your answer sentences below each problem. Where possible, use the back of this page or a separate sheet of paper to show your work.

Touchdown (TD) = 6 points
Point After (PAT) = 1 point
Field Goal (FG) = 3 points
Safety (S) = 2 points

1. Use the chart at the top of this page and determine the final score of the game:

   Central: 2 TD 1 PAT 1 FG
   Bishop: 1 TD 2 FG

2. Use the score of the championship game (from Problem 1 of this set) along with the score chart found in the story. On an average, how many more points did the Tigers score than their opponents? Give your answer to the nearest tenth of a point.

3. Use the chart in the story and the one at the beginning of this problem set. List two possible ways in which the Tigers and their opponents scored their points in the third game of the season. (Hint: The only way that you can score a PAT is to score a touchdown first.)

4. The Tigers rushed for 181 yards in the championship game. Use this information along with the statistics chart in the story. Find, to the nearest tenth of a yard, how many yards rushing did the Tigers average?

The Challenge
Problem Set C

Directions: First read the story "The Challenge." Information from the story and the statistics charts will help you to solve some of the problems that follow. Write your answer sentences below each problem. Where possible, use the back of this page or a separate sheet of paper to show your work.

Touchdown (TD)   =   6 points
Point After (PAT)   =   1 point
Field Goal (FG)   =   3 points
Safety (S)   =   2 points

1. Use the chart at the top of this page and determine the final score of the game:

   Central: 2 TD   1 PAT   1 FG
   Bishop: 1 TD   2 FG

2. Use the score chart in the story and the score from Problem 1 of this set. Draw a bar graph to show the scores of the Tigers and their opponents.

3. Use the scores in your graph from Problem 2 of this set. Find, to the nearest tenth of a point, the average number of points scored by the Tigers and their opponents.

4. Take the score of the fourth game of the season from the score chart in the story. With the use of the chart at the beginning of this problem set, list four different ways in which the Tigers could have earned their points in the fourth game of the season. (Hint: The only way to score a PAT is to score a touchdown first.)

Let's face it, this hadn't been a good year for the JV football team. The season was more than half over and they had only won two games. Injuries, particularly to the offensive line, had been heavy.

Juan Cortez, the captain of the team, was thinking about the season. The guys had never given up. This was partly due to Coach Brown, a really great guy! He worked hard and had patience with them. Another thing—he always made time to talk to anyone who needed him.

In a few weeks, the end of the season awards dinner would be held. Juan had an idea. He asked the team to stay for a few minutes after practice. He said he thought they ought to have a little something to give Coach Brown that night. The other players agreed.

Juan had found something in a catalog at home. He passed around this ad. The team members felt that something like this might be just right. It was no big deal, but it did say what they thought. Members of the team agreed to chip in. They would get the plaque and, if there was enough money, they would also buy the mug. They agreed to have Juan pass around an envelope after practice the next Monday. The order would go in early that week. They hoped to get it in time for the awards dinner.

• 101. Coach's Plaque for that person who has devoted so much time & energy to your own or your team's training! Personalized with name...supply using up to 30 characters. Perfect for all coaches in solid walnut. 7¾" × 10". 94071-8 $11.95

• 102. Coach Mug to show your appreciation! Bright and colorful in porcelain. Dishwasher, microwave safe. 10 oz. 40140-6 $4.95 Each; 2 or more $4.75 Each

To the Coach
Problem Set A

Directions: Read the story "To the Coach." You will also find needed information in the ad and on the order form below. Do the problems in order.

1. What was the total for the plaque plus the mug?

2. Look at the table for shipping and handling charges. How much should be added if the mug and plaque were ordered?

3. Will sales tax have to be added?

4. To make sure the order gets to Centerville on time, ad the amount for "rush handling." What will be the total cost?

5. Mr. Cortez said that Juan could put the order on his credit card. Juan will pay his father back with money from the team. Fill out the order form below:

PLEASE PRINT CLEARLY

PAGE NO.	NAME OF ITEM	SIX-DIGIT PRODUCT NUMBER	HOW MANY	PERSONALIZED ITEMS: Note the maximum number of letters and spaces available in the product descriptions and print the information below.	PRICE EACH	TOTAL

100% Satisfaction Guaranteed   MERCHANDISE TOTAL ▶

Name _____

Address _____

Address _____

City _____ State _____ Zip _____

CHARGE MY ORDER TO: ☐ VISA   ☐ MasterCard

VISA   **MasterCard**

Card Expires: Mo. Year

1	2	3	4	5	6	7	8	9	10	11	12	13	14	15	16

SIGNATURE:

Shipping & Handling Charges
Covers order processing, packaging, delivery costs.
Up to 10.00, add 2.60
10.01 to 15.00, add 3.45
15.01 to 25.00, add 4.00
25.01 to 35.00, add 4.60
35.01 to 50.00, add 5.20
50.01 to 75.00, add 5.85
Over 75.00, add 6.45

TOTAL ORDER ▶

SHIPPING AND HANDLING ▶
Is your order going to more than one address? If it is, add $1.00 for each additional address.

RUSH HANDLING ADD AN ADDITIONAL 50¢

SUB-TOTAL ▶

INDIANA RESIDENTS ADD 5% SALES TAX ▶

Total of Check or Money Order ☐
Total Charged to Credit Card ☐   **THANK YOU!** $

PLEASE DO NOT SEND CASH OR STAMPS.

MAILING LISTS: Sometimes we make our customer lists available to organizations whose products may be of interest to you. If you would prefer not to receive such mailings, check box.

Under "Personalized Items" put the coach's name, Leroy Brown. Check whichever credit card you decide Mr. Cortez holds.

Name _____   Period _____   Date _____

To the Coach
Problem Set B

Directions: Read the story "To the Coach." You will also find needed information in the ad and on the order form. State sales taxes are collected only from people buying in that state. Ignore the sales tax line since this order is being placed in California.

1. What is the total of prices for the plaque and the mug?

2. Juan decided to pay for "Rush Handling" to make sure that the order got to Centerville on time. How much did he add for shipping, handling and "Rush Handling"?

3. What was the total amount to be paid?

4. Mr. Cortez said that Juan could put the order on his credit card. Juan will pay his father back with money from the team. Fill out the order form below:

PLEASE PRINT CLEARLY

PAGE NO.	NAME OF ITEM	SIX-DIGIT PRODUCT NUMBER	HOW MANY	PERSONALIZED ITEMS: Note the maximum number of letters and spaces available in the product descriptions and print the information below.	PRICE EACH	TOTAL

100% Satisfaction Guaranteed   MERCHANDISE TOTAL ▶

Name _____

Address _____

Address _____

City _____ State _____ Zip _____

CHARGE MY ORDER TO: ☐ VISA   ☐ MasterCard

VISA   MasterCard

Card Expires: Mo. Year

1 2 3 4 5 6 7 8 9 10 11 12 13 14 15 16

SIGNATURE:

Shipping & Handling Charges
Covers order processing, packaging, delivery costs.
Up to 10.00, add 2.60
10.01 to 15.00, add 3.45
15.01 to 25.00, add 4.00
25.01 to 35.00, add 4.60
35.01 to 50.00, add 5.20
50.01 to 75.00, add 5.85
Over 75.00, add 6.45

TOTAL ORDER ▶

SHIPPING AND HANDLING ▶
Is your order going to more than one address? If it is, add $1.00 for each additional address.
RUSH HANDLING ▶
ADD AN ADDITIONAL 50¢

SUB-TOTAL ▶

INDIANA RESIDENTS ▶
ADD 5% SALES TAX

Total of Check or Money Order ☐
Total Charged to Credit Card ☐ **$**
THANK YOU!

PLEASE DO NOT SEND CASH OR STAMPS.

MAILING LISTS: Sometimes we make our customer lists available to organizations whose products may be of interest to you. If you would prefer not to receive such mailings, check box.

Under "Personalized Items" put in the coach's name, Leroy Brown. Check whichever credit card you decide that Mr. Cortez holds.

5. About what is the average amount the 30 team members of the JV team would need to chip in (to the nearest cent)?

To the Coach
Problem Set C

Directions: Read the story "To the Coach." Added information will be found in the ad and on the order form.

1. What is the "merchandise total" for the mug and plaque?

2. Juan decided to pay for "Rush Handling." When you add this to other charges (see order form), what is the total cost of this order?

3. Mr. Cortez said Juan could charge the order to his credit card. Juan will pay his father back with money from the team. Fill in the order form below.

PLEASE PRINT CLEARLY

PAGE NO.	NAME OF ITEM	SIX-DIGIT PRODUCT NUMBER	HOW MANY	PERSONALIZED ITEMS: Note the maximum number of letters and spaces available in the product descriptions and print the information below.	PRICE EACH	TOTAL

100% Satisfaction Guaranteed — MERCHANDISE TOTAL ▶

Shipping & Handling Charges
Covers order processing, packaging, delivery costs.
Up to 10.00, add 2.60
10.01 to 15.00, add 3.45
15.01 to 25.00, add 4.00
25.01 to 35.00, add 4.60
35.01 to 50.00, add 5.20
50.01 to 75.00, add 5.85
Over 75.00, add 6.45

Name _____
Address _____
Address _____
City _____ State _____ Zip _____

CHARGE MY ORDER TO: ☐ VISA   ☐ MasterCard

VISA   MasterCard

Card Expires:
Mo. Year

1 2 3 4 5 6 7 8 9 10 11 12 13 14 15 16

SIGNATURE:

PLEASE DO NOT SEND CASH OR STAMPS.

TOTAL ORDER ▶
SHIPPING AND HANDLING ▶
Is your order going to more than one address? If it is, add $1.00 for each additional address.
RUSH HANDLING ADD AN ADDITIONAL 50¢
SUB-TOTAL ▶
INDIANA RESIDENTS ADD 5% SALES TAX ▶

Total of Check or Money Order ☐
Total Charged to Credit Card ☐ **$**
THANK YOU!

MAILING LISTS: Sometimes we make our customer lists available to organizations whose products may be of interest to you. If you would prefer not to receive such mailings, check box.

Under "Personalized Items" put in the coach's name, Leroy Brown. Check whichever credit card you decide Mr. Cortez holds.

4. About what contribution would each of the 30 players on the team need to pay the bill?

5. "Flanker" Fong, one of the team members, had another idea. He said that Mrs. Brown, one of the other teachers and the coach's wife, was their biggest rooter. He thought it would be nice to give her flowers at the banquet. If they each put in a dollar, how much could they spend at the florist for her after paying for the coach's gift?

THE PRO GAME

Football season at Central High School was over. While Michael liked playing, he didn't miss practice too much. He really needed time to study more. He was ready to settle for pro games on TV through January.

Early in December his father said, "Michael, a friend of mine has Wildcat season tickets. He can't use them for the Driller game. He asked if you and I could use them. Would you like to go?"

"Would I?" said Michael. "I've never been to a pro game before. That game's in Jackson City. How do we get there?"

"Let's look at the map," said his father.

"Where's the stadium?" asked Michael.

"At the junction of I 117 and I 113," his father replied.

Michael saw that they could go two ways. One way would be to go through Edgewater to the freeway. The other would be to go through the mountains by Summit City. There could be snow in the mountains at this time of year, he remembered.

The Pro Game
Problem Set A

Directions: Read the story "The Pro Game" first. You will also use information from the map. You may want to use your calculator. Write your answer sentences below each problem. Where possible, use the back of this page or a separate sheet of paper to show your work.

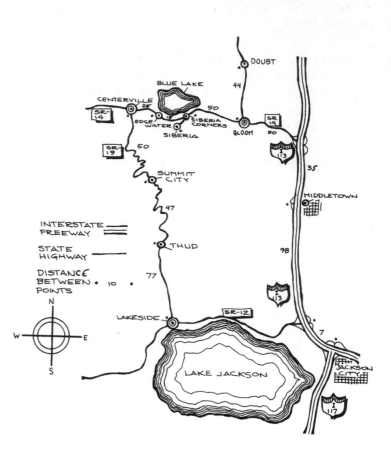

1. How far is it from Centerville to the freeway?

2. How many miles will Michael's father drive on the freeway to get to the stadium?

3. Just after the game, Michael's father called a friend in Lakeside. He and Michael were invited to dinner. They decided to go to Lakeside. What direction did they drive from Jackson City?

4. How much further did they drive from Lakeside to get home?

5. Tell how to go home from Jackson City through Lakeside. Use compass directions and highway numbers. Give directions, beginning with "Turn west at the State Route (SR) 12 freeway exit...."

Name _____   **Period** _____   **Date** _____

The Pro Game
Problem Set B

Directions: Read the story "The Pro Game" first. You will need to use some story information. You will refer to the map for most problems. You may wish to use your calculator. Write your answer sentences below each problem. Where possible, use the back of this page or a separate sheet of paper to show your work.

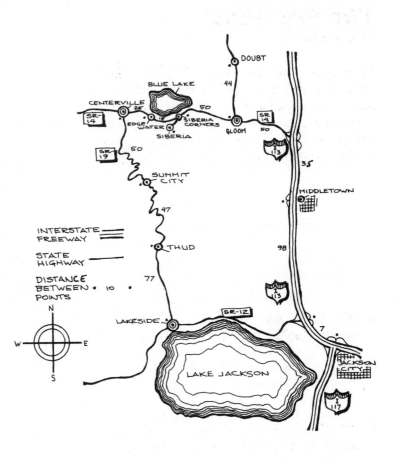

1. How far is it from Centerville to the stadium in Jackson City if they go on the freeway (I 113)?

2. How many miles would it take to go by way of Summit City to the stadium in Jackson City?

3. Which way is shorter?

4. Which way do you think will take longer? Give two reasons.

5. Tell how to go from the freeway junction in Jackson City to Centerville by way of Lakeside. Mention highway numbers and compass directions.

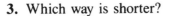

The Pro Game
Problem Set C

Directions: Read the story "The Pro Game." You will need to use the map. Your calculator will also be useful. Write your answer sentences below each problem. Where possible, use the back of this page or a separate sheet of paper to show your work.

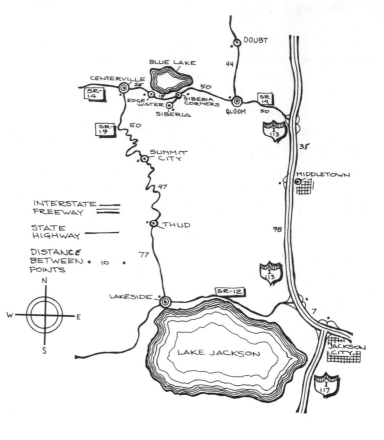

1. There are two ways to get to Jackson City from Centerville. Pick the one you think would be the faster and give two reasons for your choice.

2. They chose the faster route. Michael estimated that his father would average 50 miles per hour. They want to get to the stadium by noon. Allowing for two rest stops, about when should they leave home in order to arrive at the stadium by noon?

3. It took three hours to get to the freeway. What was their average speed to that point?

4. Michael's father called a friend in Lakeside. He invited them for dinner after the game. How far did they have to go to get home from Lakeside?

5. It was snowing above Thud. They had to put on chains at Thud and remove them at Summit City. At 30 miles per hour, how long did it take them to drive this part of the trip?

TABLE FOR EIGHT?

The prom committee met to discuss plans for decorating the gym. Raj, Erin, Marco and Wendy had the responsibility of getting enough card tables and chairs to seat everyone. The committee decided to use one table for four people. If more than two couples wanted to sit as a group, they would put tables together. Two tables together would seat six people. Three tables together would seat eight, and so on.

"How are the ticket sales going?" asked Raj.

"Well, one ticket represents two people. So far we've sold 90 tickets. I think we should plan for 120 tickets to be sold," answered Marilyn, the ticket chairperson.

"Let's not make tables for more than 12 people," suggested Erin. "I think the room will look nicer that way," she added.

"And no table should have fewer than four people," said Wendy.

"When people pick up the tickets they can reserve a table. That will make it easiest to set up," added Marco.

"Start asking around to find tables and cloths. Sounds like we'll need quite a few," said Raj.

Table for Eight?
Problem Set A/B

Directions: First read the story "Table for Eight?"
Information from the story will help solve some of
the problems below. Write your answer sentences
below each problem. Where possible, use the back
of this page or a separate sheet of paper to show
your work.

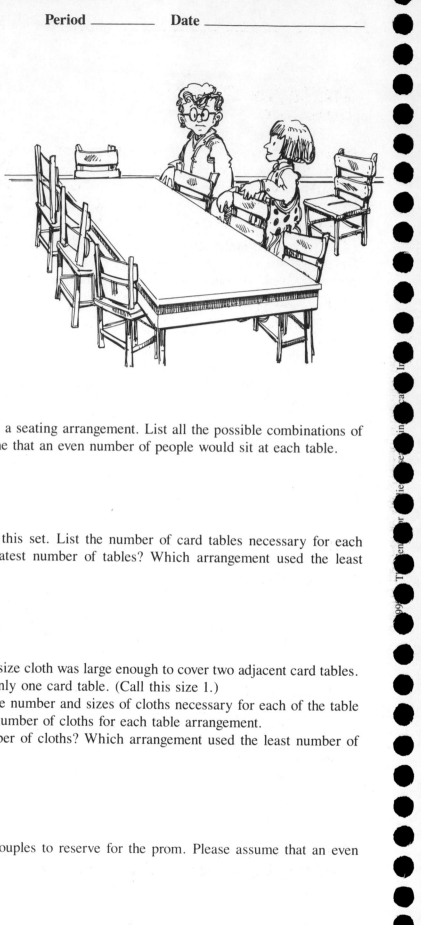

1. How many tables would be needed for ten people
   to sit together? Draw a diagram to support your
   answer.

2. A group of six couples were trying to decide on a seating arrangement. List all the possible combinations of
   table sizes that they could reserve. Please assume that an even number of people would sit at each table.

3. Refer to the table sizes listed in Problem 2 of this set. List the number of card tables necessary for each
   arrangement. Which arrangement used the greatest number of tables? Which arrangement used the least
   number of tables?

4. The table cloths were in two different sizes. One size cloth was large enough to cover two adjacent card tables.
   (Call this size 2.) The other size cloth covered only one card table. (Call this size 1.)
       Refer back to Problem 2 of this set. List the number and sizes of cloths necessary for each of the table
   arrangements in Problem 2. Use the minimum number of cloths for each table arrangement.
       Which arrangement used the greatest number of cloths? Which arrangement used the least number of
   cloths?

5. Draw three possible table arrangements for 16 couples to reserve for the prom. Please assume that an even
   number of people will sit at each table.

Table for Eight?
Problem Set C

Directions: First read the story "Table for Eight?" Information from the story will help to solve some of the problems below. Write your answer sentences below each problem. Where possible, use the back of this page or a separate sheet of paper to show your work.

1. How many tables would be needed for ten people to sit together? Draw a diagram to support your answer.

2. A group of eight couples were trying to decide on a seating arrangement. List all the possible combinations of table sizes that they could reserve. Please assume that an even number of people will sit at each table.

3. Refer to the list of table sizes in Problem 2 of this set. List the number of card tables necessary for each arrangement. Which arrangement used the greatest number of tables? Which arrangement used the least number of tables?

4. The table cloths were in two different sizes. One size cloth was large enough to cover two adjacent card tables. (Call this size 2.) The other size cloth covered only one card table. (Call this size 1.)
   Refer to Problem 2 of this set. List the number and sizes of cloths necessary for each of the table arrangements in Problem 2. Use the minimum number of cloths for each table arrangement.
   Which arrangement used the greatest number of cloths? Which arrangement used the least number of cloths?

5. If 120 couples attended the prom, what do you think would be the least number of tables necessary to seat them all? Why do you think this? Share your answer and your thoughts with your group or partner.

© 1990 by The Center for Applied Research in Education, Inc.

JAKE'S SURPRISE

Jake appeared out of place as he worked in the Andersons' kitchen. Michael and Tessa came over to help him prepare for the surprise anniversary dinner.

"It was all Jake's idea," whispered Tessa when Jake went into the next room. "He even got a 6½ pound ham for the dinner and he bought the Andersons a new lamp for $10 down and payments."

"He never seemed the type to me," Michael replied. "Why so sentimental all of a sudden?"

It did seem out of character for Jake to take such an interest in the Andersons. It had been over a year since Jake had arrived at their home. They had had several heated discussions about house rules, but the problems eventually worked out. Michael's parents had invited the Andersons over earlier to celebrate. "They should be here in a few minutes," said Jake. "Tessa, hurry and finish the table," he added. "Someone come in here—quick! I think the oven's on fire!" he cried.

Michael and Jake cleared the smoke from the kitchen just as the front door opened. The Andersons were overwhelmed by Jake's idea and offered their help in getting things onto the table. The Samuelsons and Mrs. Martin helped Tessa with the chairs.

"The dinner was a success! Thanks for including us, Jake," said Mrs. Samuelson.

Jake, Michael and Tessa finished up in the kitchen and joined the others for dessert in the family room. Soon afterwards the Samuelsons and the Martins left. Jake was unusually quiet before saying goodnight and going into his room.

"I'd better wait until tomorrow," Jake thought. "I know they won't like the idea, but I'm ready to get out on my own. I have a steady job working 35 hours a week and sometimes I'll be able to work overtime. As soon as I'm eighteen, I'll find a place and move out. Now, I just have to find a way to break the news!"

Jake's Surprise
Problem Set A

Directions: First read the story "Jake's Surprise." Information from the story will help you to solve some of the problems below. Write your answer sentences below each problem. Where possible, use the back of this page or a separate sheet of paper to show your work.

1. The ham that Jake bought was priced at $1.79 per pound. What was the total cost?

2. The ham had to bake 30 minutes per pound. How long did the ham have to bake?

3. Tessa bought flowers for the table. They cost $3.29 and she paid with $5.00. Name two ways in which the clerk could have given her the correct change.

4. Jake turned 18 on May 17. How many days did he have until his birthday if the party took place on April 3?

5. Jake bought the ham, potatoes, green beans and bread. The total price was $15.49. The ham cost $11.64, the potatoes cost $1.19 and the beans cost $.79. Estimate the cost of the bread.

Jake's Surprise
Problem Set B

Directions: First read the story "Jake's Surprise." Information from the story will help you to solve some of the problems below. Write your answer sentences below each problem. Where possible, use the back of this page or a separate sheet of paper to show your work.

1. Tessa bought flowers for the table. They cost $3.29 and she paid with $5.00. Name two ways in which the clerk could have given her the correct change.

2. Jake earned overtime when he worked more than 8 hours each day. He worked 6 hours Monday, 5 hours Tuesday, 8 hours Wednesday, 9 hours Friday and 10 hours Saturday. How many overtime hours did he work? How many regular hours did he work?

3. Jake figured he had to earn $129.50 per week in order to afford an apartment. How many regular hours (to the nearest tenth) would he have to work at $3.75 per hour in order to earn $129.50?

4. The landlord told Jake that he needed to pay two months' rent before he could move in. If the rent is $205 per month and Jake had $195 saved up, how much more did he need before he can move in?

5. The landlord also told Jake that he must plan on paying the electric bill. Over the past three months the electric bill for a similar apartment was $32.15, $19.94 and $23.50. Estimate the average cost for electricity.

Jake's Surprise
Problem Set C

Directions: First read the story "Jake's Surprise." Information from the story will help you to solve some of the problems below. Write your answer sentences below each problem. Where possible, use the back of this page or a separate sheet of paper to show your work.

1. Jake decided to cut down on personal expenses. He used to spend $37.50 per month. If he reduced his spending by 20%, how much could he now spend on personal expenses?

2. Jake lived 12.3 miles from the Burger Barn. He traveled 175 miles on his motorcycle each week and worked 5 days. Other than the miles he traveled to work and back, how many miles did he travel each week?

3. Jake bought gas for $4.76. He paid with $5.00. List all the possible coin combinations he could have received for the correct change.

4. The ham required 3¼ hours for baking. If Jake put it in at 2:52 P.M., what time was the ham done?

5. The dining table was 8 feet long. How many 18-inch place mats could be put on each side if you wanted 6 inches of table to show on both sides of every mat?

Jake had a hard day of work on his new job. He had started early in the morning. His boss, Fred, sent him out with a load to Siberia Corners. That was 45 miles out of town.

Fred told him to load the company pickup. Loading took 15 minutes of hard work. He also had to unload when he got to Siberia Corners. Jake got back to Centerville for lunch. After lunch, he worked until 5 o'clock in the hot warehouse unloading and stacking bags.

Jake took a shower when he got home. He then ate and looked at mail advertising. He saw a coat he really liked. The price was $29.95. If he sent a check with the order he would save postage and handling charges. These were $3.25 which would have been added.

Jake had written two small checks after paying his rent. This left a bank balance of $105.47. He decided to send for the coat. He would also send a check with the order. The company advertisement was "Sale by Mail."

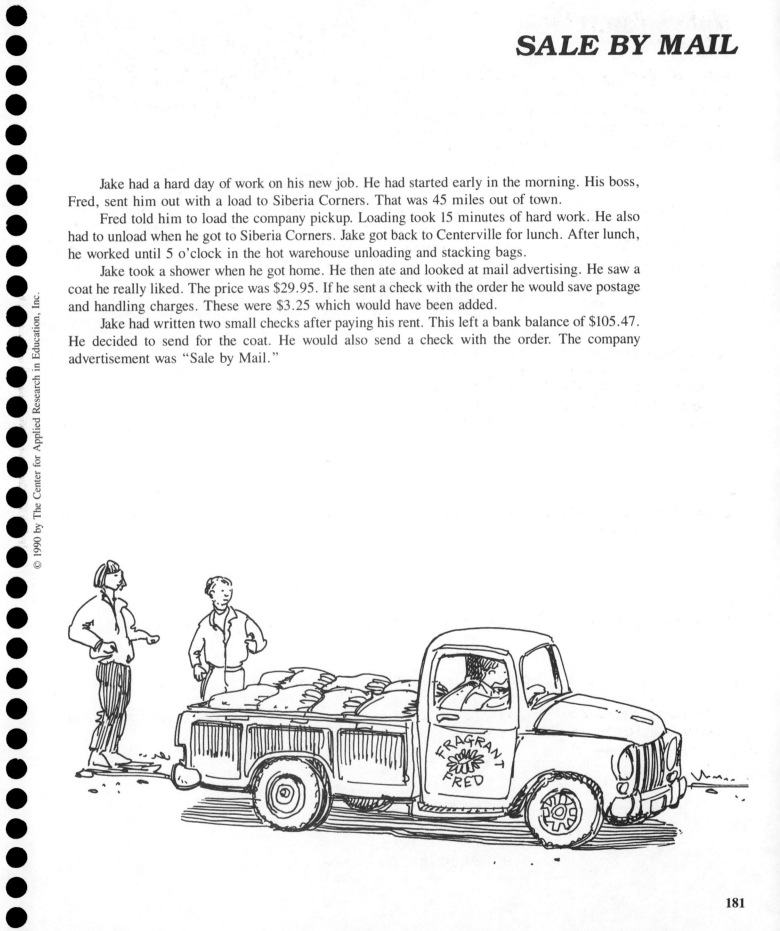

Name _____   Period _____ Date _____

Sale by Mail
Problem Set A/B/C

Directions: Read the story "Sale by Mail." Answer the problems or fill out the checks as Jake would have done. For Problem 2, write your answer sentence below the problem. Where possible, use the back of this page or a separate piece of paper to show your work.

1. Fill out Jake's check stub and the check he sent to pay for the coat. (Remember to include the 15-cent check charge on the stub.)

```
_____ 19 ___
104
$ _____
TO _____
FOR _____
           DOLLARS | CENTS
OLD
BALANCE
DEPOSITED
TOTAL
THIS CHECK
TOTAL
IF SPEC. CHECKING
CHECK CHARGE
NEW
BALANCE
```

CENTERVILLE BANK
711 MAIN ST.
CENTERVILLE, CA 95999

11-24/170
1210(8)   104

_____ 19 ___

PAY TO THE
ORDER OF _____ $ _____

_____ DOLLARS

JAKE BURTON
123 NORTH ST.
CENTERVILLE, CA 95999

_____

⑆121000248⑈785 0170 241104⑈

2. The next day Jake bought some food at the Farmer Foods store. The tag came to $25.43. He asked if he could write a check for $35.00. The manager asked for Jake's driver's license. He checked it and said "OK." How much change did Jake get?

3. Fill out Jake's check to Farmer Foods. Remember to fill out the stub first.

```
_____ 19 ___
105
$ _____
TO _____
FOR _____
           DOLLARS | CENTS
OLD
BALANCE
DEPOSITED
TOTAL
THIS CHECK
TOTAL
IF SPEC. CHECKING
CHECK CHARGE
NEW
BALANCE
```

CENTERVILLE BANK
711 MAIN ST.
CENTERVILLE, CA 95999

11-24/170
1210(8)   105

_____ 19 ___

PAY TO THE
ORDER OF _____ $ _____

_____ DOLLARS

JAKE BURTON
123 NORTH ST.
CENTERVILLE, CA 95999

_____

⑆121000248⑈785 0170 241104⑈

Sale by Mail
Problem Set A/B/C (Cont'd)

4. On November 28 Jake got a statement from the bank. It showed a balance of $70.32. Jake's checkbook showed a balance of $40.22. The statement listed:

Deposits	Date	Amount
	Nov 1	100.00
	Nov 9	137.82

Check	Amount	Check	Amount
101	115.00	103	10.00
102	6.90	105	35.00
Other charges	$ .60	Ending balance	$ 70.32

Was the statement correct? What were the "Other charges"?

5. Why did the statement balance differ from Jake's checkbook balance?

A DAY AT CLEAR LAKE

Mr. Samuelson was thinking about buying a boat. He wanted one that could safely carry 8 people. It would also be used for water skiing. The boat shop had a 2-year-old 16-foot fiberglass boat for sale. It was an inboard-outboard model with a 160-horsepower engine. It also came with a trailer. Michael really wanted his father to buy the boat and trailer. Mr. Samuelson said he might. But he wanted to try it on Clear Lake first. The boat shop agreed to let him try it out the next weekend.

Mr. and Mrs. Samuelson asked Mrs. Martin and Tessa to go along. Michael also invited two friends. He asked Maggie and Dan. Mrs. Martin said she would provide up to $50 for food and drinks. Michael, Dan, Tessa and Maggie agreed to buy and prepare it.

It was 54 miles to Clear Lake. They would need to buy gas for the van. The boat would also need gas and oil. Mr. Samuelson said he would pay these costs.

On Saturday morning everyone was up early. They were ready to leave by 7:15 A.M. They expected to get to the lake in about an hour. However, the highways were busy and it took longer. Mr. Samuelson's van usually got around 24 miles per gallon on the highway. With the slow traffic, and the extra weight of the boat, he figured his mileage would be about 1/3 less. Even though the trip took longer than expected, everyone had a good time. They enjoyed seeing the different sights and teasing each other. They even sang a couple of songs.

Luckily, when they got to the lake, the boat ramp wasn't busy. They launched the boat and had it loaded in a short time. Soon they were speeding toward the other end of the lake. Michael knew that the lake was 7 miles long. The boat speedometer read 37 mph. They would spend the day boat riding and water skiing. Later they would have a picnic. This was great!

A Day at Clear Lake
Problem Set A

Directions: First read the story "A Day at Clear Lake." You will use facts from the story to solve some of the problems. You may also need to get information from a grocery store, a service station, a boat shop and reference books. Write your answer sentences below the problems. Where it helps, use a calculator.

1. The Samuelsons and their friends left for Clear Lake at 7:15 A.M. They arrived 1 hour and 40 minutes later. What time was it when they got to the lake?

2. Mrs. Martin said she would pay up to $50 for food. Michael, Dan, Tessa and Maggie were to buy enough for lunch and snacks. They would also need enough drinks for 7 people. What kind and how much food should they have bought? Keep a list of the foods you think should have been purchased. Also figure out the cost.

3. Michael knew that Clear Lake was 7 miles long. The boat speedometer read 37 mph. About how many minutes did it take to travel the length of the lake?

4. The boat had a 160-horsepower engine. Find the term "horsepower" in a reference book and tell what it means.

5. The Samuelsons were trying a 16-foot fiberglass boat. It was an inboard-outboard model with a 160-horsepower motor. It also had nice seats, a steering wheel and running lights. About how much would such a boat cost?

A Day at Clear Lake
Problem Set B

Directions: First read the story "A Day at Clear Lake." You will use facts from the story to solve some of the problems. You may also need to get information from a grocery store, a service station, a boat shop and reference books. Write your answer sentences below the problems. Where it helps, use a calculator.

1. They left for Clear Lake at 7:15 A.M. The traffic was moving slowly. They averaged only 35 miles per hour. What time was it when they got to the lake?

2. Michael, Dan Tessa and Maggie were to buy and prepare the food. Mrs. Martin was providing up to $50 for this. They needed food for 7 people. What kind and how much food should they have bought? Keep a list of the foods you think should have been purchased. Also figure out the cost.

3. The boat speedometer read 37 mph. The lake was 7 miles long. About how many minutes did it take to travel down the lake and back again?

4. Dan noticed an outboard motor that had "9.8 horsepower" painted on it. Another was marked "45 HP." The boat that the Samuelsons were trying out had a 160-horsepower engine. Find the term "horsepower" in a reference book and tell what it means.

5. The Samuelsons were trying a 16-foot fiberglass boat. It was an inboard-outboard model with a 160-horsepower motor. It also had nice seats, a steering wheel and running lights. About how much would such a boat cost?

A Day at Clear Lake

Problem Set C

Directions: First read the story "A Day at Clear Lake." You will need to use information from the story to solve some of the problems. You may also need to gather related information from a grocery store, a service station, reference books and a boat shop. Write your answer sentences below the problems. When it helps, use a calculator.

1. Due to the extra weight of the boat and the slow traffic, Mr. Samuelson estimated that the van's mileage would be about 1/3 less. How many gallons of gasoline did the van need for the entire trip to and from Clear Lake? What would this much unleaded gasoline cost?

2. Mrs. Martin provided $50 to Michael, Dan, Tessa and Maggie so that they could purchase and prepare the food. What kind and how much food should they have bought in order to feed everyone? Keep a list of the foods you think should have been purchased and determine the final cost.

3. The boat speedometer read 37 mph and the lake was 7 miles long. At that rate, about how many minutes did it take to travel down the lake and back again? The boat salesperson had said that this boat would use approximately 5 gallons of gasoline per hour when running at fast speeds. Thus, how much gas was used when going down the lake and back? Estimate the gasoline cost for this one trip. Also estimate the cost of gasoline for the entire day of boating.

4. What does the term "horsepower" mean? Dan noticed an outboard motor that had "9.8 horsepower" painted on the side of it. Another was marked "45 HP." The boat that the Samuelsons were trying out had a 160-horsepower engine. Will the Samuelsons' boat, with its 160-HP engine, travel nearly 4 times as fast as the 45-HP motor, and approximately 16 times faster than the 9.8-HP motor? Why or why not?

5. The boat that Mr. Samuelson was trying out had nice seats, a steering wheel and running lights. What other features did this particular boat have? What is the approximate value of such a boat and a trailer to haul it? How much might be saved by purchasing a 2-year-old boat that is in good condition?

SURVEY

"For your final project in Civics class you must conduct a survey of the student body," said Mr. Wills. "The survey must cover at least 100 people, include members from classes in the school and your questionnaire must have at least four questions. This must be completed by May 15. Now, get together with your group and discuss what your survey will cover. The survey topics are due next Monday in class."

Jed's group decided that they would ask (1) the number of cars in your family, (2) the number of miles you travel one way to school, (3) what you think is the best radio station, and (4) whether you think smoking should be allowed on campus.

Trent would make out the questionnaire. Meta was responsible for writing the report. Jed and Shelly were to make the graphs. Each group member would compile the results from one question.

CIVICS CLASS PROJECT
Mr. Wills

Directions: Please complete the following questions. The results will be used in a civics class project. Thank you.

1. How many cars do your immediate family members own?

    0 1 2 3 4 5 _____
                          other

2. How many miles do you travel one way to school? Round to the nearest mile.

    0 1 2 3 4 5 _____
                          other

3. What is your favorite radio station?   _____

4. Do you think that smoking should be allowed on campus?   No   Yes

---

Name _____   Period _____   Date _____

Survey
Problem Set A

Directions: First read the story "Survey." Information from the story and the illustration will help you to solve some of the problems that follow. Write your answer sentences below each problem. Where possible, use the back of this page or a separate sheet of paper to show your work.

1. List the two questions that Jed's group asked and that required an opinion answer.

2. List the two questions that Jed's group asked and that required a factual answer.

3. Take one question in Problem 1 of this set and ask your classmates to respond. Record the results in a frequency chart.

Response	*Tally*	*Total*

4. Take one question in Problem 2 of this set and ask your classmates to respond. Record the results in a frequency chart.

Response	*Tally*	*Total*

Survey
Problem Set B

Directions: First read the story "Survey." Information from the story and the illustration will help you to solve some of the problems that follow. Write your answer sentences below each problem. Where possible, use the back of this page or a separate sheet of paper to show your work.

1. Ask your classmates to respond to one of the questions in Jed's survey that required a factual answer. Organize the results in the frequency table.

Response	*Tally*	*Total*

2. Draw a bar graph to show the results from Problem 1 of this set.

3. Ask your classmates to respond to one of the questions in Jed's survey that required an opinionated response. Record the results in the frequency chart.

Response	*Tally*	*Total*

Survey
Problem Set C

Directions: First read the story "Survey." Information from the story and the illustration will help you to solve some of the problems that follow. Write your answer sentences below each problem. Where possible, use the back of this page or a separate sheet of paper to show your work.

1. Conduct a school survey similar to the one mentioned in the story. Include two questions that require opinion answers. Also include two questions that require factual (numerical) answers.

2. Show the results to Problem 1 of this set in a frequency table.

3. Draw a bar graph to show the responses to one of the questions of your survey.

SUMMER PLANS

"I'm so sorry, Mrs. Applegate. I hope your shoes aren't ruined," said Mr. Lindsey.

"Tessa, now get the mop and clean it up," he continued.

As Tessa cleaned up the broken vinegar bottle she thought about how guilty she felt for staining Mrs. Applegate's shoes. She knew that she had better keep her mind on her job or else she'd lose it. She felt so lonely now that Maggie had moved to Oregon. Summer was near. So many plans were changed now without Maggie around.

Tessa had started working for Mr. Lindsey's grocery store two weeks ago. She was glad to finally get a job so that she had spending money. Tessa also wanted to save for a car. She knew she'd better concentrate more on the job if she hoped to keep it. Tessa had a full day ahead of her. Shipments of produce arrived. They had to be priced and displayed. She noticed that lemons were on sale at 3 for $.29, lettuce at $.59 a head and avocados at 2 for $.79.

Daily Specials			
Lettuce	$.59	Beans	$.79/2 lb.
Squash	$.89/lb.	Butter	$1.19/lb.
Potatoes	$.29/lb.	Avocado	2 for $.79

During their break that day Michael and Tessa talked about Maggie. They started planning a trip to Oregon. They decided to check into bus and plane fares. Each could only get one week off. Even that was without pay. Michael said he'd volunteer himself and Tessa for overtime to earn extra money. Overtime would pay $5.25 per hour.

Tessa returned home after work. Later she talked over the vacation plans with her mom. She could hardly wait to write to Maggie and tell her of their plans. After dinner she sat down and began her letter. The summer just might turn out all right after all.

Name _____   Period _____   Date _____

Summer Plans
Problem Set A

Directions: First read the story "Summer Plans." Information from the story and illustration will help you to solve some of the problems below. Write your answer sentences below each problem. Where possible, use the back of this page or a separate sheet of paper to show your work.

1. Tessa unpacked four crates of oranges. Each crate contained four dozen oranges. How many oranges did Tessa unpack in all?

2. How much would it cost to buy 2½ pounds of green beans?

3. At the marked price, how much will one lemon cost?

4. Each bunch of broccoli weighed 3/4 pound. How many bunches were needed for 5 pounds of broccoli?

5. Peanuts sold for $1.20 per pound. How many pounds could you buy with $5.00?

Daily Specials			
Lettuce	$.59	Beans	$.79/2 lb.
Squash	$.89/lb.	Butter	$1.19/lb.
Potatoes	$.29/lb.	Avocado	2 for $.79

Summer Plans
Problem Set B

Directions: First read the story "Summer Plans." Information from the story and illustration will help you to solve some of the problems below. Write your answer sentences below each problem. Where possible, use the back of this page or a separate sheet of paper to show your work.

1. Green peppers sold for $.59 per pound. How much would three peppers cost if they each weighed 1/4 pound?

2. How many heads of lettuce could you buy with $3? How much change would you receive?

3. Green grapes sold 3 pounds for $1.79. Purple grapes sold 2 pounds for $1.15. Which grapes had the lower price per pound?

4. Apples sold by the bag with a dozen and a half per bag. How many bags would you have to buy to get 75 apples?

5. Carrots normally sold for $.27 per pound. On sale they sold for $.19 per pound. How much would you save in all by buying 10 pounds of carrots on sale?

Daily Specials			
Lettuce	$.59	Beans	$.79/2 lb.
Squash	$.89/lb.	Butter	$1.19/lb.
Potatoes	$.29/lb.	Avocado	2 for $.79

Summer Plans
Problem Set C

Directions: First read the story "Summer Plans." Information from the story and illustration will help you to solve some of the problems below. Write your answer sentences below each problem. Where possible, use the back of this page or a separate sheet of paper to show your work.

1. The bus company ran a special. If you bought one adult ticket at regular fare, another adult could travel for half-fare. A one-way ticket normally cost $33.40. How much would Michael and Tessa pay in all for two round-trip tickets? Assume that they took advantage of the special.

2. Tessa's regular pay was $3.40 per hour. If she worked 25 regular hours and 5 overtime hours, how much would she earn?

3. Michael earned $3.50 per hour for his regular pay. Monday he worked 4.5 hours, Tuesday 5.2 hours, Wednesday 6.1 hours and Saturday 10.4 hours. How much did he earn in all?

4. Tessa earned $93.50 in gross wages. How many hours did she work at regular rate ($3.40 per hour)?

5. Michael earned $3.50 per hour for his regular pay. He worked 6 overtime hours and earned $105 in gross pay. How many regular hours did he work?

THE DINOSAURS ROCK

"Mike, how about turning on KUKU? Let's see what's on. Maybe they'll play that new Dinosaurs album."

"Good idea, Jed," replied Michael, "In three seconds, you'll hear from my dad." He was almost right. Jed timed Mr. Samuelson's bellow of "Turn it down!" at five seconds after the radio went on.

Michael had just lowered the volume a bit when great news came on: "Flash! KUKU is first to let you know! The Dinosaurs will appear in person! One time only! Middletown fairgrounds will be the place. May 23 is the date. The concert will be from two to five that day. $12.50 tickets will be on sale at Dizzy Dave's Disk and Tape. Don't miss this one!"

Did Michael and Jed want to go? Does the sun rise in the east? All that was left was to figure out the answer to a few problems. Would their folks let them go? Could they get a car? Who would go with them? What would it cost? How would they pay for it?

They got out a map to see how far it was to Middletown. It would also show them how to get there.

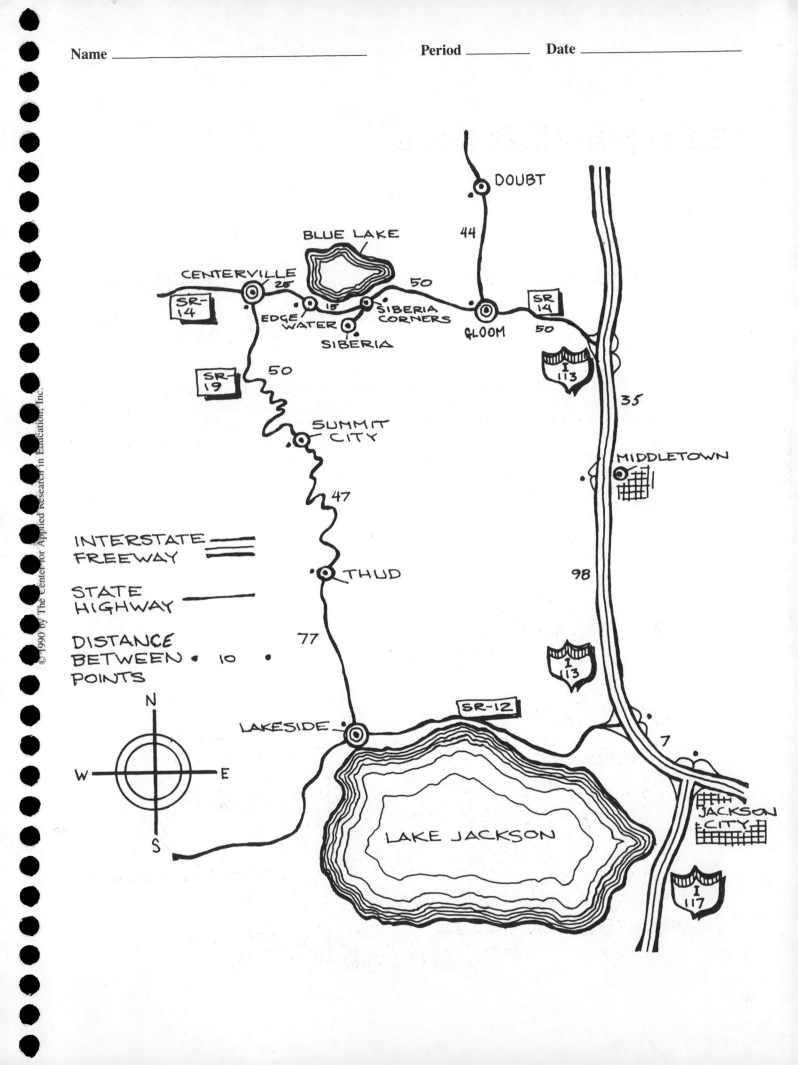

The Dinosaurs Rock
Problem Set A

Directions: Read the story "The Dinosaurs Rock." You will also need information from the map. For estimates, the calculator will help. Use local prices for Problem 5.

1. Michael and Jed decided to ask Tessa, Maggie and Jack to go with them. How much would the tickets cost for this group?

2. How far would they have to drive from Centerville to Middletown and back?

3. Weather should be good in May. If they averaged 45 miles an hour, about how long would it take each way? 4 hours? 6 hours? 8 hours?

4. They hoped to average 22 miles to a gallon of gas. How much would the round trip take (to the nearest gallon)?

5. Nobody expected to starve. If they left after breakfast they would eat before and after the concert. If you were going, how much money would you need to take for food? List what you would eat below. Use local prices.

Before the Concert		After the Concert	
Items	Prices	Items	Prices
Total			

I would need to take at least $_____ (top off the nearest dollar).

The Dinosaurs Rock
Problem Set B

Directions: Read the story "The Dinosaurs Rock." You will also need to refer to the map. Your calculator will be helpful in making estimates. Do the problems.

1. Michael and Jed invited Tessa, Maggie and Jake to go with them. In addition to the ticket price, there was a $2 service charge for any ticket order. If Jed bought all the tickets in one order, how much would he pay altogether?

2. Jed's mother said he could use the car. He figured they would drive 10 miles in town in picking up and leaving people at their homes. He then checked the map to find round-trip miles between Centerville and Middletown. How far did he expect to drive in all?

3. It took half an hour to pick up Jed's friends. If he could average 45 miles per hour between Centerville and Middletown, how long would he drive one way after leaving the house?

4. Jed felt he could average 22 miles to the gallon. If this is right, about how many gallons of gas would he need (look at your answer to Problem 2)?

5. Jed began with an almost full tank of gas. He filled up when they got back to Centerville. The other four shared the cost of the gas among them. The price was 95.9 cents per gallon. What would be fair for each of them to pay? About $4.00? About $3.50? About $5.50?

The Dinosaurs Rock
Problem Set C

Directions: Read the story "The Dinosaurs Rock." You will also need to refer to the map. Your calculator will be useful for estimates as you do the problems.

1. Jed and Michael invited Tessa, Maggie and Jake to go with them. Dizzy Dave charged a $2 service charge per ticket order. How much would they each save if they bought their tickets in one order?

2. They averaged 42 miles per hour to the I 113 junction. How long did this drive take?

3. When they left SR 14, they drove from the I 113 junction on the freeway to Middletown. They got to Middletown in 50 minutes after leaving SR 20. About what was their average speed on this part of the trip?

4. Assume that you would eat before and after the concert. Using local prices, list by item the cost of food you would buy on a trip like this.

Before the Concert		After the Concert	
Items	Prices	Items	Prices
Total			
Total Food Cost			

5. They averaged 22 miles per gallon. The price of gas was 95.9 cents per gallon. Jed filled the tank when they got home. He had started with a full tank. If four of them split the cost of the gas, about what did each pay? $3? $4? $5?

CASSETTE BY CREDIT

"Look at this, Mom," said Maggie. "Here are three great movies we missed. The Video Center is renting them for a special price of 99 cents each. I sure wish we had a VCR."

"I know, dear," her mother replied. "I wish we had one too, but I just don't have the cash to buy one now."

"But Mom, look at this ad. Both Cheapo's and Below Cost are having specials and they're top brands too. Cheapo's will include one free tape. Below Cost will give coupons at Video Center for three free movies. These are really good deals."

"Well, I don't know. How much is the full price?"

"Get this, Mom, the one at Cheapo's is $299.95. Below Cost's price is $298.98. Besides, you could just put it on your credit card."

"Maggie, do you know what that costs?"

"What do you mean?"

"The bank charges 18% annual rate. This means that I pay interest each month on any balance after my payment. I have to pay at least 10% of the balance and interest on the rest. I want to think about this some more. I'll talk with Dad when he gets home."

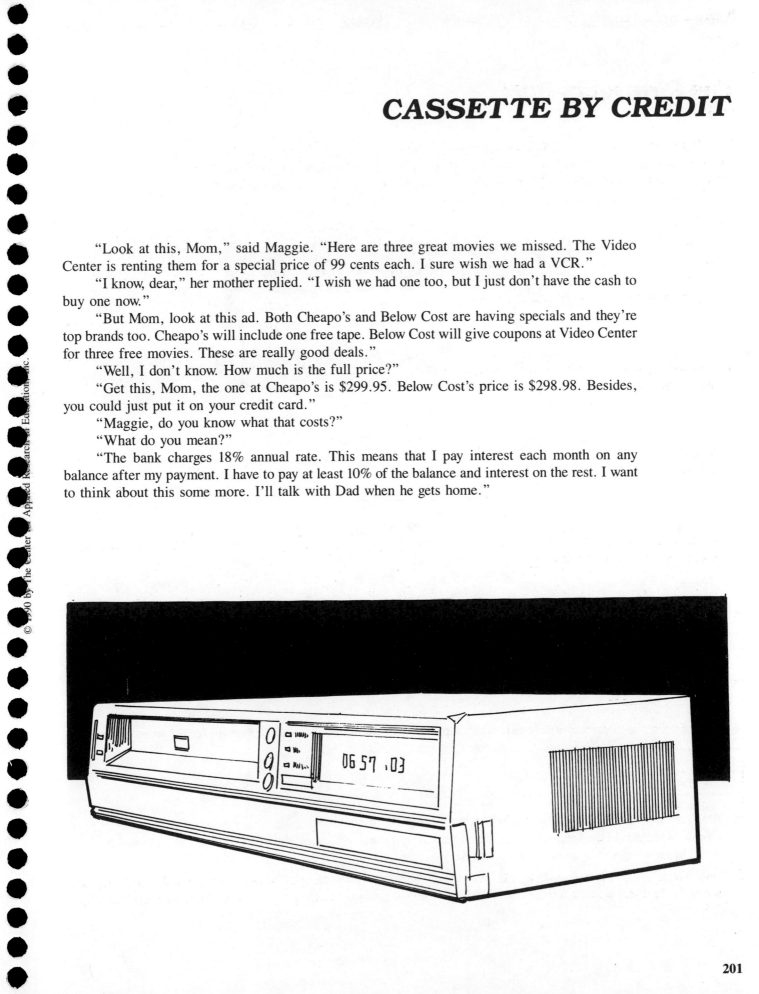

Cassette by Credit
Problem Set A

Directions: Read the story "Cassette by Credit." Story information will be needed. Do the problems in order. Some information from Problems 1 and 2 will be useful in Problems 4 and 5. Write your answer sentences below each problem. Where possible, use the back of this page or a separate piece of paper to show your work.

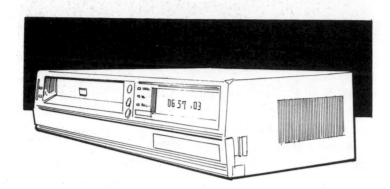

1. If they buy the VCR from Cheapo's, how much will the 6% sales tax add to the total price?

2. The "free tape" advertised by Cheapo's is worth $4.98. What is the "real price" of the VCR?

3. Below Cost includes the free rental of three VCR movies from Video Center. Which store offers the best deal? (Assume they would buy tapes and rent movies if they bought the VCR.)

4. With an 18% annual rate of interest, what percent would the monthly interest rate be on the unpaid balance?

5. Maggie's mother had other charges on her credit card bill. She paid these off. If she didn't pay on the VCR for a month, what would the interest charge be on her Cheapo purchase? (Remember to add 6% sales tax to Cheapo's price in figuring the amount of the purchase.)

Cassette by Credit
Problem Set B

Directions: Read the story "Cassette by Credit." You will use story information when doing the problems. Write your answer sentences below each problem. Where possible, use the back of this page or a separate piece of paper to show your work.

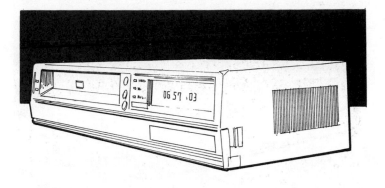

1. Add 6% sales tax to the price advertised by each store. What is the difference in total cost?

2. Cheapo's "free tape" is worth $4.98. Below Cost includes three free VCR movie rentals at the Video Center worth 99 cents each. What is the net cost of the VCR at each store before adding sales tax? (Assume that if they buy the VCR they will buy tapes and rent movies anyway.)

3. The annual interest rate on credit card balance is 18%. What is the monthly interest rate on unpaid balance on the credit card?

4. Maggie's parents have other charges on the credit card. They can't pay anything on the Cheapo bill this month. What will be the interest cost of their Cheapo purchase next month? (Remember to add the sales tax to the price as you did in Problem 1.)

5. The next month they would pay $32 on the Cheapo bill. What would they still owe because of the VCR (purchase plus interest minus payment)?

Cassette by Credit
Problem Set C

Directions: Read the story "Cassette by Credit." Do the problems in order. Useful facts will be found in both the story and the early problems. Your calculator will be helpful. Write your answer sentences below each problem. Where possible, use the back of this page or a separate piece of paper to show your work.

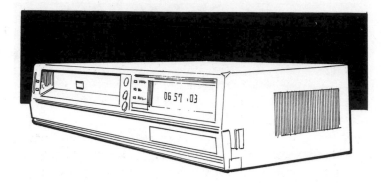

1. Add sales tax of 6% to the price advertised by each store. What is the difference between the totals?

2. Cheapo's "free tape" is worth $4.98. Maggie went into Below Cost and told them that Cheapo had a better deal. How much better was it?

3. What was the monthly credit card interest rate charged on the unpaid balance?

4. The manager at Below Cost said, "OK, but what if you buy ours and I give you 90 days to pay?"
   Maggie said, "At what interest?"
   "None," he replied, "if you pay it all in 90 days."
   How much credit card interest charges would be saved during the three months, based on the Below Cost price (plus sales tax)?

5. Maggie's dad used his credit card on the road a lot. His monthly balance averaged $500. What would the balance be if the VCR from Cheapo's was added? If he made his usual $500 payment and added $150 for the VCR, what would be the next interest charge?

OREGON OR BUST!

Tessa and Michael couldn't have been more excited! They had just phoned Maggie in Oregon. They told her that they could come to visit after all. They could get two weeks' vacation from their jobs at the grocery store. They had enough money for plane flights. Maggie got excited too. She said that she would take them to see some really neat places in Oregon, Idaho and California. She said something about Crater Lake, an old time fiddle contest and a redwood forest. Michael almost shouted, "Wow, it's Oregon or bust!"

They talked about the trip for quite a long time. Then Michael said, "Let's get out a map of Oregon and see where some of those places are." Tessa found a map in an encyclopedia. Michael located a road map. They began to search for the places Maggie had talked about.

Name _____ **Period** _____ **Date** _____

Oregon or Bust!
Problem Set A

Directions: First read "Oregon or Bust!" Locate and use several maps of Oregon and the bordering states. You may also need to use reference books and/or talk to a pilot. Write your answer sentences below each problem. Where possible, use the back of this page or a separate sheet of paper to show your work.

1. What states and ocean border Oregon?

2. Maggie lives in Salem, Oregon. She plans to pick up Michael and Tessa at the airport in Portland. How many miles is it from Salem to Portland? You may read the mileage from a map or use the map scale to find the approximate distance.

3. Maggie really wants to take them to Crater Lake National Park. If they drive from Salem, about how many miles will they travel? They will only average 40 mph, since some of the driving is on mountain roads. About how much time will they spend driving? What special features does Crater Lake have?

4. Maggie knows that Michael really likes fiddle music. She has a friend who is willing to fly them from Portland to the National Old Time Fiddle Contest in Weiser, Idaho. How many miles will they fly? If her friend's single engine airplane travels 125 mph, how long will they be in the air?

5. Select one site that you would like to visit in Oregon or a bordering state. Why would you like to go there? How far is it from where you live? How long would it take to drive there?

Oregon or Bust!
Problem Set B

Directions: Read the story "Oregon or Bust!" Use several maps of
Oregon and the bordering states. Also locate and use reference books
and/or talk to people who know about travel arrangements and the
Oregon area. Write your answer sentences below each problem. Where
possible, use the back of this page or a separate sheet of paper to show
your work.

1. What four states and three major waterways make up Oregon's
    borders? About how many miles of the border are waterways?

2. After picking up Tessa and Michael at the airport in Portland, Maggie will bring them to her home in Salem,
    Oregon. After staying there a couple of days, they plan to drive to Crater Lake National Park and then to
    Ashland to see a play at the Oregon Shakespearean Festival. Next they want to go to Oregon Caves National
    Monument and then to Redwood National Park near Crescent City, California. How many miles from Portland
    will they have traveled to this point? How many days should be allowed for this part of their vacation? Locate
    information about these vacation sites and share it with the class.

3. Maggie knows that Michael really likes fiddle music. She has a friend who is willing to use his single engine
    airplane to fly them from Portland to the National Old Time Fiddle Contest in Weiser, Idaho. How many miles
    will they fly one way and approximately how long will they be in the air? If they were to drive instead, how
    many miles would they need to travel and about how many driving hours would be necessary? You may need to
    talk to a pilot and use several maps to find reasonable solutions. Also, locate information about this fiddle
    contest and share it with the class.

4. What is the land like in Oregon? What are the highest and lowest points and what are their elevations? Name the
    major mountain ranges. How are the climate and land in eastern and western Oregon different?

5. Select one site that you would like to visit in Oregon or a bordering state. Why would you like to go there? How
    far is it from where you live? Would you drive or fly there and how long would it take?

Oregon or Bust!
Problem Set C

Directions: Read the story "Oregon or Bust!" Use several maps of
Oregon and bordering states. Also locate and use reference books and/
or talk to people who know about travel arrangements and the Oregon
area. Write your answer sentences below each problem. Where
possible, use the back of this page or a separate sheet of paper to show
your work.

1. What states and major waterways make up Oregon's borders? About
   how many miles of the border are waterways? About how many
   miles of border does Oregon share with each of its neighboring
   states?

2. After picking up Tessa and Michael at the airport in Portland, Maggie will bring them to her home in Salem,
   Oregon. After staying there a couple of days, they plan to drive to Crater Lake National Park and then to
   Ashland to see a play at the Oregon Shakespearean Festival. Next, they want to go to Oregon Caves National
   Monument and then to Redwood National Park near Crescent City, California. Then they will travel up U.S.
   Highway 30 to get back to Portland. How many days should be allowed for this part of their vacation? Locate
   information about these vacation sites and share it with the class.

3. Fiddle music is what Michael really likes. Maggie has a friend who is willing to use his single-engine airplane
   to fly them from Portland to the National Old Time Fiddle Contest in Weiser, Idaho. How many miles will they
   fly one way and approximately how long will they be in the air? If they were to drive instead, how many miles
   would they need to travel and about how many driving hours would be necessary? You may need to talk to a pilot
   and use several maps to find reasonable solutions. Also, locate information about this fiddle contest and share it
   with the class.

4. What is the land like in Oregon? What are the highest and lowest points and what are their elevations? Name the
   major mountain ranges. How are the climate and land in eastern and western Oregon different?

5. Select one site that you would like to visit in Oregon or a bordering state. Why would you like to go there? How
   far is it from where you live? How much time would it take, and what would the total cost be, to drive there? If
   you were to fly instead, what would the single-engine airplane flight cost be, and how much time would it take?

ANSWER KEY
(WITH EXPLANATIONS)

Which Way for Jake?—Answers
Problem Set A (Story on page 3)

1. 4 hours 45 minutes *AM TO 12:30 PM*
~~12:30 P.M. to 7:45~~ *BM* = 4 hr. 45 min.

2. 2 hours
1/2 hr. + 3/4 hr. + 1/2 hr. + 1/4 hr. = 2 hr.

3. ~~38⁵/₈~~ inches
~~12~~ 12¹/₂ in. + 18³/₄ in. + 7³/₈ in. = ~~28~~⁵/₈ in.

4. 162.02 cm
27.5 cm + 32.65 cm + 101.87 cm = 162.02 cm

5. 99 apples
$\dfrac{9 \text{ apples}}{6 \text{ peaches}} = \dfrac{n \text{ apples}}{66 \text{ peaches}}$

Which Way for Jake?—Answers
Problem Set B (Story on page 3)

1. 130 people
18 + 7 + 23 + 11 + 16 + 23 + 29 + 3 = 130

2. 7/6 ratio
$\dfrac{7 + 11 + 23 + 29}{18 + 23 + 16 + 3} = \dfrac{70}{60} = \dfrac{7}{6}$

3. 130 people per day
2600 ÷ 20 = 130

4. 988 people got jobs
2,600 × .38 = 988

5. Combination 1: 3 quarters + 1 dime
Combination 2: 3 quarters + 2 nickels
Combination 3: 2 quarters + 3 dimes + 1 nickel
Combination 4: 2 quarters + 2 dimes + 3 nickels
Other combinations are possible.

Which Way for Jake?—Answers
Problem Set C (Story on page 3)

1. $65.65 spent
$88.75 − $23.10 = $65.65   *AVGE = $\dfrac{65.65}{13}$ = $5.05*

2. $7.70 spent, $15.40 left
$23.10 ÷ 3 = $7.70
$23.10 − $7.70 = $15.40

3. Combination 1: 3 quarters + 1 dime
Combination 2: 3 quarters + 2 nickels
Combination 3: 2 quarters + 3 dimes + 1 nickel
Combination 4: 2 quarters + 2 dimes + 3 nickels
Other combinations are possible.

4. 31 bags
65 ft. × 95 ft. = 6,175 sq. ft. ÷ 200 = 31 bags

5. $7.49 fee charged; tip = $.55
$.75 × 5 = $3.75 + $.55 × 6.8 = $3.74 = $7.49
15% of $7.49 = $.55

The Caper—Answers
Problem Set A (Story on page 8)

1. 25 minutes
12:07 − 11:42 = 25 min.

2. $380 estimate, $374.75 actual
$180 + $200 = $380
$177.80 + $196.95 = $374.75

3. $187.38
$374.75 ÷ 2 = $187.38

4. 1 year 9 months
August 1971 to August 1972 = 1 yr.
August 1972 to May 1973 = 8 mo.

5. $15.00
$3.75 × 4 = $15.00

The Caper—Answers
Problem Set B (Story on page 8)

1. $2.73
$1.45 + $.69 + $.59 = $2.73

2. $.60 more
$1.75 + $.49 + $.89 = $3.13; $1.19 + $.69 + $.65 = $2.53
Then $3.13 − $2.53 = $.60

3. $6.69
$1.15 + $.49 + $.59 = $2.23 × 3 = $6.69

4. Order 1: Double Burger, Medium Shake—$1.75 + $.69 = $2.44
Order 2: Burger Deluxe, Fries, Large Drink—$1.15 + $.49 + $.65 = $2.29
Other answers are possible.

5. $.39 change
Combination 1: 3 dimes + 1 nickel + 4 pennies
Combination 2: 2 dimes + 3 nickels + 4 pennies
Other combinations are possible.

The Caper—Answers
Problem Set C (Story on page 8)

1. $4.32 total, $.68 change
$1.45 + $.59 = $2.04 × $.06 = $.12 tax; $2.04 + $.12 = $2.16
$2.16 × 2 = $4.32
$5.00 − $4.32 = $.68 change

2. $6.84 total, $13.16 change
3 ($1.19) + 2 ($.69) + 3 ($.50) = $6.45 total × .06 = $.39 tax
$6.45 + $.39 = $6.84
$20.00 − $6.84 = $13.16 change

3. 146 people
(20 × 4 = 80) + (6 × 6 = 36) + (15 × 2 = 30) = 146

4. Student drawings representing 41 tables

5. Order 1: Juicy Burger, Drink, Fries—$.99 + $.35 + $.69 = $2.03
+ tax $.12
Order 2: Fish Burger, Shake $1.45 + $.89 = $2.34
+ tax $ .14
Order 3: Burger Deluxe, Shake, Fries $1.15 + $.59 + $.49 = $2.23
+ tax $ .13

A Sigh of Relief—Answers
Problem Set A (Story on page 12)

1. Estimate (individual); actual $18,900; show the difference between own estimate and actual annual salary.
12 × $1,575 = $18,900

2. 45 minutes
(2:35 to 3:00 = 25 min.) + (3:00 to 3:20 = 20 min.) = 45 min.

3. $44,651
$47,650 − $2,999 = $44,651

4. 9,900 square feet
110 ft. × 90 ft. = 9,900 sq. ft.

5. $2,679.06
6% of $44,651 (see Problem 3) = .06 × $44,651 = $2,679.06

A Sigh of Relief—Answers
Problem Set B (Story on page 12)

1. 12 feet by 15 feet
1 in. = 12 ft.; 1¼ in. = 15 ft.

2. 180 square feet
12 ft. × 15 ft. = 180 sq. ft. (see Problem 1)

3. 12 feet by 12 feet, perimeter is 48 feet
1 in. = 12 ft.
4 × 12 = 48 feet

4. $400
180 (see Problem 2) ÷ 9 (1 sq. yd.) = 20
20 × $22 = $440

5. $439.80
180 sq. ft. (see Problem 2) ÷ 9 sq. ft. (1 sq. yd.) = 20
20 × $21.99 = $439.80

A Sigh of Relief—Answers
Problem Set C (Story on page 12)

1. 16 square yards
Bathroom 1: 6′ (1/2 in.) × 9′ (3/4 in.) = 54 sq. ft.
Bathroom 2: 6′ (1/2 in.) × 15′ (1¼ in.) = 90 sq. ft.; 54 + 90 = 144 sq. ft.; 144 ÷ 9 (1 sq. yd.) = 16 sq. yd.

2. $55.09
15% of $47.90 = .15 × $47.90 = $7.185 = $7.19; $47.90 + $7.19 = $55.09

3. 1,378 square feet
48 ft. (4 in.) × 33 ft. (2¾ in.) = 1,584 square feet
This made the entire house a rectangle. Now subtract the cutout section: 12 ft. (1 in.) × 18 ft. (1½ in.) = 216 sq. ft.
1,584 − 216 = 1,378 square feet.

4. Show a different floor plan; show the square footage of your plan.

Future Forecast—Answers
Problem Set A (Story on page 16)

1. 145 credits
220 − 75 = 145

2. 30 hours
$112.50 ÷ $3.75 = 30 hr.

3. Estimate about $11; actual $10.96
About 10 gal. × about $1.10 = $11.00
9.7 gal. × $1.14 = $10.96

4. 3½ cups
2 × 1¾ cups = 3½ cups

5. Two ways of measuring 3½ cups with 1/2 and 1/4 cup measures:
1. Fill the half-cup measure 7 times. 2. Fill the half-cup measure 6 times and the quarter cup measure twice. Other answers are possible.

Future Forecast—Answers
Problem Set B (Story on page 16)

1. Estimate 1,300 to 1,500; actual 1,435
(2 × 187 = 374) + (2 × 103 = 206) + (1 × 25 = 25) + (1 × 110 = 110) + (1 × 400 = 400) + (2 × 160 = 320) = 1,435

2. He consumed fewer calories than Michael. Estimate 300 to 400 less; actual 335 less.
$(187 + 103 = 290) + (2 \times 400 = 800) + (2 \times 5 = 10) = 1,130$
$1,435$ (see Problem 1) $- 1,100 = 335$

3. She could have any combination of food totalling 290 calories or less.
$450 - 160 = 290$
She could have chicken and rice $(187 + 103 = 290)$; chicken, beans and coffee $(187 + 25 + 5 = 217)$; rice, beans, bread and coffee $(103 + 25 + 110 + 5 = 253)$. Other answers are possible.

4. Estimate 100; actual 73 calories
$378 + 187 + 103 + 400 + 5 = 1,073 - 1,000 = 73$ cal.

5. List choices; estimate calories; add actual calories. This is a matter of personal choice or weight goal, if any.

Future Forecast—Answers
Problem Set C (Story on page 16)

1. $93.75
$25 \times \$3.75 = \$93.75$

2. Ratio of 11:14 or 11 to 14 or 11/14.
$2,500 - 1,400 = 1,100$; $1,100$ to $1,400 = 11$ to 14.

3. Combination 1: 15 classrooms of 20 desks and 50 rooms of 30 desks
Combination 2: 30 classrooms of 20 desks and 40 rooms of 30 desks
Combination 3: 45 rooms of 20 desks and 30 rooms of 30 desks
Other answers are possible.

4. 12 rooms of 20 desks and 52 rooms of 30 desks would be the minimum number of rooms to house 1,800 students.

5. The maximum number of rooms would be 85: 10 rooms of 30 desks each and 75 rooms of 20 desks each.

Harper's Surprise—Answers
Problem Set A (Story on page 20)

1. 45 minutes
7:15 to 8:00 = 45 min.

2. 1½ cups
$3/4 \times 2 = 1½$ cups

3. Combination 1: 3 half-cups
Combination 2: 2 half-cups and 2 quarter-cups
Other answers are possible.

4. An estimate of $6.00 to $6.30
$\$.90 + \$1.70 + \$.70 + \$.90 + \$.80 + \$.30 + \$1.00 = \$6.30$

5. Combination 1: 3¾ divided by 1/2; 7 half-cups plus 1 quarter-cup
Combination 2: 15 quarter-cup measures
Other combinations are possible.

Harper's Surprise—Answers
Problem Set B (Story on page 20)

1. 16.8 miles
12.5-mi. detour + 4.3-mi. = 16.8 mi.

2. 24.6 miles
$16.8 + 7.8 = 24.6$ mi.

3. 14 boys
Set up a proportion showing the ratio of $\frac{7}{5} = \frac{x}{10}$
Cross multiply to solve.

4. No
24 at the party (see Problem 1) ÷ teams of 4 = 6 teams. Neither 14 nor 10 is equally divisible by 6.

5. 9.4%
9 is what % of 96? $9 \div 96 = .0937 = 9.4\%$

Harper's Surprise—Answers
Problem Set C (Story on page 20)

1. 36 songs
$90 \div 2.5 = 36$ songs

2. 11:25 P.M.
$2 \times 90 = 180$ min. 180 min. = 3 hr. 8:25 + 3 hr. = 11:25 P.M.

3. Plan for 60 people: need 3 pkg. napkins = $3 \times .79 = \$2.37$; need 4 pkg. of plates = $4 \times \$1.19 = \$4.76$; total is $\$2.37 + \$4.76 + \$.43$ (tax) = $\$7.56$

4. No
Set up a proportion showing $\frac{7}{5} = \frac{x}{10}$
Cross multiply to solve.
The proportion shows that there were 14 boys, for a total of 24 people at the party. This made 6 teams of 4. Neither 10 nor 14 is equally divisible by 6, so there could not be an equal number of boys or girls on each team.

5. $6.28
Sales tax on $23.70 = $.06 \times \$23.70 = \$1.42$
Total selling price of the earrings = $\$23.70 + \$1.42 = \$25.12$
$\$25.12 \div 4$ people = $\$6.28$ each

Our Daily Bread—Answers
Problem Set A (Story on page 24)

1. Answers will vary. Check for reasonableness. After the students survey other class members, allow time for a discussion.

2. Direct a discussion about the averages.

3. Answers will vary. Reasonable averages will likely be between 10 and 25 slices per loaf.

4. Answers will vary. A typical solution:
6 slices/person $\times$ 60,000 people ÷ 22 slices/loaf = approx. 16,364 loaves of bread eaten each day

5. Answers will vary. The average prices will likely be between $.50 and $3.00 per loaf. A typical solution for the total spent on bread in the story might be:
$1.65 per loaf $\times$ 16,364 loaves = approx. $27,000

Our Daily Bread—Answers
Problem Set B (Story on page 24)

1. Answers will vary. Check for reasonable averages or means. After the students survey other class members, allow time for a discussion.

2. Direct a discussion about the means, medians and modes found by the students. Have several reproduce their charts on the chalkboard and compare their findings. (In this instance the mean = the arithmetic average of the bread prices, the mode = the bread price that they found the greatest number of times, and the median = the bread price in the middle of those surveyed.)

3. Answers will vary. Reasonable means, medians and/or modes (see definitions in Answer 2 above) will likely be between 10 and 25 slices per loaf. Discuss the students' findings.

4. Answers will vary. Discuss reasonable outcomes such as the following solution. 6 slices per person × 60,000 people ÷ 22 slices per loaf = approx. 16,364 loaves of bread eaten each day.

5. Answers will vary. The mean, median or mode bread prices will likely be between $.50 and $3.00 per loaf. A typical solution, for the total spent on bread in the story, might be $1.65 per loaf × 16,364 loaves = approx. $27,000.

Our Daily Bread—Answers
Problem Set C (Story on page 24)

1. Answers will vary. Check for reasonable averages or means. After the students survey other class members, allow time for a discussion.

2. Direct a discussion about the means, medians and modes found by the students. Have several reproduce their charts on the chalkboard and compare their findings. (In this instance the mean = the arithmetic average of the bread prices, the mode = the bread price that they found the greatest number of times, and the median = the bread price in the middle of those surveyed.)

3. Answers will vary. Reasonable means, medians and/or modes (see definitions in Answer 2 above) will likely be between 10 and 25 slices per loaf. Discuss the students' findings.

4. Answers will vary. Discuss the reasonableness of the students' findings. Their solutions should include number of slices/person × number of people ÷ number of slices/loaf = number of loaves of bread eaten each day.

5. Results will vary. Have groups of students use large graphs or charts to present their findings to the class.

Sweet Spending—Answers
Problem Set A (Story on page 29)

1. Ryan spent 20 cents.
1. 1 chocolate drop; 2. 1 sucker, 1 turtle; 3. 2 sticks.
Other answers are possible.

2. 15 cents is the least; 3 suckers

3. 45 cents is the greatest amount (since that is all she had): 1. 3 turtles; 2. 2 chocolate drops, 1 sucker; 3. 1 candy ball, 2 sticks. Other answers are possible.

4. 1 turtle, 1 stick, 1 sucker = 30 cents
1 chocolate drop, 1 stick, 1 turtle = 45 cents
Other answers are possible.

Sweet Spending—Answers
Problem Set B (Story on page 29)

1. Combination 1: 1 quarter
Combination 2: 2 dimes, 1 nickel
Combination 3: 1 dime, 3 nickels
Combination 4: 5 nickels

2. Combination 1: 1 chocolate drop, 1 stick, 1 sucker
Combination 2: 1 turtle, 2 sticks
Combination 3: 2 suckers, 1 candy ball
Other answers are possible

3. Combination 1: 1 candy ball, 1 chocolate drop
Combination 2: 3 turtles
Combination 3: 4 sticks, 1 sucker
Combination 4: 1 candy ball, 4 suckers
Combination 5: 9 suckers
Other answers are possible

Sweet Spending—Answers
Problem Set C (Story on page 29)

1. Combination 1: 2 suckers = 10 cents
Combination 2: 1 turtle, 1 stick = 25 cents
Combination 3: 1 chocolate drop, 1 sucker = 25 cents
Combination 4: 3 sticks = 30 cents
Other answers are possible.

2. Combination 1: 1 quarter, 2 dimes
Combination 2: 1 quarter, 1 dime, 2 nickels
Combination 3: 1 quarter, 4 nickels
Combination 4: 4 dimes, 1 nickel
Other answers are possible.

3. Combination 1: 1 candy ball, 1 chocolate drop
Combination 2: 1 candy ball, 2 sticks
Combination 3: 1 candy ball, 4 suckers
Combination 4: 1 candy ball, 1 turtle, 1 sucker
Combination 5: 1 candy ball, 1 stick, 2 suckers
Combination 6: 2 chocolate drops, 1 sucker
Combination 7: 1 chocolate drop, 1 turtle, 1 stick
Combination 8: 1 chocolate drop, 2 sticks, 1 sucker
Other answers are possible.

The County Fair—Answers
Problem Set A (Story on page 33)

1. $2.40 each
4 × $1.00 each for gas + $1.50 for parking + 2 × $2.00 for 2 more gate passes = $9.50 ÷ 4 = $2.375, which rounds to $2.40/person

2. 30 tickets
Maggie, 7 + Michael, 7 + Dan, 8 + Tessa, 8 = 30

3. $8.90, $11.20, $2.70, $14.10
89 dimes = $8.90, 112 dimes = $11.20, 27 dimes = $2.70 and 141 dimes = $14.10

4. $5.50 for their food
2 × $1.50 (egg rolls) + $.75 (root beer) + $.50 (small coke) + $1.25 (hot dog) = $5.50

5. Estimates will vary. The expenses noted so far appear to be more than $30, and it appears Michael, Maggie, Tessa and Dan aren't finished; thus, estimates above $40 should be expected.

The County Fair—Answers
Problem Set B (Story on page 33)

1. $2.40 each
4 × $1.00 each for gas + $1.50 for parking + 2 × $2.00 for 2 more gate passes = $9.50 ÷ 4 = $2.375, which rounds to $2.40/person

2. 24 tickets needed, but 30 will likely be purchased for $10.
4 people × 6 tickets each = 24 tickets needed. Tickets are sold in groups of 15 for $5; thus, two sets will likely be purchased at 2 × $5 = $10.

3. $9.20 or $9.30 to win a large teddy bear
89 + 112 + 27 + 141 = 369 × $.10 = $36.90 ÷ 4 = $9.225, but since dimes are being tossed, the total would be either $9.20 or $9.30. (Further, it must be realized that the mean is the arithmetic average.)

4. $11.50 for their food
2 × $1.50 (egg rolls) + $.75 (root beer) + $.50 (small coke) + $1.25 (hot dog) + 2 × 1.25 (pizza) + $1.00 (large coke) + $1.75 (hamburger) + $.75 (milk) = $11.50

5. Estimates will vary. The expenses noted so far total over $40, and it appears Michael, Maggie, Tessa and Dan aren't finished; thus, estimates of $50 or more should be expected.

The County Fair—Answers
Problem Set C (Story on page 33)

1. $2.40 each
4 × $1.00 each for gas + $1.50 for parking + 2 × $2.00 for 2 more gate passes = $9.50 ÷ 4 = $2.375, which rounds to $2.40/person

2. 24 tickets needed, but 30 will likely be purchased for $10
4 people × 6 tickets each = 24 tickets needed. Tickets are sold in groups of 15 for $5; thus, two sets will likely be purchased at 2 × $5 = $10.

3. $10.40 (mean), $11.20 (median), or $14.50 (mode) to win a large teddy bear
145 + 112 + 27 + 145 + 89 = 518 × $.10 = $51.80 ÷ 5 = $10.36, but since dimes are being tossed, the mean or arithmetical average would be $10.40. When arranged from high to low, the numbers of dimes tossed were 145, 145, 112, 89, and 27; thus, the middle or median amount was 112 dimes = $11.20. The most frequently occurring amount is 145; thus, the mode is 145 dimes = $14.50.

4. $5.50 for their food
2 × $1.50 (egg rolls) + $.75 (root beer) + $.50 (small coke) + $1.25 (hot dog) + 2 × 1.25 (pizza) + $1.00 (large coke) + $1.75 (hamburger) + $.75 (milk) = $11.50 + $.69 (6% sales tax) = $12.19

5. Estimates will vary. The expenses noted so far total over $40, and it appears Michael, Maggie, Tessa and Dan aren't finished; thus, estimates of $50 or more should be expected.

Square Cents—Answers
Problem Set A/B/C (Story on page 38)

1.

Q	N	D
N	D	Q
D	Q	N

Other arrangements are possible.

H = half-dollar
Q = quarter
D = dime
N = nickel
P = penny

2. There are many methods that could be used. Students must use logical thinking and eliminate possibilities as they complete the square.

3.

P	N	D	Q
D	Q	P	N
Q	D	N	P
N	P	Q	D

Other arrangements are possible.

4. Several different arrangements are possible. Be sure to check the diagonals to see that only one of each coin is represented in the diagonals, rows and columns.

5. The same method could be used. Problem 3 has the added criterion that the diagonals also are to be considered.

6.

P	D	Q	H	N
D	N	H	P	Q
H	Q	D	N	P
N	H	P	Q	D
Q	P	N	D	H

Other arrangements are possible.

7. Have the students carefully discuss their methods for arranging the coins. There are several different arrangements, all variations of the one given in Problem 6 of this set. The teacher may request that students draw their arrangements, posting them on the bulletin board or displaying them on the blackboard.

Halloween—Answers
Problem Set A/B (Story on page 40)

1.

	C	R	H	W
T	X			
M	X	X	X	
J	X		X	
E				

Clue 3: Jake is not the clown. Mark an X to show that.

Clue 4: Michael is not the hobo or the rabbit. Mark an X in each box to show that.

2. Conclusions: Erin is the clown, since from the Xs shown, no one else could be the clown.
Michael is the witch, since he has an X in the box of each of the other costumes.

3.

	C	R	H	W
T	X			X
M	X	X	X	O
J	X		X	X
E	O	X	X	X

Erin is not wearing the rabbit, hobo or witch costume since she is the clown. Mark an X in each box showing that information.

Tessa, Jake and Erin are not wearing the witch costume since Michael is wearing it.

4.

	C	R	H	W
T	X	X	O	X
M	X	X	X	O
J	X	O	X	X
E	O	X	X	X

Clue 5: Tessa is not the rabbit, so she is the hobo. Jake is not the hobo. Jake is the rabbit.
Clue 6: Erin is not the witch.

Halloween—Answers
Problem Set C (Story on page 40)

1.

	C	R	H	W
T	X	X		X
M	X	X	X	
J	X		X	X
E		X	X	X

Clue 1: Neither Tessa nor Michael is the clown.
Clue 2: Jake is not the hobo.
Clue 3: Jake is not the clown.
    Erin must be the clown.
    Erin is not the rabbit, hobo or witch.
Clue 4: Michael is not the hobo or the rabbit.
    Michael must be the witch.
    The witch is not Tessa, Jake or Erin.
Clue 5: Tessa is not the rabbit.
    Tessa must be the hobo.
    Jake is the rabbit.
Clue 6: Erin is not the witch.

2.

	D	C	A	G	S
Donna	X	X	X	O	X
Craig	O	X	X	X	X
Artie	X	X	X	X	O
Greg	X	X	O	X	X
Sandy	X	O	X	X	X

Clue 1: Donna is not the dancer; Craig is not the cowboy; Artie is not the artist; Greg is not the ghost; and Sandy is not the scarecrow.
Clue 2: Neither Greg nor Sandy is the dancer.
Clue 3: Craig is not the scarecrow.
Clue 4: Sandy is not the ghost or the artist.
    Sandy must be the cowboy.
    Donna, Craig and Greg are not wearing the cowboy costume.
Clue 5: Donna is not the scarecrow or the artist.
    Donna must be the ghost.
    Neither Craig nor Artie is the ghost.
Clue 6: Artie is not the dancer or the cowboy.
    Artie is the scarecrow.
    Greg is not the scarecrow.
    Greg is the artist.
    Craig is not the artist.
    Craig is the dancer.

Amazing Measurements—Answers
Problem Set A (Story on page 44)

1. A cubit = 18 to 22 inches. Answers will vary depending on the dimensions of your classroom.

2. A fathom is about 6 feet, and it is used in nautical measurement internationally.

3. The Roman mile = 1,000 paces or double steps
A mile = 5,280 feet
Answers will vary, but check for approximate accuracy.

4. In 1150 A.D. King David I of Scotland ruled that the inch was the mean measure of the thumbs of 3 different-size men. In 1324, King Edward II of England declared that 3 barleycorns taken from the middle of the ear and placed end to end would be 1 inch. During the 1700s the barleycorns were replaced by 12 poppyseeds, and each seed equalled 12 human hairs.

5. The United States of America is the only industrial country that has not converted to the metric system. The meter measurements will depend on the dimensions of your classroom, but check for reasonableness.

Amazing Measurements—Answers
Problem Set B (Story on page 44)

1. Each pyramid had a perimeter of 2,000 cubits. The cubit is now standardized at 18.24 inches. (Cubit = 18 to 22 inches.)

2. A fathom = about 6 feet
The nautical units are:
1 span (9 inches) = 1/8 fathom
1 fathom (6 feet) = 1/120 cable's length
1 cable's length = 240 yards

3. The Roman mile = 1,000 paces or double steps
A statute mile = 5,280 feet
A meridian or nautical mile = 6,076.115 feet
Answers will vary, but check for approximate accuracy.

4. In 1150 A.D. King David I of Scotland ruled that the inch was the mean measure of the thumbs of 3 different-size men. In 1324, King Edward II of England declared that 3 barleycorns taken from the middle of the ear and placed end to end would be 1 inch. During the 1700s the barleycorns were replaced by 12 poppyseeds, and each seed equalled 12 human hairs.

5. Span = originally an Egyptian measure of the distance between the outstretched thumb and little finger tips, or 9 inches
Palm = the breadth of 4 fingers, or about 3 inches
Rod = originally a double fathom or 12 feet, but now 1/4 chain or 16.5 feet
Yard = initially 1/2 fathom, or 3 feet, or 36 inches
Furlong = 1/8 mile for horse racing
League = 3 miles
Acre = 1/640 section or 4,840 square yards

Amazing Measurements—Answers
Problem Set C (Story on page 44)

1. Each pyramid had a perimeter of 2,000 cubits.
2,000 cubits = 1/2 meridian mile

2. A fathom = about 6 feet
The nautical units are:
1 span (9 inches) = 1/8 fathom
1 fathom (6 feet) = 1/120 cable's length
1 cable's length = 240 yards
1 nautical mile = approx. 1.15 statute mile

3. The Roman mile = 1,000 paces or double steps
A statute mile = 5,280 feet
A meridian or nautical mile = 6,076.115 feet
The nautical mile was originally intended to be 1/60 of 1° of any imaginary line circling the earth; however, since the earth is not a perfect sphere this figure varies. Thus, the international nautical mile is now defined as 1,852 meters.

4. In 1150 A.D. King David I of Scotland ruled that the inch was the mean measure of the thumbs of 3 different-size men. In 1324, King Edward II of England declared that 3 barleycorns taken from the middle of the ear and placed end to end would be 1 inch. During the 1700s the barleycorns were replaced by 12 poppyseeds, and each seed equalled 12 human hairs.

5. Ell = 5 spans for measuring cloth
Span = originally an Egyptian measure of the distance between the outstretched thumb and little finger tips, or 9 inches
Rod = originally a double fathom or 12 feet, but now 1/4 chain or 16.5 feet
Furlong = 1/8 mile for horse racing
League = 3 miles
Chain = 1/80 mile or 66 feet or 4 rods
Acre = 1/640 section or 4,840 square yards
Cord = 128 cubic feet of firewood often stacked 4 feet by 4 feet by 8 feet
Board foot = 1/12 cubic foot of lumber usually as 1 inch by 12 inches by 12 inches
Peck = 1/4 bushel or 8 dry quarts or 8.810 liters
Gill = 1/2 cup or 4 fluid ounces
Hogshead = 2 liquid barrels or 63 gallons or 238.474 liters
Long ton = 2,240 pounds or 1.016 metric tons

Metric Airplane Contest—Answers
Problem Set A/B/C (Story on page 49)

1. Answers will vary according to the individual. Check for reasonableness. For example, a person 1 m 65 cm tall = 1,650 mm = 165 cm = 16.5 dm = 1.65 m = .165 dam = .0165 hm = .00165 km.

2. Answers will vary. Compare results and check for reasonableness. The items should likely be measured in the following units: floor = sq. m; book cover = sq. cm or sq. dm; basketball court = sq. m; town = sq. km; shoe sole = sq. cm.

3. 28 cm (length) × 21.6 cm (width) = approx. 604.8 sq. cm (area) for a "regular" sheet of typing paper.
The diagonal measure is approximately 35.5 centimeters. You may wish to direct a discussion about possible paper airplane features.

4. Plans will vary. Check for accurate measurements and descriptions.

5. Have each student keep his or her own records. When everyone is finished, have a discussion about why certain airplanes flew farther or were more accurate than others.

Take Me to Your Liter—Answers
Problem Set A/B/C (Story on page 53)

1.

1 cl	= (10) ml	3 dl	= (300) ml
1 dl	= (100) ml	5 cl	= (50) ml
1 l	= (1,000) ml	5 dl	= (500) ml

2. Gasoline is sometimes measured in (liters).
You can get Coke in 2-(liter) bottles.
Liquid medicine is often measured in (milliliters).
A quart of milk is nearly a (liter).
A cubic centimeter or cc is the same as a (milliliter).

3. Results will vary. Check that correct amounts of water are poured and recorded.

Give a Gram—Answers
Problem Set A/B/C (Story on page 58)

1.

1 kg	= 1,000 g	1 g	= 1,000 mg	500 g	= .5 kg
1 hg	= 100 g	1 dg	= 100 mg	2 hg	= 200 g
1 dag	= 10 g	1 cg	= 10 mg	10 g	= 1 dag

2. Your own weight is measured in kg.
Medicine is often measured in mg.
The mass of a cubic centimeter of water is one g.
An automobile is weighed in kg or tonnes.
A metric tonne equals 1,000 kg.

3. For everyday purposes mass and weight are considered equivalent. Technically, they are different. Mass measures the actual quantity of matter, whereas weight is the force on an object due to the pull of gravity. As such, an object will weigh less on the moon, but its mass will be constant. For example, on a balance scale, if a mass of 60 kilograms will balance a person on earth, that same mass will do so on the moon. However, using a spring scale the same person will weigh 60 kilograms on earth, but only 10 kilograms on the moon. Technically, mass and weight are only equivalent at sea level.

4. The objects and their masses will vary. Have the students keep a record of them on the chart provided.

5. The results will vary.
For a class of 30 students the calculation 30 × 43 = 1,290 kg which is more than a metric ton. This same class would weigh 1,290 × 2.2 = 2,838 pounds.

Measurement Madness—Answers
Problem Set A/B/C (Story on page 60)

Results on the Measurement Madness grid will vary. Check some of each student's line segments for accuracy.

The Invitation—Answers
Problem Set A (Story on page 63)

1. 77
70 + 6 + 1 = 77

2. $15,246

$77 \times \$99 \times 2 = \$15,246$

3. $600

$2 \times 2 \times \$150 = \$600$

4. 18

$70 \div 5 = 14 + 4 = 18$

5. $2,700

$18 \times 3 \times \$50 = \$2,700$

The Invitation—Answers
Problem Set B (Story on page 63)

1. $15,246

$70 + 6 + 1 = 77 \times \$99 \times 2 = \$15,246$

2. $1,732

$(\$566 \times 2 = \$1,132) + (2 \times 2 \times \$150 = \$600) = \$1,732$

3. $900

$70 \div 5 = 14 + 4 = 18$ rooms $\times \$50 = \$900$

4. $1,116.50

$\$5.00 + \$2.25 = \$7.25 \times 2 \times 77 = \$1,116.50$

5. $3,816.50

3 nights $\times \$900 = \$2,700 + \$1,116.50$ (see Problem 4) = $3,816.50

The Invitation—Answers
Problem Set C (Story on page 63)

1. $16,978

$(70 + 6 + 1 = 77$ people$) \times (\$99 \times 2 = \$198$ airfare each$) = \$15,246$ ($\$566 \times 2$ for buses to and from Jackson City = $1,132) + (2 \times \$300$ for buses in Washington = $600) + \$15,246 = \$16,978

2. $2,700

$(70 \div 5 = 14 + 4 = 18$ hotel rooms$) \times (\$50 \times 3 = \$150) = \$2,700$

3. $1,212.75

$(2 \times \$2.25 = \$4.50) + (2 \times \$5 = \$10)$
$\$4.50 + \$10 + \$1.25 = \$15.25 \times 77 = \$1,212.75$

4. $20,890.75

Transportation	$16,978.00
Hotel	2,700.00
Meals	1,212.75
Total	$20,890.75

5. This amount would be determined by individual consumption patterns. Use local prices as a guide. What would be reasonable for your students?

On to D.C.—Answers
Problem Set A (Story on page 67)

1. $1,132

$2 \times \$566$

2. $94.50

$\$15.75 \times 6 = \$94.50$

3. $1,226.50

$\$1,132 + \$94.50 = \$1,226.50$ (see Problems 1 and 2)

4. $19,774

Using Bill's estimate of $21,000, subtract $1,226. (Accept $1,227 as an answer.)

5. One inch of the thermometer should be filled in.

$\$19,774 \div \$3,320 =$ approx. 1/6 the amount to be raised

On to D.C.—Answers
Problem Set B (Story on page 67)

1. $1,226.50

$2 \times \$566 = \$1,132$ (bus saving) $6 \times \$15.75$ (meal saving) = $94.50
$\$1,132 + \$94.50 = \$1,226.50$

2. $19,774 (or $19,775)

Bill's estimate of $21,000 $- \$1,226 = \$19,774$ (see Problem 1).

3. $2,820

$\$3,320 - \$500 = \$2,820$

4. One inch of the thermometer should be filled in.

$\$19,774 \div \$3,320 =$ about 1/6 the amount to be raised

5. $3,296

At one-inch intervals, weekly goals should be marked on the thermometer. Goal amounts are $3,296, $6,592, $9,887, $13,183, $16,479, $19,774. Divide the $19,774 by 6. Enter the amounts to the nearest dollar at the appropriate one-inch intervals.

On to D.C.—Answers
Problem Set C (Story on page 67)

1. $19,774 (accept $19,773)

(bus savings $\$566 \times 2 = \$1,132$) + (meal savings $\$15.75 \times 6 = \$94.50$) = $1,226.50
Subtract this amount from Bill's estimate of $21,000.

2. 1½ inches filled in.

$\$19,774 \div \$4,862 =$ about 25%; $.25 \times 6$ in. = 1½ in.

3. $3,155

$\$19,774 - \$4,000 = \$15,774 \div 5 = \$3,155$

4. 2%

$\$193 + 200 = \$393 \div \$19,774 = .0199$ or 2%

5. $1,922; 9.72% or 10%

$\$19,774 - \$17,822 = \$1,922$
$\$19,744 \div \$1,922 = .0972$

The Job Crisis—Answers
Problem Set A (Story on page 71)

1. $77.05

$\$3.35 \times 23 = \$77.05$

2. 22.3 hours
18 + 22 + 27 = 67 ÷ 3 hr. = 22.3 hr.

3. $60
$83.00 − $68.25 = $14.75/week ($15 estimate)
$15 × 4 = $60

4. 2 feet 5 inches
12 ft. − 9 ft. 7 in. = 2 ft. 5 in.

5. 5 pieces and 5 ft. left over
40 ft. ÷ 7 ft. = 5 pieces + 5 ft.

The Job Crisis—Answers
Problem Set B (Story on page 71)

1. $7.45 total
$1.49 × 5 = $7.45

2. 2,160 shingles
240 × 9 = 2,160

3. 22 boxes; $1,900
2,160 ÷ 100 = 21.60 or 22 boxes
Estimate $90 × 20 = $1,800, so $1,900 is best choice

4. $49.65 tax
$827.55 × .06 = $49.65

5. $81.45 deposited
$56.77 + 39.68 = $96.45 − $15.00 = $81.45

The Job Crisis—Answers
Problem Set C (Story on page 71)

1. $116.23 total
($5.99 × 9 = $53.91) + ($9.29 × 6 = $55.74) = $109.65 +
6% tax ($6.58) = $116.23

2. Student drawing showing 15 cabinets. 9 should be the same size
and smaller than the other 6.

3. 66 miles
3.7 mi. + 2.9 mi. = 6.6 mi. × 2 = 13.2 mi. round trip; 13.2 ×
5 = 66 mi.

4. $408.83
$453.75 × .06 = $27.23 tax; $453.75 + 27.23 = $480.98
$480.98 × .15 = $72.15; $480.98 − $72.15 = $408.83

5. $136.39 saved
$514.66 × .06 = $30.88; $514.66 + $30.88 = $545.54;
$545.54 × .25 = $136.39 saved

Tickets—Answers
Problem Set A (Story on page 75)

1. 50 prizes
1 first prize + 4 second prizes + 10 third prizes + 34 fourth
prizes

2. 600 tickets
$1,200 ÷ $2 = 600

3. 50/600 or 1/12
Of 600 tickets, 50 of them will win a prize.

4. 1/600
There are 600 tickets and only one first prize. You have one chance
to win the first prize with only one ticket. The probability is 1/600
× 1 or 1/600.

5. 5/600
There are a total of 5 prizes between first and second place. The
probability of winning is 5/600, since 600 tickets were sold.

Tickets—Answers
Problem Set B (Story on page 75)

1. 8.3% will win a prize
50/600 = .083 = 8.3%

2. 50/600 or 1/12; 50/600 or 1/12
The probability is written as a fraction representing the number of
prizes over the total number of tickets sold.

3. 5/600 or 1/120
One first prize added to 4 second prizes totals 5 prizes out of 600
tickets sold.

4. 10/600 or 1/60
There are 10 third prizes offered.

5. (a) 2/600 or 1/300; (b) 100/600 or 1/6; (c) 500/600 or 5/6

Tickets—Answers
Problem Set C (Story on page 75)

1. 1/600
$1,200 represents 600 tickets at $2 each. There is only one first
prize offered.

2. 2/600 or 1/300
1/600 × 2. Multiply the chance of winning first prize by the
number of tickets held by one person.

3. 50/600 or 1/12
50 prizes/600 tickets × 1 = 50/600 or 1/12

4. 50/300 or 1/6
50/600 × 2 = 100/600 or 1/6

5. Methods for writing the answers should include fractional
representation. The numerator represents the number of favorable
outcomes. The denominator represents the number of possible
outcomes. (For example, the number of wins as the numerator with
the number of tickets sold as the denominator.)

Jake Turns the Corner—Answers
Problem Set A/B/C (Story on page 79)

This is primarily a check-writing exercise. There is only one set of
problems.

1. $137.82
Jake's paycheck was $167.82. He took $30 in cash and deposited
the rest: $167.82 − $30.00 = $137.82.

2. On the deposit slip, enter the date [November 10(?)] under check listings, the bank number (11-24), gross amount ($167.82), $167.82 as "TOTAL," $30.00 as "CASH RECEIVED," the "NET DEPOSIT" of $137.82 and Jake's signature.

3. On the check stub, the entries are the date, $115.00, Barbara Allan, rent, $100.00, $137.82, $237.82, $115.00, $122.82, 15 cents, and the new balance of $122.67.

4. On the check, enter the date, Barbara Allan as payee, $115.00, One hundred fifteen and no/100, and Jake's signature.

5. $240.00
$72.18 (total deductions) + $167.82 (net paycheck) = $240.00

It's Simply Interest—Answers
Problem Set A (Story on page 82)

1. 1/4
3/12 = 1/4

2. 3%
1/4 × 12% = 3%

3. $3,000
3% × $100,000 = $3,000

4. $103,000
$100,000 (principal) + $3,000 (interest, see Problem 3) = $103,000.

5. $12,000
The yearly rate is 12%. 12% × $100,000 is $12,000

It's Simply Interest—Answers
Problem Set B (Story on page 82)

1. 3%
Three months is 3/12 = 1/4 of a year: 1/4 × 12% = 3%.

2. $103,000
$100,000 (principal) × .03 (interest, see Problem 1) = $3,000 + $100,000 = $103,000

3. $106,000
Six months is 6/12 or 1/2 of a year. One half of 12% is 6%. 6% of $100,000 is $6,000. Add that to the $100,000 principal = $106,000.

4. $3,090
The new loan amount would be $103,000 (see Problem 2) × .03 = $3,090

5. $90
$103,000 (Problem 2) + $3,090 (Problem 4) = $106,090 − $106,000 (Problem 3) = $90

It's Simply Interest—Answers
Problem Set C (Story on page 82)

1. $3,000
Three months is 1/4 of a year. 1/4 of 12% = 3%. $100,000 × .03 = $3,000.

2. $12,000
$100,000 × 12% = $12,000

3. $12,550.88

	Beginning Balance	+ interest	= new balance
Third quarter	$106,090.00	$3,182.70	$109,272.70
Fourth quarter	$109,272.70	$3,278.18	$112,550.88

Either add the interest column or subtract the original loan from the final entry in "new balance."

4. $550.88
$12,550.88 (compound interest) − $12,000 (simple interest) = $550.88

5. $1,500
1/2 × $100,000 = $50,000 × .03 = $1,500 additional interest

An Interesting Loan—Answers
Problem Set A (Story on page 86)

1. $16.44
$273.95 × .06 = $16.44

2. $290.39
$273.95 + $16.44 = $290.39 (see Problem 1)

3. $270.00
$290.39 − $20.39 = $270.00 (see Problem 2)

4. $16.20
$270.00 × .06 = $16.20 (see Problem 3)

5. $8.10
Either 1/2 × $16.20 (see Problem 4) or 1/2 × .06 = 3% × 270 = $8.10

An Interesting Loan—Answers
Problem Set B (Story on page 86)

1. $290.39
Price was $273.95 × .06 = $16.44. $273.95 + $16.44 = $290.39

2. $270.00
$290.39 − $20.39 = $270.00 (see Problem 1)

3. $8.10
Six months is 1/2 of a year. 1/2 × 6% = 3%; .03 × $270 = $8.10

4. $278.10
$270.00 + $8.10 = $278.10

5. $4.05
Either 1/2 of the interest for 6 months (see Problem 3) or 1/4 × 6% = 1.5%. $270 × .015 = $4.05

An Interesting Loan—Answers
Problem Set C (Story on page 86)

1. $270.00
$273.95 (bike price) + .06 × $273.95 (sales tax) of $16.44 = $290.39

$290.39 − $20.39 = $270.00

2. $298.49
Six months is 1/2 of a year. 1/2 × 6% is 3%. 3% × $270.00 (loan amount) = $8.10. $273.95 (bike price) + $16.44 (tax) + $8.10 (interest) = $298.49

3. $.01644
Principal × rate × time = interest
$100.01634 × .06 = $6.0009804 × 1/365 = $.01644

4. $.01644
Principal × rate × time = interest
$100.01634 × .06 ÷ 365 = $.01644

5. He would get compound interest while paying simple interest.

Homecoming—Answers
Problem Set A (Story on page 90)

1. $238
$119 × 2 = $238

2. $112
$350 − $238 = $112

3. June 16
July 7 − 7 days = June 30; June 30 − 7 days = June 23; June 23 − 7 days = June 16.

4. Any two combinations equal to $8.02 that do not include a $5 bill.
Combination 1: 8 $1 bills and 2 pennies
Combination 2: 4 $2 bills and 2 pennies
Other combinations are possible.

5. 89 miles each way or 178 miles round trip.
741 − 652 = 89 mi.

Homecoming—Answers
Problem Set B (Story on page 90)

1. $2.50
1:35 to 2:00 = 25 min.; 2:00 to 2:50 = 50 min.; 50 min. + 25 min. = 75 min. or 1 hr. 15 min.; 1 hr. costs $2.00; part of another hr. costs $.50; total cost $2.50

2. 3:35 P.M.
1:35 to 2:35 = 1 hr.; 2:35 to 3:35 = additional hr. Two hours would be the maximum time allowed for a fee of $2.50.

3. $13.50
(1 hr. at $2.00) + (23 hr. at $.50 = $11.50) = $13.50

4. $41.55
$119 (flight one way) − $77.45 (bus one way) = $41.55

5. $30 per week
20 × $1.50 = $30

Homecoming—Answers
Problem Set C (Story on page 90)

1. $7.40
$5.00 for first 20 miles; 12 miles at $.20 per mile = $2.40; $5.00 + $2.40 = $7.40

2. 70 miles or more
($15 − $5 = $10) + ($10 ÷ $.20 = 50 mi.); (first 20 mi. = $5.00) + (next 50 miles mi. × $.20 per mi. = $10) = the total for 70 mi. of $15.00

3. $7.04
1:05 to 1:37 = 32 min.; (first 3 min. = $.95) + (32 min. − 3 = 29 min. × $.21 = $6.09) = $7.04

4. $2.96 for the call; $4.08 difference in the charge.
32-minute call (see Problem 3); first 3 minutes cost $.35; 29 minutes at $.09 each = $2.61; $.35 + $2.61 = $2.96 total; $7.04 (see problem #3) − $2.96 = $4.08

5. $4.52 Mon.–Fri. 8 A.M. to 11 P.M.
(First 3 minutes = $.95) + (20 min. − 3 min. = min. × $.21 = $3.57) = $4.52

Pendulum Project—Answers
Problem Set A/B/C (Story on page 95)

1. Have the students try different pendulum cord lengths and bobs, but insist that they keep systematic records of their findings. Results will be easier to interpret if only one item (cord length or pendulum bob amount) is changed at a time. Also, it helps if the cord lengths are standard (1 ft., 2 ft., 3 ft., etc.), and the bob amounts are in increments (2 oz., 4 oz., etc., or 1 washer, 2 washers, etc.). [Caution: do not use bobs that are extremely light weight (such as styrofoam) or that may disrupt air flow (such as window screen).]

2. The length of the arc becomes shorter, but it still requires the same amount of time to make each swing (period of the pendulum), because the pendulum travels more slowly as the swings become shorter.

3. A heavier bob will keep a pendulum swinging for a longer time. A longer cord will cause the pendulum to swing more slowly.

4. The pendulum periods are: 1 foot = 1 second, 4 feet = 2 seconds, 9 feet = 3 seconds, 16 feet = 4 seconds, etc. A beginning rule might be: short pendulums have short periods and swing slowly. A more precise rule is, the period of a pendulum is directly proportional to the square root of its length.

5. (a) The Foucault Pendulum was more than 200 feet long with a bob that traced a line in loose sand on each swing. It proved that the Earth turns by demonstrating its rotation.
(b) Twin pendulums that hang from a revolving shaft and act as speed controls are called "governors."
(c) A "metronome" is a device used by musicians to keep steady tempo.
(d) Mechanical clocks have a special device called an "escapement" that gives the pendulum a tiny push at regular intervals. The escapement has to be wound with a special key.
(e) Momentum, gravity, time, distance and acceleration are the five principles of physics that a swinging pendulum demonstrates.

Take a Chance—Answers
Problem Set A/B (Story on page 98)

1. 1; 1/36

2. The probability of winning a TV is 1/36
The probability of winning a telephone is 2/36 or 1/18.

3. The probability of winning any prize is 16/36 or 4/9.

4. The probability of not winning a prize is 20/36 or 5/9.

5. The probability of not winning the TV is 35/36.

6. Have the students carefully record the information onto the frequency chart. Possible discussion questions that might develop include: How do our outcomes compare with the predicted outcomes given in Problems 1-4 of this set? How do you account for any differences between the actual outcomes and the predicted ones?

Take a Chance—Answers
Problem Set C (Story on page 98)

1. 1; 1/36

2. The probability of winning the TV is 1/36.
The probability of winning the telephone is 2/36 or 1/18.

3. The probability of winning the TV is 1/36.
The probability of winning the telephone is 2/36 or 1/18.
The probability of winning candy is 7/36.
The probability of winning an animal is 6/36 or 1/6.
The probability of not winning a prize is 20/36 or 5/9.

4. Students' responses should be recorded in a table or chart showing the prize and the number of times it was selected.

5. Student comparisons should be made between the results of Problems 3 and 4 of this set.

6. Student comparisons should be made between the results of Problem 3 and the combined responses of Problems 4 and 6 of this set.

7. Examples of student predictions:
(a) More people will draw candy than any other prize.
(b) More people will draw no prize than will draw a prize.
(c) Actual probabilities get closer to the predicted ones with more spins (or draws) made.
(d) Other predictions are possible.

831 Monroe Street—Answers
Problem Set A (Story on page 102)

1. 831, 813, 381, 318, 138, 183

2. 83, 81, 38, 31, 18, 13

3. System: (a) largest to smallest; (b) smallest to largest; (c) all 80s, all 30s, all teens. Other systems are possible.

4. 831, 813, 381, 318, 183, 138

831 Monroe Street—Answers
Problem Set B (Story on page 102)

1. 831, 813, 381, 318, 183, 138

2. System: (a) largest to smallest; (b) smallest to largest; (c) all 800s, all 300s, all 100s; (d) other systems are possible.

3. 752, 725, 572, 527, 275, 257

4. Answers will vary. Sample predictions: 775, 772, 757, 755, 752, 727, 725, 722, 577, 575, 572, 557, 552, 527, 525, 522, 277, 275, 272, 257, 255, 252, 227, 225.

831 Monroe Street—Answers
Problem Set C (Story on page 102)

1. 831, 813, 381, 318, 183, 138

2. Systems: (a) largest to smallest; (b) smallest to largest; (c) all 800s, all 300s, all 100s. Other systems are possible.

3. Answers will vary. Sample predictions: 883, 881, 838, 833, 831, 818, 813, 811, 388, 381, 383, 338, 331, 318, 313, 311, 188, 183, 181, 138, 133, 131, 118, 113.

4. Answers will vary. Sample predictions: 888, 883, 881, 838, 833, 831, 818, 813, 811, 388, 381, 383, 338, 333, 331, 318, 313, 311, 188, 183, 181, 138, 133, 131, 118, 113, 111.

The Pattern Game—Answers
Problem Set A (Story on page 106)

1.

1	7	3	0	5	2	4	6
2	14	6	0	10	4	8	12

Rule: The bottom number is twice the top number.

2. (a) Double the top number to get the bottom number.
(b) Add the top number to itself to get the bottom number.
(c) Students may have other answers.

3.

2	0	6	3	5	1	4	7
4	0	36	9	25	1	16	49

Rule: Square the top number to get the bottom number.
Multiply the top number by itself to get the bottom number.
Students may have other answers.

4. Answers will vary. Be sure to have students describe the pattern or rule in verbal and written form.

The Pattern Game—Answers
Problem Set B (Story on page 106)

1.

1	7	3	0	5	2	4	6
2	14	6	0	10	4	8	12

Rule: Take the top number and double it to get the bottom number.
Add the top number to itself to get the bottom number.
Students may have other answers.

2.

1	5	3	6	0	2	7	4
3	15	9	18	0	6	21	12

Rule: Take the top number and multiply it by three to get the bottom number.

Take the top number and add it to twice itself to get the bottom number.

Students may have other answers.

3.

12	4	6	2	5	9
10	2	4	0	3	7

Rule: Take the top number and subtract two to get the bottom number.

Students may have other answers.

4. Answers will vary. Be sure to have students express their patterns or rules in verbal and written form.

The Pattern Game—Answers
Problem Set C (Story on page 106)

1.

1	7	3	0	5	2	4	6
2	14	6	0	10	4	8	12

Rule: Take the top number and double it to get the bottom number. Take the top number and add it to itself to get the bottom number. Students may have other answers.

2.

2	5	8	0	1	3	7	4	6
6	12	18	2	4	8	16	10	14

Rule: Take the top number, double it and add two to get the bottom number.

Students may find other answers.

3.

9	2	7	15	0	5	12
13	6	11	19	4	9	16

Rule: Take the top number and add 4 to get the bottom number. Students may find other answers.

4. Answers will vary. Be sure to have students express their patterns or rules in verbal and written form.

Unlucky Friday—Answers
Problem Set A (Story on page 109)

1. $142.50
$38 \times \$3.75 = \$142.50$

2. 5 months
$\$566.40 \div \$120.00 = 4.72$ months, or 5 months

3. $107.50
$\$275.00 - \$167.50 = \$107.50$

4. $25
$4 \times \$75 = \$300; \$300 - \$275 = \$25$

5. $337.12
$\$275.00 + \$32.25 + \$29.87 = \$337.12$

Unlucky Friday—Answers
Problem Set B (Story on page 110)

1. $5.63
$\$3.75 \times .5 = \$1.875 + \$3.75 = \$5.625$ or $\$3.75 \times 1.5 = \$5.625$

2. $41.25
$(8 \times \$3.75 = \$30.00) + [2 \times \$5.625$ (see Problem 1) $= \$11.25]$
$= \$41.25$

3. About 10 hours
$\$50.00 \div \$5.625 = 8.89 +$ hr.

4. Regular pay plus overtime
$25 \times \$3.75 = \$93.75; 16 \times \$3.75 = \$60.00$ plus $7 \times \$5.25$
(see Problem 1) $= \$39.375; \$60.00 + \$39.38 = \$99.38$

5. 25 hours
$\$93.59 \div \$3.75 = 24.96$, or 25 hours

Unlucky Friday—Answers
Problem Set C (Story on page 110)

1. $14.68
$\$1.19 + \$1.19 + \$1.40 + \$1.40 + \$6.00 + \$3.50 = \$14.68$

2. 1.2 hours
$(\$45.05 - \$14.68 = \$30.37) \div \$26.50 = 1.2$ hr.

3. Close, but $3.24 short
$5 \times \$15 = \$75.00; \$36.95 + \$41.29 = \$78.24$

4. 7 cans
$\$7.50 \div \$1.30 = 5.7$ cans (only enough for 5 cans); 5 paid cans gives 2 cans free, or 7 cans in all.

5. 50.5 miles per gallon
$94.5 \div 2.1 = 45$ mph; $90.9 \div 1.8 = 50.5$ mpg

Lucky Seven—Answers
Problem Set A (Story on page 114)

1.

	Red	Green
Time 1	6	1
Time 2	1	6
Time 3	5	2
Time 4	2	5
Time 5	4	3
Time 6	3	4

2.

	Red	Green
Time 1	3	1
Time 2	1	3
Time 3	2	2

3.

	Red	Green
Time 1	5	1
Time 2	1	5
Time 3	4	2
Time 4	2	4
Time 5	3	3

4. There are more ways to get a sum of 7 than any other sum. Answers will vary. Sample predictions:

	Red	Green
Time 1	6	4
Time 2	4	6
Time 3	5	5

Lucky Seven—Answers
Problem Set B (Story on page 114)

1.

	Red	Green
Time 1	5	1
Time 2	1	5
Time 3	4	2
Time 4	2	4
Time 5	3	3

2.

	Green Die					
Red Die	1	2	3	4	5	6
1	2	3	4	5	6	7
2	3	4	5	6	7	8
3	4	5	6	7	8	9
4	5	6	7	8	9	10
5	6	7	8	9	10	11
6	7	8	9	10	11	12

There are 36 boxes in the chart.

3. 6; there are more 7s than any other sum

4. 36; 6/36 or 1/6; 6/36 or 1/6; also written 6 in 36 or 1 in 6.

Lucky Seven—Answers
Problem Set C (Story on page 114)

1.

	Green Die					
Red Die	1	2	3	4	5	6
1	2	3	4	5	6	7
2	3	4	5	6	7	8
3	4	5	6	7	8	9
4	5	6	7	8	9	10
5	6	7	8	9	10	11
6	7	8	9	10	11	12

There are 36 boxes in all.

2. 4/36; 4/36; 6/36 or 1/6
6/36 represents the sum of 2, 3 and 4.

3. 18/36 or 1/2
18/36 represents the sum of 2, 4, 6, 8, 10 and 12.

4. 21/36 or 7/12
21/36 represents the sum of 7, 8, 9, 10, 11 and 12.

5. There are more boxes showing a sum of 7 than any other sum.

Busing for Bucks—Answers
Problem Set A (Story on page 118)

1. 36 hours
$7:30 - 9:30 = 2$ hr., $12 - 2 = 2$ hr., $6 - 8 = 2$ hr.: 6 hr./day in all. They work 6 days/week: $6 \times 6 = 36$.

2. $120.60
36 hr. (see Problem 1) at $3.35/hr. = $120.60

3. 6
$30 \div 5 = 6$

4. $3
$5 + $5 + $10 = $20; $20 \times .15 = $3

5. $30 \times $3 = $90; 20\% \times $90 = $18

Busing for Bucks—Answers
Problem Set B (Story on page 118)

1. $120.60
$7:30 - 9:30 = 2$ hr., $12 - 2 = 2$ hr., $6 - 8 = 2$ hr.; 6 hr./day in all. They work 6 days/week. $6 \times 6 = 36$ hr. $\times $3.35 = $120.60

2. $90
$5 + $5 + $10 = 20×30 people = $600; $600 \times .15 = $90

3. $18
$90 (see Problem 2) $\times .20 = $18

4. $38.10
6 hours $\times $3.35 = $20.10 + $18 (see Problem 2) = $38.10

5. $228.60
$6 \times $38.10 = $228.60 (see Problem 4)

Busing for Bucks—Answers
Problem Set C (Story on page 118)

1. $120.60
They worked 3 2-hour shifts each day in a 6-day week: $3 \times 2 \times 6 = 36$ hr.; $3.35 (hourly rate) $\times 36 = $120.60.

2. $90
($10 + $5 + $5 = 20×30 people = $600) $\times .15 = $90

3. $228.60
[$90 (see Problem 2) $\times 6 = $540 \times .20 = $108] + $120.60 (see Problem 1) = $228.60

4. $6.35
$228.60 \div 36$ hr. = $6.35

5. $48.15
$6.35 (see Problem 4) $\times 1.5$ (time and a half) $\times 6 = $48.15 or $(1.5 \times 6 = 9$ hr.) $\times $6.35 = $48.15

Far Out Funds—Answers
Problem Set A (Story on page 122)

1. $225
$450 \div 2 = $225

2. $9
$2.50 + $2.75 + $3.75 = $9

3. $8
[$9 (see Problem 2) × 7 = $63] − $55 = $8

4. 5 trips
They took the bus to Centerville at the end of the first, third, fifth, seventh and ninth weeks.

5. $87.10
5 trips × $17.42 = $87.10

Far Out Funds—Answers
Problem Set B (Story on page 122)

1. $63
($2.50 + $2.75 + $3.75 = $9.00) × 7 = $63

2. The meal ticket.
They would use the meal ticket for 13 days every two weeks. The cost would be $110. If they paid for each meal, the cost would be $9 per day for 13 days or $117.

3. $87.10
They traveled by bus at the end of the first, third, fifth, seventh and ninth weeks = 5 trips: 5 × $17.42 = $87.10.

4. $90.00
$3.35 × 36 = $120.60 − $30.60 = $90.00

5. $35.00
$90.00 (see Problem 4) − $55.00 = $35.00

Far Out Funds—Answers
Problem Set C (Story on page 122)

1. The meal ticket
Individual meals: $2.50 + $2.75 + $3.75 = $9.00/day; 13 days × $9.00 = $117.00. The meal ticket would cost $55 × 2 = $110 every 2 weeks.

2.

	First Two Weeks	Ten Weeks
Deductions		$126.00
Income Tax		180.00
Meals	$110.00	550.00
Bus fare		87.10
Launderette		17.50
Phone calls to Centerville		30.00
Personal		50.00
Estimate of total reductions		1,040.60

3. $1,200
Estimated income $2,250 − $1,041 (see Problem 2) = $1,209 or $1,200 to nearest $100

4. $700
$278 + $200 = $478; $1,200 (see Problem 3) − $478 = $722 or $700 to the nearest $100

5. $600
$636 + $200 = $836; $1,200 (see Problem 3) − $836 = $364 or $400 to the nearest $100

Maggie's Secret—Answers
Problem Set A (Story on page 126)

1. 4 hours and 45 minutes (4¾ hours)
12:45 to 1 P.M. = 15 min.; 1:00 to 5:30 = 4½ hr.; 4½ hr. + 15 min. = 4¾ hr.

2. Combination 1: 2 quarters, 1 nickel
Combination 2: 1 quarter, 3 dimes
Combination 3: 3 dimes, 5 nickels
Other combinations are possible.

3. $4.30
$20.00 − $15.70 = $4.30

4. Combination 1: 4 dollar bills, 1 quarter, 1 nickel
Combination 2: 4 dollar bills, 3 dimes
Other combinations are possible.

5. 1 hour and 45 minutes
11:20 to 12:00 = 40 min.; 12:00 to 1:05 = 1 hr. 5 min.; 1 hr. 5 min. + 40 min. = 1 hr. 45 min.

Maggie's Secret—Answers
Problem Set B (Story on page 126)

1. $510
12% of $4,250 = $510

2. 27 women
Proportion: $4/3 = 36/x$

3. 53
(60 − 12 = 48) + 5 = 53

4. 14.7 years
(5 × 18 = 90) + (3 × 17 = 51) + (1 × 16 = 16) + (3 × 13 = 39) + (2 × 9 = 18) + (1 × 7 = 7) = 221 ÷ 15 = 14.73, or 14.7 yr.

5. $236
$221 (total years from Problem 4) + $15 (15 children each 1 year older) = $236

Maggie's Secret—Answers
Problem Set C (Story on page 126)

1. $4,000
$480 is 12% of _____; 480 ÷ .12 = $4,000

2. 322.3 miles
347 + 299 + 318 + 325 = 1,289 ÷ 4 = 322.25, or 322.3

3. $4.80
60% of $12.00 = $7.20; $12.00 − $7.20 = $4.80
Or
100% − 60% = 40%; 40% of $12.00 = $4.80

4. 28,946 people
18% of 35,300 = 6,354; 35,300 − 6,354 = 28,946 people
Or
100% − 18% = 82%; 82% of 35,300 = 28,946

5. $11.55 or $11.56
$.65 × 3 = $1.95 + $8.95 = $10.90 × .06 = $.654, or $.65 + $10.90 = $11.55

The Frantic Drive—Answers
Problem Set A (Story on page 131)

1. 1 hour and 48 minutes
8:10 − 6:22 = 1:48

2. Combination 1: 1 quarter and 3 dimes
Combination 2: 5 dimes and a nickel
Combination 3: 4 dimes and 3 nickels
Other combinations are possible.

3. November 16
October 27 to October 31 = 5 days; 21 − 5 = 16

4. Combination 1: 3 single dollar bills and 3 pennies
Combination 2: 2 single dollar bills, 4 quarters and 3 pennies
Other combinations are possible.

5. Combination 1: fish burger, small shake, small fries—$1.45 + $.59 + $.49 = $2.53
Combination 2: burger deluxe with cheese, medium shake, large fries—$1.35 + $.69 + $.69 = $2.73
Other combinations are possible.

The Frantic Drive—Answers
Problem Set B (Story on page 131)

1. Water and Maple (refer to map)

2. 1¾ miles
7 in. on map at 1/4 mi./in. = 1¾ mi.

3. Driving: Drive north to Hickory; turn left and go 2 blocks to Water St. Turn left and drive south 3 blocks on Water St. The stadium is at the corner of Olive and Water Streets.
Walking: Walk south, turn right on Cyprus. Turn left on Main; turn right on Olive. The stadium is at the corner of Olive and Water Streets.
Other routes are possible (refer to map).

4. 2 miles
$10.00 − $8.30 = $1.70 taxi fare. $1.70 ÷ $.85 = 2 mi.; could also be calculated by measuring distance on map (8 in. = 2 mi.).

5. Two routes from Oak and Pine to Walnut and Water (Hickory is closed):
Route 1: Go north to Spruce. Turn left (west) on Spruce. Go two blocks and turn left (south) on Water. Go two blocks south on Water.
Route 2: Go north to Spruce. Turn left (west) on Spruce. Go one block and turn left (south) on Main. Go two blocks south on Main. Turn right (west) on Walnut and go one block to Water.
Other answers are possible (refer to map).

The Frantic Drive—Answers
Problem Set C (Story on page 131)

1. One mile
4 in. on the map at 1/4 mi./in. = 1 mi.

2. About 1 mi.
4 in. on the map at 1/4 mi./in. = 1 mi.

3. Directions to bus station. Drive from Elm and Main to Maple and Water. Elm St. and Water St. are blocked off. Drive south on

Main for 1 block. Turn left (east) on Cyprus. Go one block on Cyrpus. Turn left (north) on Pine until you get to Maple. Turn left (west) on Maple and go two blocks to Water.
Other routes are possible (refer to map).

4. Maple and Pine.
Shorter directions: Drive 1 block east on Hickory. Turn left (north) on Pine. Go 2 blocks north on Pine.

5. 1-1/16 miles
4¾ in. × 1/4 in./mi. = 1-1/16 mi.

Tessa's Grounding—Answers
Problem Set A (Story on page 136)

1. 24 hours
The speeding ticket was $47. Divide this by the $2 per hour she makes by babysitting. 47 divided by 2 = 23.5, rounded to the nearest hour = 24 hours.

2. 6 weeks
She sat about once a week for four hours at $2 per hour. This made $8 per week. Divide 47 by 8 = 5.825, or six weeks.

3. $442.05
Multiply $421 by .05 = $21.05. Add $21.05 to $421 = $442.05

4. $486.26
Multiply $442.05 (Problem 3 answer) by 10% = $44.21. Add these two numbers. $442.05 + $44.21 = $486.26

5. $65.26
Subtract $421.00 from $486.26 (Problem 4)

Tessa's Grounding—Answers
Problem Set B (Story on page 136)

1. 24 hours
$47 (speeding ticket) ÷ $2/hr. (for babysitting) = 23.5 hr., or 24 hr.

2. 37 hours
Add the number of hours shown on Tessa's records.

3. $74
37 hr. × $2/hr.

4. 37
$74 ÷ 2 = $37

5. 5 hours
$47 fine − $37 = $10 ÷ $2/hr. = 5 hr.
$37 earnings in November—$31 paid to her mother = $6 to spend in November
This leaves $10. Divide by $2 per hour = 5 hours.

Tessa's Grounding—Answers
Problem Set C (Story on page 136)

1. $37
37 (total number of hours) × $2/hr. = $74 ÷ 2 mo. = $37

2. $28
$8.00 (two movies @$4.00) + $10.50 (30 days of drinks @ 35

cents) + $9.00 (four Burger Barn visits @$2.25) = $27.50, or
$28

3. 14 hours
$28 expenses ÷ $2/hr. earned = 14 hr.

4. $31, $16
$47 ticket ÷ 1.5 months = $31.33
She would have to save about $31 out of her November earnings
and about $16 from her December earnings to pay her mother in a
month and a half.

5. $6
$37 − $31 = $6

Geometry in the Park—Answers
Problem Set A (Story on page 140)

1. 120,000 square feet of land
400 ft. × 300 ft. = 120,000 sq. ft. of land in the park

2. 8,256 (8,400) sq. ft. of sidewalks.
(400 ft. × 6 ft. × 2 = 4,800) + [(300 ft. − 12) × 6 ft. × 2 =
3,456] = 8,256 sq. ft.
Note: You may wish to allow 8,400 sq. ft. as an answer; if so,
however, the overlapping corners have not been accounted for.

3. Acceptable terms are equilateral, equiangular, congruent, isosceles, acute.

4. 20 ft. is the approx. diameter.
Use $C = \pi d$ and change 62 ft. 10 in. to 754 in.
Then
754 ÷ 3.14 = 240.13 in. and 240.13 ÷ 12 = 20.01 ft.
Thus, the diameter of the flower circle is approximately 20 feet.

5. The gazebo height is 25 feet. Diagrams should be similar to the
one shown here. Estimates may vary from 15 to 35 feet.

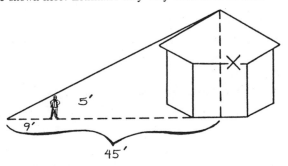

Geometry in the Park—Answers
Problem Set B (Story on page 140)

1. 13,333⅓ square yards of land
133⅓ yd. × 100 yd. = 13,333⅓ sq. yd.

2. Approximately 11,692 sq. yds. Estimates may vary from
10,000 to 12,500 square yards of grass area in the park.

3. Acceptable terms are equilateral, equiangular, congruent, isosceles, acute.

4. Diameter = 20 feet; radius = 10 feet; area = 314 square feet.
Use $C = \pi d$ and change 62 ft. 10 in. to 754 in.
Then
754 ÷ 3.14 = 240.13 in. and 240.13 ÷ 12 = 20.01 ft.

Thus, the diameter of the flower circle is approximately 20 feet
and the radius is about 10 feet. Since $A = \pi r^2$, then 3.14 × 10 feet
× 10 feet = 314 square feet is the approximate area of the flower
circle.

5. 25 ft. = gazebo height
Diagrams should be similar to the one shown here. Estimates may
vary from 15 to 35 feet. The actual gazebo height is 25 feet, which
may be found by using the ratio 5:9 as x:45.

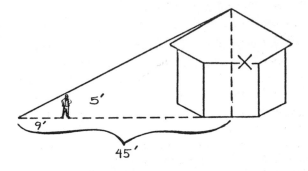

Geometry in the Park—Answers
Problem Set C (Story on page 140)

1. 1,564 square yards of sidewalks.
133⅓ yd. × 2 yd. × 2 = 533⅓ and (100 − 4 yd.) × 2 yd. × 2
= 384
So 533⅓ + 384 = 917⅓ square yards of sidewalks along the
edges of the park. (Note: The −4 yds. takes into account the
overlapping corners.) Then by using $c^2 = a^2 + b^2$ you will find the
length of each central sidewalk to be approximately 166⅔ yards.
Next, for the sidewalk in the center of the park: (166⅔ + 166⅔ −
10 yd.) × 2 yd. = 646⅔ sq. yd. (Note: The −10 yards takes into
account the overlapping portions.) Finally, for the sidewalks in the
park:
917⅓ + 646⅔ = 1,564 sq. yd.

2. 11,692 square yards of grass.
133⅓ yd. × 100 yd. = 13,333⅓ sq. yd. in the park
Since the sidewalks take up 1,564 square yards, the approximate
grass areas is:
13,333⅓ − 1,564 = 11,769⅓ sq. yd.
Finally, if the gazebo and the flower circle are also considered,
another 77 square yards must be subtracted, leaving approximately
11,692 square yards.

3. 25 feet is the gazebo height.
Estimates may vary from 15 to 35 feet. A diagram, similar to the
one shown here, should be drawn. The actual gazebo height is 25
feet, which may be found by using the ratio 5:9 as x:45.

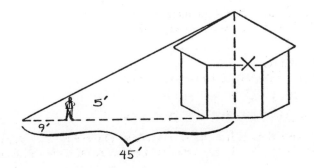

4. The gazebo floor has the greatest area.

Use $C = \pi d$ and change 62 feet 10 inches to 754 inches. Then $754 \div 3.14 = 240.13$ in.

Thus, the diameter of the flower circle is approximately 20 feet and the radius is about 10 feet. Since $A = \pi r^2$, then the approximate area of the flower circle is:

3.14×10 ft. $\times 10$ ft. $= 314$ sq. ft.

Use $A = 1/2bh$ to find the area of each triangle formed by drawing lines between opposite vertexes of the hexagon. Then:

$1/2 \times 12$ ft. $\times 10\frac{1}{2}$ ft. $= 63$ sq. ft.

The gazebo floor area is: $63 \times 6 = 378$ sq. ft.

5. Answers will vary. Students may work in teams as they gather data for this problem.

String Triangles—Answers
Problem Set A (Story on page 145)

1. Check to see that the vertexes are labeled.

2. 64 JKL = ABC

There are 64 triangles the size of JKL in ABC. By noting similar triangles, it can be determined tht GHI contains 4 triangles the size of JKL, and so do DHG, HIE and FGI, making 16 in DEF; since FGI contains 16, so do BDE, ADF and CEF, making a total of 64.

3. 4 = DEF; 16 = GHI

By noting the similar triangles we find that there are 4 triangles the size of DEF in ABC, and 16 the size of GHI.

4. HJK, GJL or IKL = JKL. GHI, DGH, EHI or FGI = 4 × JKL. ABC = 64 × JKL

It can be demonstrated that HJK, GJL and IKL are congruent to JKL. All of the similar triangles GHI, DGH, EHI and FGI have areas that are 4 times greater than JKL. Triangle ABC has an area that is 64 times greater than JKL.

5. 4^n = the number of triangles (n = the number of subdivisions). Triangle ABC = 4^0 = 1 triangle; when string is stretched to points D, E and F, we note that 4 triangles the size of DEF result, so 4^1 = 4 triangles; then when string is stretched GHI the outcome equals 16 triangles, so 4^2 = 16 triangles, and so on.

String Triangles—Answers
Problem Set B (Story on page 145)

1. 64 JKL = ABC

There are 64 triangles the size of JKL in ABC. By noting similar triangles it can be determined that GHI contains 4 triangles the size of JKL, and so do DHG, HIE and FGI, making 16 in DEF; since FGI contains 16, so do BDE, ADF and CEF, making a total of 64.

2. 4 = DEF; 16 = GHI; area DEF = 4 × GHI; area ABC = 4 × DEF and 16 × GHI

By noting the similar triangles, we find that there are 4 triangles the size of DEF in ABC, and 16 the size of GHI.

3. 256 MNO = ABC

There will be 4 triangles the size of MNO in each triangle the size of JKL; thus, 4 × 64 = 256. (Note: See Problem 1 above for further explanation.)

4. 4^n = the number of triangles (n = the number of subdivisions). Triangle ABC = 4^0 = 1 triangle; when string is stretched to points D, E and F, we note that 4 triangles the size of DEF result, so 4^1 = 4 triangles; then when string is stretched GHI, the outcome equals 16 triangles, so 4^2 = 16 triangles, and so on.

5. PST = 4 × PQR; PUV = 9 × PST; PXW = 16 × PST. There will be 9 additional triangles the size of PST for a total of 25.

String Triangles—Answers
Problem Set C (Story on page 145)

1. 64 JKL = ABC

There are 64 triangles the size of JKL in ABC. By noting similar triangles, it can be determined that GHI contains 4 triangles the size of JKL, and so do DHG, HIE and FGI, making 16 in DEF; since FGI contains 16 so do BDE, ADF and CEF, making a total of 64.

2. 4 = DEF; 16 = GHI; area DEF = 4 × GHI; area ABC = 4 × DEF and 16 × GHI

By noting the similar triangles we find that there are 4 triangles the size of DEF in ABC, and 16 the size of GHI.

3. 256 MNO = ABC; 4^n = the number of triangles (n = the number of subdivisions)

There will be 4 triangles the size of MNO in each triangle the size of JKL; thus 4 × 64 = 256. (Note: See Problem 1 above for further explanation.)

Triangle ABC = 4^0 = 1 triangle; when string is stretched to points D, E and F, we note that 4 triangles the size of DEF result, so 4^1 = 4 triangles; then when string is stretched GHI, the outcome equals 16 triangles, so 4^2 = 16 triangles, and so on.

4. PST = 4 × PQR; PUV = 9 × PST; PXW = 16 × PST
There will be 9 additional triangles the size of PST for a total of 25.

5. E^2 = total number of triangles (E = extensions)
By constructing a chart we find:

Number of Extensions	Number of Additional Triangles	Total Number of Triangles
1 (PQR)	0	1
2 (PST)	3	4
3 (PUV)	5	9
4 (PWX)	7	16
5 (etc.)	9	25
etc.		

By looking at the number of additional triangles column, it can be seen that, for each extension, we can add 2 to the previous result to get the "new" additional amount. For example, with 3 extensions, we can look back and see that there were 3 the time before. So we can now add 2 more to the 3 to equal 5. We can also combine the 5 with the 4 to obtain a total of 9.

However, there is a more efficient rule. It is E^2 = total number of triangles (E = extensions). For example, notice that for 1 extension (which is the original triangle PQR), we get 1^2 = 1 triangle; for 2 extensions (or triangle PST) we obtain 2^2 = 4 total triangles the size of PQR; for 3 extensions we have 3^2 = 9 triangles; for 4 extensions we get 4^2 = 16; next 5^2 = 25; and 6^2 = 36; and so forth.

Geometry Project—Answers
Problem Set A (Story on page 149)

1. Triangles should have the greatest strength and stability.

2. Triangles can often be seen in the exposed frameworks of bridges.

3. The design of bridge frameworks may vary; check that the length equals 45 centimeters and the width 6 centimeters or more.

4. Costs will vary; however, the total should be less than $3.

5. Bridge construction will vary; however, all should support at least 1 kilogram. Give extra points for pleasing design, decoration, paint, and other features.

Geometry Project—Answers
Problem Set B (Story on page 149)

1. Triangles are often used to provide strength and stability to bridge frameworks.

2. Triangles can often be seen in the exposed frameworks of bridges.

3. The design of bridge frameworks may vary; check that the length equals 45 centimeters and the width 6 centimeters or more.

4. Answers will vary.
Number of beams × $7.23 = _____
The bridge shown in the diagram would cost 39 beams × 7.23 = $281.97.

5. Bridge construction will vary; however, all should support at least 1 kilogram. Give extra points for pleasing design, decoration, paint, and other features.

Geometry Project—Answers
Problem Set C (Story on page 149)

1. Testing procedures and results will vary, but two- and three-dimensional triangle frameworks should have the greatest strength and stability.

2. Triangles are often used to provide strength and stability to bridge frameworks.

3. The design of bridge frameworks may vary; check the scale drawing for an approximate length of 15 centimeters and width of 2 centimeters.

4. Costs will vary, but check for reasonableness. The students will need to check prices at a lumber yard or building supply store or from newspaper ads.

5. Bridge construction will vary; however, all should support at least 1 kilogram. Give extra points for pleasing design, decoration, paint, and especially for bridges that support more than 3 kilograms.

What's the Score?—Answers
Problem Set A (Story on page 153)

1. Dots represent the SAT scores by years; 24 years are covered by the graph.

2. 24 points difference
502 − 478 = 24

3. An estimate is 470–474.

4. Student observations should be similar to these:
(a) The average SAT math score has been higher than the average SAT verbal score.
(b) SAT scores generally dropped from 1963 to 1980.
(c) The SAT scores were higher on the average in 1963 than in 1986.
Other observations are possible.

What's the Score?—Answers
Problem Set B (Story on page 153)

1. An estimate is 45 points.

2. An estimate is 25 points.

3. Observations could be similar to these:
(a) The SAT scores were lower in 1986 than in 1963.
(b) The 1986 average math score is approximately the same as the 1963 verbal score.
(c) Math scores are generally higher than the verbal scores.
(d) SAT scores in general decreased from 1963 to 1980.
Other observations are possible.

4. Predictions could be similar to these:
(a) The 1990 scores will be lower than the 1963 scores.
(b) the 1990 math score will be higher than the 1990 verbal score.
Other predictions are possible.

What's the Score?—Answers
Problem Set C (Story on page 153)

1. Trends could be similar to these:
(a) Verbal scores are lower than math scores.
(b) Scores generally decrease from 1963 to 1980.
(c) Scores generally increase from 1980 to 1986.
Other trends are possible.

2. Predictions could be similar to these:
(a) Math scores will be higher than verbal scores
(b) Scores will be lower in 1990 than in 1963.
Other predictions are possible.

3. Observations could be similar to these:
(a) SAT scores were lower in 1986 than in 1963.
(b) The 1986 math score is approximately the same as the 1963 verbal score.
(c) Math scores are generally higher than verbal scores.
(d) SAT scores in general decreased from 1963 to 1980.
Other observations are possible.

4. Questions could be similar to these:
(a) About what was the SAT verbal score in 1975?
(b) About how large is the average difference in math and verbal SAT scores shown on the graph?

(c) In what year was the SAT math score the lowest? What was that score?

What is the Average?—Answers
Problem Set A (Story on page 157)

1. 17 is the mode.
The mode is the age that occurs most often. This is found in the frequency chart by the age with the most tallies.

2. 16 is the median.
The median is the age exactly in the middle of all the ages represented by the survey. Since there are 101 students represented, the median would be the age of the 51st student when arranged from youngest to oldest. Count down the tallies until you reach the 51st tally. This represents the median age.

3. 15.9 is the mean age.
$1,610 \div 101 = 15.9$

4. Student results should be recorded in a chart similar to the one in the story.

What is the Average?—Answers
Problem Set B (Story on page 157)

1. 15.9 is the mean; 16 is the median; 17 is the mode.
$1,610 \div 101 = 15.9$, or the mean. The median age is that of the 51st student (exactly in the middle of all the students when arranged from youngest to oldest). The mode is the age that occurs most often.

2. Each height should be rounded to the nearest inch. Student results should be in a frequency chart similar to the one shown in the story.

3. The mean is calculated by dividing the total sum of the students' heights by the number of students.

4. The median height is that height of the student who falls exactly in the middle when lined up from shortest to tallest. If there is an even number of students, average the middle two heights.

The mode height is that height that occurs most often. It is possible to have more than one mode. Do not average the modes if there is more than one.

What is the Average?—Answers
Problem Set C (Story on page 157)

1. Student results should be recorded in a frequency chart similar to the one in the story.

2. Be sure to arrange the information from the smallest to largest in the frequency table.

3. Mean is average. Calculate by dividing the total sum of ages or heights by the total number of students.
Median is determined by finding the exact middle of the class when they are arranged from the lowest age or height to the largest. The age or height that corresponds to the student in the middle is the median. If an even number of students are in your class, you must average the middle two ages or heights to find the median.

Mode is the age or height that occurs most often. There might be more than one mode. In that case you write them all, do not average them.

4. A bar graph can have either horizontal or vertical bars. The scale shown should be evenly calculated. The graph should be labeled and titled.

The Challenge—Answers
Problem Set A (Story on page 161)

1. Central 16; Bishop 12
Central: $(2 \times 6) + (1 \times 1) + (1 \times 3) = 16$
Bishop: $(1 \times 6) + (2 \times 3) = 12$

2. 127 yards
$(100 + 65 + 160 + 170 + 140) \div 5 = 127$

3. 18.8 points
$(16 + 8 + 24 + 21 + 28 + 16) \div 6 = 18.8$

4. 6.2 points more per game
Take the difference between the scores per game and total them. Then find the average:
$(4 + 8 + 10 + 4 + 7 + 4) \div 6 = 6.2$

5. Combination 1: 1 TD, 1 PAT and 3 FG
Combination 2: 2 TD, 2 PAT and 1 safety
Combination 3: 2 TD, 1 PAT and 1 FG
Other combinations are possible.

The Challenge—Answers
Problem Set B (Story on page 161)

1. Central 16; Bishop 12
Central: $(2 \times 6) + (1 \times 1) + (1 \times 3) = 16$
Bishop: $(1 \times 6) + (2 \times 3) = 12$

2. 6.2 points more per game
Take the difference between each of the scores. Find the total of the differences and then the average.
$(4 + 8 + 10 + 4 + 7 + 4) \div 6 = 6.2$

3. Tigers: 4 TD; or 3 TD and 2 FG
South: 2 TD, 2 PAT; or 1 TD, 1 safety, and 2 FG
Other combinations are possible

4. 155.2 yards
$(125 + 100 + 150 + 175 + 200 + 181) \div 6 = 155.2$

The Challenge—Answers
Problem Set C (Story on page 161)

1. Central 16; Bishop 12
Central: $(2 \times 6) + (1 \times 1) + (1 \times 3) = 16$
Bishop: $(1 \times 6) + (2 \times 3) = 12$

2.

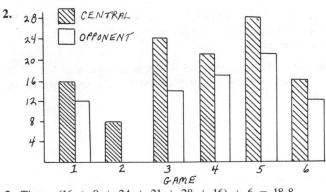

3. Tigers: (16 + 8 + 24 + 21 + 28 + 16) ÷ 6 = 18.8
Opponents: (12 + 0 + 14 + 17 + 21 + 12) ÷ 6 = 12.7

4. 21 points can be scored in the following ways:
(a) 3 TD, 3 PAT
(b) 3 TD, 1 PAT, 1 safety
(c) 2 TD, 3 FG
(d) 2 TD, 1 PAT, 1 safety, 2 FG
Other combinations are possible.

To the Coach—Answers
Problem Set A (Story on page 165)

1. $16.90
$11.95 + $4.95 = $16.90

2. $4.00
See order form.

3. No
Order form says: "Indiana residents add 5% sales tax." Juan Cortez is a California resident.

4. $21.40
See order form. For "Rush handling," add 50 cents to the order.
$16.90 + $4.00 + $.50 = $21.40

5. Filled-out order form:

Name of item	Six-digit #	How Many	Personalized Items	Price each	Total
Coach's Tribute Plaque	94071-8	1	Leroy Brown	11.95	11.95
#1 Coach Mug	40140-6	1		4.95	4.95
			Merchandise Total		16.90
			Total order		16.90
			Shipping and Handling		4.00
			Rush handling		.50
			Sub-total		21.40
Check either Visa or Master Card			Total charged to credit card		21.40

To the Coach—Answers
Problem Set B (Story on page 165)

1. $16.90
$11.95 + 4.95 = $16.90

2. $4.50
$4.00 + $.50 = $4.50
See order form.

3. $21.40
$11.95 + 4.95 + $4.00 + $.50 = $21.40

4. Filled-out order form

Name of item	Six-digit #	How Many	Personalized Items	Price each	Total
Coach's Tribute Plaque	94071-8	1	Leroy Brown	11.95	11.95
#1 Coach Mug	40140-6	1		4.95	4.95
			Merchandise Total		16.90
			Total order		16.90
			Shipping and Handling		4.00
			Rush handling		.50
			Sub-total		21.40
Check either Visa or Master Card			Total charged to credit card		21.40

5. 71 cents
$21.40 ÷ 30 = 71 cents (to the nearest cent)

To the Coach—Answers
Problem Set C (Story on page 165)

1. $16.90
$11.95 + $4.95 = $16.90

2. $21.40
$16.90 (see Problem 1) + $4.00 + $.50 (see order form) = $21.50

3. Filled out order form

Name of item	Six-digit #	How Many	Personalized Items	Price each	Total
Coach's Tribute Plaque	94071-8	1	Leroy Brown	11.95	11.95
#1 Coach Mug	40140-6	1		4.95	4.95
			Merchandise Total		16.90
			Total order		16.90
			Shipping and Handling		4.00
			Rush handling		.50
			Sub-total		21.40
Check either Visa or Master Card			Total charged to credit card		21.40

4. 71 cents
$21.90 ÷ 30 = 71 cents (to the nearest cent)

5. $8.60 or $8.70
30 × $1 = $30 − $21.40 (cost of order) = $8.60
Or
$1.00 − $.71 = $.29 × 30 = $8.70

The Pro Game—Answers
Problem Set B (Story on page 169)

1. 140 miles
Add the total of the "distances between points" from Centerville to the SR 14/I 113 junction.
25 + 15 + 50 + 20 = 140

2. 140 miles
Add the total of the "distances between points" from the SR 14/I-113 junction to the junction of I-113 and I-117 (the location of the stadium).
35 + 98 + 7 = 140

3. West
Michael's father will drive from Jackson City to Lakeside. The compass direction shown on the map is west.

4. 174 miles
Add the "distances between points" from Lakeside to Centerville.
77 + 47 + 50 = 174

5. Turn west at the SR 12 freeway exit. Go on SR 12 for 140 miles to Lakeside. Turn north on SR 19. Stay on SR 19 for 174 miles until you get to Centerville.

The Pro Game——Answers
Problem Set C (Story on page 169)

1. 280 miles
Add the total of the "distances between points" from Centerville to the stadium at the junction of I 113 and I 117.
25 + 15 + 50 + 50 + 35 + 98 + 7 = 280

2. 321 miles
Add the total of the "distances between points" from Centerville through Summit City and on to the junction of I 113 and I 117 (the location of the stadium).

3. Freeway
The freeway route is 280 miles; the Summit City route is 321

4. The Summit City route
Accept any two reasons: (1) It is longer. (2) Part of the way is a crooked mountain road. (3) You can drive faster on a freeway than on a State Highway. (4) You could run into snow and have to use chains in the mountains.

5. Turn west at the SR 12 freeway exit. Go on SR 12 to Lakeside. Turn north on SR 19. Stay on SR 19 until you get to Centerville.

The Pro Game—Answers
Problem Set A (Story on page 169)

1. By way of the freeway (or) SR 14/I 113 (or west to the freeway and so on.
Accept any two reasons: (1) It is shorter. (2) You can go faster on the freeway. (3) Summit City way has crooked mountain road. (4) It could be snowing in the mountains.

2. About 6 A.M.
Add the "distances between points" from Centerville to the junction of I 113 and I 117 (the location of the stadium).
25 + 15 + 50 + 50 + 35 + 98 + 7 = 280
Then divide:
280 mi. ÷ 50 mph = 5 hr. 36 min.
Add 2 10-minute rest stops, giving a total of about 6 hours. Subtract 6 hours from the planned arrival at noon.

3. 46.7 mph
Add the "distances between points" from Centerville to the freeway.
25 + 15 + 50 + 50 = 140
Divide:
140 mi. ÷ 3 hr. = 46.7 mph

4. 174 miles
Add the total of the "distances between points" between Lakeside and Centerville.
77 + 47 + 50 = 174

5. 2 hours
See the "distances between points" between Thud and Summit City. Then add 13 miles:
47 + 13 = 60
Divide: 60 mi. ÷ 30 mph = 2 hr.

Table for Eight—Answers
Problem Set A/B (Story on page 173)

1. Four tables would be needed for 10 people.

	Person 1	Person 2	Person 3	Person 4	
Person 5					Person 6
	Person 7	Person 8	Person 9	Person 10	

2.

Number of Persons per Table	12	10	8	6	4
Method 1	1				
Method 2			1		1
Method 3				2	
Method 4					3

3. Method 1: 5 tables
Method 2: 4 tables
Method 3: 4 tables
Method 4: 3 tables
Method 1 uses the greatest number of tables; method 4 uses the lowest number of tables.

4. Method 1: 2 size #2 cloths, 1 size #1 cloth
Method 2: 1 size #2 cloth, 2 size #1 cloths
Method 3: 2 size #2 cloths
Method 4: 3 size #1 cloths

5. 16 couples = 32 people. Table arrangements could be:
Arrangement 1: 8 tables for 4
Arrangement 2: 2 tables for 12 and a table for 8
Arrangement 3: 4 tables for 8
Arrangement 4: 2 tables for 10 and a table for 12
Arrangement 5: 4 tables for 6 and a table for 8
Arrangement 6: 2 tables for 8, 1 of 12, and 1 of 4
Other arrangements possible.

Table for Eight—Answers
Problem Set C (Story on page 173)

1. Four tables would be needed to seat 10 people.

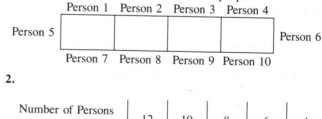

	Person 1	Person 2	Person 3	Person 4	
Person 5					Person 6
	Person 7	Person 8	Person 9	Person 10	

2.

Number of Persons per Table	12	10	8	6	4
Method 1	1				1
Method 2		1		1	
Method 3			2		
Method 4			1		2
Method 5				2	1
Method 6					4

3. Method 1: 6 tables
Method 2: 6 tables

Method 3: 6 tables
Method 4: 5 tables
Method 5: 5 tables
Method 6: 4 tables
Methods 1, 2 and 3 use the greatest number of tables. Method 6 uses the least number of tables.

4. Method 1: 2 size #2 cloths, 2 size #1 cloths
Method 2: 3 size #2 cloths
Method 3: 2 size #2 cloths, 2 size #1 cloths
Method 4: 1 size #2 cloth, 3 size #1 cloths
Method 5: 2 size #2 cloths, 1 size #1 cloth
Method 6: 4 size #1 cloths
Methods 1, 3 and 6 use the greatest number of cloths, Methods 2 and 5 use the lowest number of cloths.

5. The minimum number of tables used for 240 people would be 60, with 4 at each table.

Jake's Surprise—Answers
Problem Set A (Story on page 173)

1. $11.64
$1.79 × 6.5 = $11.635 or $11.64

2. 3¼ hours, or 3 hours 15 minutes
1/2 hr. × 6½ = 3¼ hr.

3. Two ways of giving $1.71 in change:
$5.00 − $3.29 = $1.71
Combination 1: 1 dollar bill, a 50-cent piece, 2 dimes and 1 penny
Combination 2: 1 dollar bill, 2 quarters, 2 dimes and 1 penny
Other combinations are possible.

4. 44 days
April 3 until April 30 equals 28 days, plus 16 days in May for 44 days total.

5. Estimate: $1.50/$2.00; actual $1.87
$11.64 + $1.19 + $.79 = $13.62
$15.49 − $13.62 = $1.87

Jake's Surprise —Answers
Problem Set B (Story on page 176)

1. Two ways in which $1.71 in change could be given
$5.00 − $3.29 = $1.71
Combination 1: 1 dollar bill, a 50-cent piece, 2 dimes and 1 penny
Combination 2: 1 dollar bill, 2 quarters, 2 dimes and 1 penny
Other combinations are possible.

2. 3 overtime hours; 35 regular hours
9 − 8 = 1; 10 − 8 = 2; 2 + 1 = 3 overtime hours; 6 + 5 + 8 + 8 + 8 = 35 regular hours.

3. 34.5 hours
$129.50 ÷ $3.75 = 34.53, or 34.5 hr.

4. $215
$205 × 2 = $410; $410 − $195 = $215

5. Estimate $25.00
$32 + 20 + 24 = $76 ÷ 3 = approx. $25

Jake's Surprise—Answers
Problem Set C (Story on page 176)

1. $30
$37.50 − (20% of $37.50 = $7.50) = $30.00
Or
100% − 20% = 80%; 80% of $37.50 = $30.00

2. 52 miles
175 − (12.3 × 2 = 24.6 × 5 = 123) = 52

3. All possible combinations of coins to equal 24 cents.
$5.00 − $4.76 = $.24
Combination 1: 2 dimes, 4 pennies
Combination 2: 1 dime, 2 nickels, 4 pennies
Combination 3: 1 dime, 4 nickels, 4 pennies
Combination 4: 1 dime, 1 nickel, 9 pennies
Combination 5: 1 dime, 19 pennies
Combination 6: 3 nickels, 9 pennies
Combination 7: 2 nickels, 14 pennies
Combination 8: 1 nickel, 19 pennies
Combination 9: 24 pennies

4. 6:08 P.M.
2:52 P.M. + 3 hrs. 15 min. = 6:08

5. Three on each side (with a minimum of 6 inches showing on each side of a mat). If you put 4 on a side, you would have a little less than 6 inches showing on each side of each mat. Three mats to a side would, of course, give more space between mats.

Sale by Mail—Answers
Problem Set A/B/C (Story on page 181)

This is primarily a check-writing exercise and has only one set of problems.

See Next Page for Check Answers

Sale by Mail—Answers
Problem Set A/B/C (Story on page 181) (Cont'd)

1. Check stub

ANY DATE IN NOVEMBER 19___		
104 $ 29 95		
TO Sale by Mail		
FOR Coat		
	DOLLARS	CENTS
OLD BALANCE	105	47
DEPOSITED		
TOTAL	105	47
THIS CHECK	29	95
TOTAL	75	52
IF SPEC. CHECKING CHECK CHARGE		15
NEW BALANCE	75	37

CENTERVILLE BANK
711 MAIN ST.
CENTERVILLE, CA 95999

11-24/170
1210(8)

104

ANY DATE IN NOVEMBER 19___

PAY TO THE ORDER OF Sale by Mail $ 29 95

Twenty-nine and 95/100   DOLLARS

JAKE BURTON
123 NORTH ST.
CENTERVILLE, CA 95999

Jake Burton

⑈1210002481:788 0170 241780⑈

2. $9.57
$35.00 check − $25.43 purchase = $9.57 change

3. Check stub

ANY DATE IN NOVEMBER 19		
104 $ 35 00		
TO Farmer Foods		
FOR Food		
	DOLLARS	CENTS
OLD BALANCE	75	37
DEPOSITED		
TOTAL	75	37
THIS CHECK	35	00
TOTAL	40	37
IF SPEC. CHECKING CHECK CHARGE		15
NEW BALANCE	40	22

CENTERVILLE BANK
711 MAIN ST.
CENTERVILLE, CA 95999

11-24/170
1210(8)

105

ANY DATE IN NOVEMBER 19___

PAY TO THE ORDER OF Farmer Foods $ 35 00

Thirty-five and no/100   DOLLARS

JAKE BURTON
123 NORTH ST.
CENTERVILLE, CA 95999

Jake Burton

⑈1210002481:783 0170 241780⑈

4. Yes, the statement was correct. The "other charges" were 4
check charges at 15 cents each.

5. The statement differed from Jake's checkbook balance because
check #104, which he sent to pay for the coat, had not yet cleared
and was not charged to his account by the statement date.

A Day at Clear Lake—Answers
Problem Set A (Story on page 184)

1. It was 8:55 A.M. when they arrived at the lake.

2. Food lists and costs will vary. The students will need to visit a grocery store or use newspaper ads to obtain current prices. Check for reasonableness and totals of no more than $50.

3. Approximately 11½ minutes
Distance = Rate × Time
7 mi. = 37 mph × time in hr.
Time = .1891891 hr., or 11½ min. (.1891891 × 60 min./hr. = 11.351346 min.)

4. Horsepower is a unit for measuring how much work an engine can do. James Watt, the man who developed the first useful steam engines, needed a way to tell people how powerful his engines were. As such, a 10-horsepower engine was said to have as much power as 10 strong horses. Today, 1 horsepower is standardized as the rate of work equivalent to lifting 550 pounds a distance of 1 foot in 1 second.

5. $10,000 to $30,000
To obtain current boat prices, the students may need to contact a boat shop or marina. The cost of such boats will vary according to construction features and optional equipment. The price of a good used boat may be one-quarter to one-half off.

A Day at Clear Lake—Answers
Problem Set B (Story on page 184)

1. They got to the lake at 8:48 A.M.
54 mi. ÷ 35 mph × 60 min./hr. = 92.571426 = approx. 93 min.
Then
7:15 A.M. + 93 min. = 8:48 A.M.

2. Food lists and costs will vary. The students will need to visit a grocery store or use newspaper ads to obtain current prices. Check for reasonableness and totals of no more than $50.

3. Approximately 23 minutes
Distance = Rate × Time
14 mi. = 37 mph × time in hr.
Time = .3783783 hr., or approx. 23 min. (.3783783 × 60 min./hr. = 22.702898 min.)

4. Horsepower is a unit for measuring how much work an engine can do. James Watt, the man who developed the first useful steam engines, needed a way to tell people how powerful his engines were. As such, a 10-horsepower engine was said to have as much power as 10 strong horses. Today, 1 horsepower is standardized as the rate of work which is equivalent to lifting 550 pounds a distance of 1 foot in 1 second.

5. $10,000 to $30,000
To obtain current boat prices, the students may need to contact a boat shop or marina. The cost of such boats will vary according to construction features and optional equipment. The price of a good used boat may be one-quarter to one-half off.

A Day at Clear Lake—Answers
Problem Set C (Story on page 184)

1. Approximately 7 gallons of gas.
7 gal. × price of unleaded gasoline = $_____
24 mpg − (24 × 1/3) = 16 mpg
108 mi. ÷ 16 mpg = 6.75 or approx. 7 gal.
Use the current price for unleaded gasoline times 7 gallons to get the cost.

2. Food lists and costs will vary. The students will need to visit a grocery store or use newspaper ads to obtain current prices. Check for reasonableness and totals of no more than $50.

3. Approximately 23 minutes; almost 2 gallons of gasoline. 2 gal. × current gasoline price = $_____.
Estimate: 4 to 6 hr. × 5 gal. gas/hr. × current price/gal. = $_____.
Distance = Rate × Time
14 mi. = 37 mph × time in hr.
Time = .3783783 hr., or approx. 23 min. (.3783783 × 60 min./hr. = 22.702898)
Then multiply the time in hours by the fuel consumption rate. Thus:
.3783783 hrs. × 5 gal./hr. = 1.89189, or approx. 2 gal.
2 gal. used × current price/gal. = cost
Student answers will vary, but with time out for launching, picnicking, drifting, and other activities, you can estimate 4 to 6 hours actual running time; thus: 4 to 6 hrs. × 5 gal. gas/hr. × current price = boat gasoline cost for the day.

4. Horsepower is a unit for measuring how much work an engine can do. James Watt, the man who developed the first useful steam engines, needed a way to tell people how powerful his engines were. As such, a 10-horsepower engine was said to have as much power as 10 strong horses. Today, 1 horsepower is standardized as the rate of work which is equivalent to lifting 550 pounds a distance of 1 foot in 1 second. Theoretically the boat with the 160-horsepower engine could go 16 times faster than the one with 9.8 horsepower, but it most likely would not due to number of variables including weight, design resistance, pitch and/or number of propeller blades, and other factors.

5. The boat was a 16-foot, fiberglass, inboard-outboard model with a 160-horsepower engine. The boat might cost from $10,000 to $30,000, and the trailer another $1,500 to $4,000. Used models might cost one-quarter to one-half less.

Survey—Answers
Problem Set A (Story on page 188)

1. What is your favorite radio station? Do you think that smoking should be allowed on campus?

2. How many cars do your immediate family members own? How many miles do you travel one way to school?

3. Student results should be shown in a frequency chart similar to this:

Station	Number of Students	Smoking	Number of Students
K210		Yes	
WYTX		No	

4. Student results should be shown in a frequency chart similar to this:

Number of Miles	Number of Students	Total
0		
1		
2		

Number of Cars	Number of Students	Total
0		
1		
2		

Survey—Answers
Problem Set B (Story on page 188)

1. Factual questions are (a) the number of cars in a family and (b) the number of miles traveled to school.
The frequency chart should look similar to this:

Number of Miles	Number of Students	Total
0		
1		
2		

Number of Cars	Number of Students	Total
0		
1		
2		

2. The bar graph can have either vertical or horizontal bars. The scale should be evenly calculated. The sides should be labeled. The graph should have a title.

3. Be sure to check students' surveys for factual versus opinion questions. The frequency table should include opinion information and student tally and totals.

Survey—Answers
Problem Set C (Story on page 188)

1. Be sure to check students' surveys for factual versus opinion questions.

2. Frequency table should include factual information and student tally and totals.

3. A bar graph could have either horizontal or vertical bars. The scale should be evenly calculated. The sides should be labeled and the graph should be titled.

Summer Plans—Answers
Problem Set A (Story on page 192)

1. 192 oranges
$4 \times 4 \times 12 = 192$

2. $1.98
$2\frac{1}{2} \times \$.79 = 2.5 \times \$.79 = \$1.98$

3. $.10
$\$.29 \div 3 = \$.10$

4. $6\frac{2}{3}$ bunch
$5 \text{ lb.} \div 3/4 = 6\frac{2}{3}$ bunch

5. 4.2 pounds
$\$5.00 \div \$1.20/\text{lb.} = 4.2 \text{ lb.}$

Summer Plans—Answers
Problem Set B (Story on page 192)

1. $.44
$\$.59 \times 3/4 = \$.59 \times .75 = \$.44$

2. 5 heads of lettuce; $.05 change
$\$3.00 \div \$.59$
$\$.59 \times 5 = \$2.95; \$3.00 - \$2.95 = \$.05$

3. 2 pounds for $1.15
$\$1.79 \div 3 = \$.596$ or $\$.60/\text{lb.}$
$\$1.15 \div 2 = \$.575$ or $\$.58/\text{lb.}$

4. 4 full bags
$1\frac{1}{2}$ doz. = 18 apples; $75 \div 18 = 4$ full bags

5. $.80 saved
$10 \times .27 = \$2.70; 10 \times .19 = \$1.90; \$2.70 - \$1.90 = \$.80$

Summer Plans—Answers
Problem Set C (Story on page 192)

1. $100.20 for 2 adults
$\$33.40 \times 2 = \$66.80$ round trip + $\$33.40$ (1/2 fare) = $\$100.20$

2. $111.25
$(\$3.40 \times 25) + (\$5.25 \times 5) = \$111.25$

3. $91.70 total pay
$4.5 + 5.2 + 6.1 + 10.4 = 26.2$ hours;
$\$3.50 \times 26.2 = \$91.70$

4. 27.5 hours
$\$93.50 \div \$3.40 = 27.5$ hrs.

5. 21 regular hours
$\$5.25 \times 6 = \$31.50; \$105 - \$31.50 = \$73.50;$
$\$73.50 \div \$3.50 = 21$ hrs.

The Dinosaurs Rock—Answers
Problem Set A (Story on page 196)

1. $62.50
$\$12.50$ ticket price $\times 5$ tickets = $\$62.50$

2. 360 miles
Add the "distances between points" between Centerville and Middletown and multiply by 2 for the round trip: $25 + 15 + 50 + 50 + 35 + 5 = 180 \times 2 = 360$ mi.

3. 4 hours
180 mi. (one-way distance, see Problem 2) $\div$ 45 mph = 4 hr.

4. 16 gallons
360 mi. (round-trip distance, see Problem 2) $\div$ 22 mpg = 16.36 gal.
This is 16 gallons to the closest full gallon.

5. Answers here will depend on the individual. Entries should be made for each item of food and its price. The total of expected food expenses will include purchases before and after the concert. Check for reasonableness in relation to local prices and patterns of consumption.

The Dinosaurs Rock—Answers
Problem Set B (Story on page 196)

1. $64.50
$12.50 ticket price × 5 = $62.50 + $2 service charge = $64.50

2. Add the "distances between points" between Centerville and Middletown and multiply by 2 for the round trip: 25 + 15 + 50 + 50 + 35 + 5 = 180 × 2 = 360
Add 10 for pick-up and drop-off mileage, for a total of 370 miles.

3. 4½ hours
180 mi (one-way distance to Middletown, see Problem 2) ÷ 45 mph = 4 hrs. + 1/2 hr. (in-town pick-up) = 4½ hr.

4. About 17
370 mi. (total distance, see Problem 2) ÷ 22 mpg = 16.82, or about 17 gal.

5. About $4.00
17 gal. (Problem 4) × 95.9 cents = $16.30 ÷ 4-about $4.00 each

The Dinosaurs Rock—Answers
Problem Set C (Story on page 196)

1. $1.60
If the 5 shared the $2.00 service charge, it would cost 40 cents each. Subtract 40 cents from $2.00 they would pay if they each bought tickets separately.

2. 3 hours 20 minutes
Add the "distances between points" from Centerville to the SR 14/I 113 junction and divide by the miles per hour:
140 mi. ÷ 42 mph = 3.33 hr., or 3 hr. 20 min.

3. 48 miles per hour
Add the "distances between points" between the SR 14/I 113 junction (40 miles). They made this portion of the trip in 50 minutes, or 5/6 of an hour.
40 mi. ÷ 5/6 = 48 mph
$$\frac{40}{1} \div \frac{5}{6} = \frac{40}{1} \times \frac{6}{5} = \frac{240}{5} = 48$$

4. Check for reasonable individual consumption and local prices. The answer is a total of food costs before and after the concert.

5. $4.00
Add the distances between points from Centerville to Middletown and back and multiply by 2 for the round trip: 25 + 15 + 50 + 50 + 35 + 5 = 180 × 2 = 360
Divide by 22 miles per gallon to find gas consumption of 16.36 gallons. Multiply by 95.9 cents per gallon for a total cost of $15.69. Then divide by 4 for a per-person cost of $3.92, or about $4.00 each.

Cassette by Credit—Answers
Problem Set A (Story on page 201)

1. $18
$299.95 × .06 = $17.997, or $18.00

2. $294.97
$299.95 − $4.98 = $294.97

3. Cheapo's
Cheapo's $294.97 (see Problem 2)
Below Cost: $298.98 − (3 × 99 cents for movies) $2.97 = $296.01

4. 1½% per month
18% credit card interest rate ÷ 12 mo. = 1½%/mo.

5. $4.77
Multiply Cheapo's cost ($299.95 + $18.00 = $317.95) by 1½% = $4.77.

Cassette by Credit—Answers
Problem Set B (Story on page 201)

1. $1.03
Cheapo's: ($299.95 × .06 = $18.00) + $299.95 = $317.95
Below Cost: ($298.98 × .06 = $17.94) + $298.98 = $316.92
$317.95 − $316.92 = $1.03

2. Cheapo's: $294.97; Below Cost: $296.01
Cheapo's $299.95 − $4.98 = $294.97
Below Cost: $298.98 − $2.97 (3 movie rentals) = $296.01

3. 1½% per month
18% ÷ 12 mo. = 1½%/mo.

4. $4.77
$317.95 (see Problem 1) × 1½% = $4.77

5. $290.72
$317.95 + $4.77 = $322.72 − $32.00 = $290.72

Cassette by Credit—Answers
Problem Set C (Story on page 201)

1. $1.03
Cheapo's: ($299.95 × .06 = $18.00) + $299.95 = $317.95
Below Cost: ($298.98 × .06 = $17.94) + $298.98 = $316.92
$317.95 − $316.92 = $1.03

2. $1.04
Cheapo's: $299.95 − $4.98 (free cassette) = $294.97
Below Cost: $298.98 − $2.97 (3 free movie rentals) = $296.01
$296.01 − $294.97 = $1.04

3. 1½% per month
18% ÷ 12 mo. = 1½%/mo.

4. $14.26
The Below Cost price, with tax, is $316.92 (see Problem 2). 1½%/mo. × 3 mo. = 4½% = $14.26

5. $817.95; $2.52
$500.00 + $317.95 (see Problem 1) = $817.95
$817.95 − $500.00 − $150.00 = $167.95
$167.95 × 1½% = $2.52

Oregon or Bust!—Answers
Problem Set A (Story on page 205)

1. California, Nevada, Idaho, Washington and the Pacific Ocean border Oregon.

2. It is about 50 miles from Portland to Salem, Oregon.

3. 240 miles; 6 hours; in a volcano and the deepest lake in U.S. Since some of the driving is on mountain roads, it will take about 6 hours to drive 240 miles. Crater Lake National Park was created around the deepest lake in the United States (1,932 feet), formed in an extinct volcano.

4. Approximately 285 miles; 2 to 3 hours
One way air mileage from Portland to Weiser, Idaho is approximately 285 miles and might take between 2 and 3 hours, depending on the type of airplane being flown and weather conditions. Airspeed for a single-engine Cessna might be 125 mph; thus:
285 mi. ÷ 125 mph = approx. 2 hr. 18 min.

5. Vacation sites will vary. Check for reasonable travel times.

Oregon or Bust!—Answers
Problem Set B (Story on page 205)

1. California, Nevada, Idaho, Washington, Columbia River, Snake River and the Pacific Ocean border Oregon. Approximate miles of waterway border are:
Pacific Ocean = 340 mi.
Columbia River = 300 mi.
Snake River = 190 mi.

2. Approximately 560 miles; 13 hours; at least 4 days plus 2 in Salem.
The approximately 560 miles from Portland to Redwood National Park will require nearly 13 hours driving time. At least 4 days should be allowed for driving and sightseeing.
Information about these interesting places should be located in encyclopedias and other reference materials.

3. Approximately 285 miles requiring 2 to 3 hours flight time; driving for 445 miles takes nearly 10 hours.
One-way air mileage from Portland to Weiser, Idaho is approximately 285 miles and might take between 2 and 3 hours, depending on the type of airplane being flown and weather conditions. (Airspeed for a single-engine Cessna might be 125 mph; thus:
285 mi. ÷ 125 mph = approx. 2 hr. 18 min.
Highway mileage of approximately 445 will require nearly 10 hours of driving.
Competition for the best fiddle players from the U.S. and Canada is held at the National Old Time Fiddlers Contest during the third full week in June. For details write the Chamber of Commerce, Weiser, Idaho 83672.

4. Much of Oregon is mountainous and approximately half of the state is forestland. The Coast Range and the Cascade Range divide the state north to south. There are numerous high peaks including Mt. Hood which, at 11,245 feet, is the highest point in the state. The lowest elevation is sea level where Oregon meets the Pacific Ocean. Eastern Oregon is high tableland with the land in the south-central merging with the desert-like Great Basin. Western Oregon, near the Pacific Ocean is very wet and rainy; eastern Oregon is quite dry with parts being desert-like. Consult encyclopedias and other reference books for further information.

5. Selected vacation sites will vary. Check for reasonable travel times. If you plan to drive, the time in minutes will be approximately double the number of miles. (For example, a trip of 45 miles, especially if on mountain highways, might take 90 min-

utes.) Flight times will vary depending on weather conditions and the type of airplane being used. However, single-engine airplanes generally travel between 100 and 180 mph, with 125 mph being a typical speed.

Oregon or Bust!—Answers
Problem Set C (Story on page 205)

1. California, Nevada, Idaho, Washington, Columbia River, Snake River and the Pacific Ocean border Oregon. Approximately 830 miles of waterway border are:
Pacific Ocean = 340 mi.
Columbia River = 300 mi.
Snake River = 190 mi.
Approximate state border distances are:
Washington = 400 mi.
Idaho = 340 mi.
Nevada = 160 mi.
California = 225 mi.

2. Approximately 1,050 mi.; at least 7 days plus 2 in Salem.
The approximately 1,050 mile trip from Portland through Salem, then as far south as Redwood National Park, then along the Pacific Coast, and back to Portland will require about 25 hours driving time. They should allow at least 7 days for traveling and sightseeing plus 2 days in Salem.
Information about these interesting places should be located in encyclopedias and other reference materials.

3. Approximately 285 miles requiring 2 to 3 hours flight time; driving 445 miles takes nearly 10 hours.
One-way air mileage from Portland to Weiser, Idaho is approximately 285 miles and might take between 2 and 3 hours, depending on the type of airplane being flown and weather conditions. (Airspeed for a single-engine Cessna might be 125 mph; thus:
285 mi. ÷ 125 mph = approx. 2 hr. 18 min.
Highway mileage is approximately 445 and will require nearly 10 hours of driving.
Competition for the best fiddle players from the U.S. and Canada is held at the National Old Time Fiddlers Contest during the third full week in June. For details write the Chamber of Commerce, Weiser, Idaho 83672.

4. Much of Oregon is mountainous and approximately half of the state is forestland. The Coast Range and the Cascade Range divide the state north to south. There are numerous high peaks including Mt. Hood which, at 11,245 feet, is the highest point in the state. The lowest elevation is sea level where Oregon meets the Pacific Ocean. Eastern Oregon is high tableland with the land in the south-central merging with the desert-like Great Basin. Western Oregon, near the Pacific Ocean is very wet and rainy; eastern Oregon is quite dry with parts being desert-like. Consult encyclopedias and other reference books for further information.

5. Selected vacation sites will vary. Check for reasonable travel times. If you plan to drive, the time in minutes will be approx. double the number of miles. (For example, a trip of 45 miles, especially if on mountain highways, might take 90 minutes.) Flight times will vary depending on weather conditions and the type of airplane being used. However, single-engine airplanes generally travel between 100 and 180 mph, with 125 mph being a typical speed. Contact a local aviation or flight service to determine costs for your area.

SELECTED REFERENCES

Burns, Marilyn. "Why California Said NO to 14 Math Textbook Series," *Learning*, 15(5):50, January, 1987.

California State Department of Public Instruction. *Mathematics Framework For California Public Schools Kindergarten Through Grade Twelve*. Sacramento, CA; Superintendent of Public Instruction, 1985.

Carpenter, Thomas P., Henry Kepner, Mary Kay Corbitt, Mary Montgomery Lindquist, and Robert E. Reys. "Results of the Second NAEP Mathematics Assessment: Secondary School," *Mathematics Teacher*, 73(5);338, May, 1980.

Fry, Edward B. *Elementary Reading Instruction*. New York: McGraw-Hill Book Co., 1977.

McKnight, Curtis C., Kenneth J. Travers, F. Joe Crosswhite, and Jane O. Swafford. "Eighth-Grade Mathematics in U.S. Schools: A Report from the Second International Mathematics Study," *Arithmetic Teacher*, 32(8):20–26, April 1985.

National Council of Teachers of Mathematics. *Recommendations for School Mathematics of the 1980's: An Agenda for Action*. Reston, VA: National Council of Teachers of Mathematics, 1980.

Overholt, James L. *Dr. Jim's Elementary Math Prescriptions: Activities/Aids/Games to Help Children Learn Elementary Mathematics*. Chicago: Scott, Foresman and Company, 1978.

"Turnaround seen in routine math skills but problem solving stumps many students." *National Assessment of Educational Progress Newsletter*, Vol. XVI, No. 2, Spring, 1983.

CENTENNIAL S.S.
MATH. DEPT.